Family in America

Family in America

Advisory Editors: David J. Rothman

Professor of History,
Columbia University

Sheila M. Rothman

THE ILLEGITIMATE FAMILY
IN NEW YORK CITY

Its Treatment by
Social and Health Agencies

BY

RUTH REED

ARNO PRESS & THE NEW YORK TIMES

New York   1972

Reprint Edition 1972 by Arno Press Inc.

Reprinted from a copy in
The University of Illinois Library

LC# 78-169397
ISBN 0-405-03874-7

Family in America
ISBN for complete set: 0-405-03840-2
See last pages of this volume for titles.

Manufactured in the United States of America

THE ILLEGITIMATE FAMILY IN NEW YORK CITY

ITS TREATMENT BY SOCIAL AND HEALTH AGENCIES

THE ILLEGITIMATE FAMILY
IN NEW YORK CITY

Its Treatment by
Social and Health Agencies

BY

RUTH REED

PUBLISHED FOR

THE WELFARE COUNCIL OF NEW YORK CITY

BY

COLUMBIA UNIVERSITY PRESS

1 9 3 4

Studies of the Research Bureau of
the Welfare Council

NUMBER ELEVEN

PRINTED IN THE UNITED STATES OF AMERICA
GEORGE GRADY PRESS   NEW YORK

PREFACE

BECAUSE it strikes at those roots of family life and of child care and protection that inhere in the coöperation of parents at the time of the birth and during the rearing of a child, illegitimacy never ceases to arouse the interest of social workers and of citizens generally. Astonishingly little authentic, current information on the number of illegitimate births and the social treatment of the members of such families is available however; and this statement applies especially to New York City. How many illegitimate children are born in New York City in a year? How many of these mothers are residents of New York City? How many New York City residents went elsewhere for maternity service? Are unmarried mothers older or younger, taken as a group, than they formerly were? How are illegitimacy rates changing in the several racial and cultural groups? Is the proportion of unmarried fathers ineligible to marry the mothers of their children growing larger or smaller? What proportion of these children are the results of unions so casual that mothers do not know who the fathers of their children are? To none of these questions can the community furnish accurate answers.

With regard to treatment, we might like to know from year to year the social and legal procedures involved in such cases. What proportion of these couples achieve legitimation of their children and at least a partial solution through marriage? What proportion of these children are accepted into their natural families? What proportion are separated from their families without effort to keep the child with his own blood kin? How do the various cultural groups regard illegitimate parenthood and the obligations of parents—especially fathers? In what proportion of these cases are the laws for establishing paternity invoked? And with what results?

How well did the various parts of the community's machinery work together in safeguarding the interests of these children and of their parents? How were the resources for maternity care, social case work, legal and court service, and child placement aligned for these people and their children? In fact, what becomes of these children? Are they, on the average, social assets or liabilities?

And what becomes of unmarried mothers? What kind of women and girls survive the experience and derive some growth of character and personality from it? What kind are wrecked by it? What kind of aid really helps the mother to see the whole of the situation in which she is, to plan her next steps in the light of that picture, and to function fully as a mother to her child? What results attend the efforts of those who provide some incidental service to help the mother cover up the episode?

How best can the children who come from parents wholly unable to meet the obligations of parenthood be cared for? Are they good candidates for adoption? Should they become wards of the city or state? Or can voluntary agencies assume responsibility for them?

Why is it that such a large number of agencies are dealing piecemeal with a type of situation in which both specialized knowledge and integrated service are highly important? Why is it that within services provided by the city government there is a range in method of treatment on a given case that goes from possessive and hampering secrecy to complete and gruelling publicity?

The answers to these and many other questions suggest themselves as necessary before there can be an understanding of illegitimacy and an appraisal of the community's treatment of it.

In the study which follows answers were sought to some of these questions for one year's grist of births out of wedlock.

There is reason to believe that almost all illegitimate children and their mothers are known to hospitals and a high proportion to social agencies. More such children were known in fact to hospitals and social agencies than were reported in birth registration statistics! But in the present somewhat chaotic state of care of these children and their parents, it is futile to ask some of the most significant questions, because the answers cannot be secured for the run of the cases. The study sets forth in detail what can and what can not be learned on the basis of existing records. It is obvious that some of the most important information—for example how many of these children die during their first year of life—will never be forthcoming until there is general recognition among the people who deal with these cases, that it is significant and important to ascertain and record such salient facts as a regular matter of routine accounting.

For children accepted by an agency for care away from their families there is ample authority for the State Department of Social Welfare to secure information as long as the child is in foster care other than adoption. But until the child is accepted for foster care and for all of these children not so accepted, there is no way to secure information either currently or in special studies.

It is hard to escape from the conclusion that the community will never be able to know about this problem or exercise any kind of control over it without some form of centralization of information—not necessarily service—which begins with the birth registration and extends to the time at which there is assurance that the child is receiving care which will give him a chance to reach adult life with reasonably good physical and mental health. Everywhere health departments, welfare departments, and public school systems are seeing the importance of building up services which are comprehensive of all the eligible children, which are systematic and responsible and which try to articulate their many kinds of service into a rounded effort, mindful of each child's many-sided needs. Children born out of wedlock are a relatively small but an especially needy segment of the child population. A comprehensive and systematic program in their behalf would seem to be especially in order. They are now receiving a grand hodgepodge of services that yield little or no information on the community's problem and that carry no assurance whatever that, as a class, these children are getting systematic and appropriate care. Some promising beginnings have been made in coördination in this field of social service, but a long road to be traveled lies ahead, before it can be said that, from the point of view of community management of the aggregate of care furnished, a good service is being rendered.

The study which follows was undertaken at the request of the Committee on the Care of the Unmarried Mother of the Welfare Council's Section on Dependent Children. This committee helped the Research Bureau's staff to define the scope of this inquiry and to make effective contacts with the agencies which have information. A subcommittee of the Council's Research Committee paid particular attention to the methods of study employed. The personnel of both of these groups are listed elsewhere.

The staff of the Research Bureau on whom direct responsibility rests for this piece of work includes Dr. Ruth Reed, who had the major part in collecting and analyzing data and in writing the report; Mrs. Evelyn Krohn, who collected data from the Jewish agencies; and Mrs. Gertrude Ollendorff, who tabulated the materials with great patience and accuracy.

Mrs. Mabel Mattingly of Cleveland, Ohio, who was originally appointed to serve as the head of this study, gave very valuable service in devising the early plans and in securing understanding among the coöperating agencies as to its purposes and methods. When, for personal reasons, she was forced to withdraw, Dr. Reed was able to step into the breach and carry the study through to completion.

Since this effort was directed toward the construction of a comprehensive picture of illegitimacy in New York City, it was thought desirable to append to the study a digest of the laws relating to the subject. The United States Children's Bureau, which has collected information on such legislation throughout the country, responded to our request, and furnished the digest, prepared by Mr. Carl A. Heisterman, which appears as Appendix 2.

It was also thought that those who are to receive and study the findings of the inquiry with a view to recommending action, would be better implemented for their task if the report included an annotated bibliography on the subject. This was prepared by Miss Clare Butler and Miss Agnes Burnham.

This piece of work was made possible by grants to the Research Bureau from the Rockefeller Foundation, the Commonwealth Fund, and the Josiah Macy, Jr. Foundation.

NEVA R. DEARDORFF

CONTENTS

Appendices

Indexes

TABLES

Part One

INTRODUCTION

I

THE NATURE AND PURPOSE OF THE STUDY

The Purpose

THIS study was undertaken at the request of the social agencies constituting the Committee on the Care of the Unmarried Mother of the Welfare Council of New York City. Its objectives were to enumerate the agencies engaged in the care of the illegitimate family in New York City; to describe the types of services being rendered by these agencies; and to state the chief characteristics of the illegitimate family itself as considered during a limited interval of time. There has been no attempt to evaluate or measure the quality of the work of particular agencies or to appraise the purposes or procedures of those engaged in this type of social work; it is intended simply to state in terms of current usage in social work the nature and extent of the work being done for clients with the problem here considered. It was believed that a general survey of the care and the characteristics of the illegitimate family would be of service to the agencies requesting the study, because it would help them to see the significance of illegitimacy as it presents itself in the social economy of New York City. It was hoped, too, that a better understanding of the more general aspects of the problem might enable the coöperating agencies to appraise their own work in view of its relation to the total situation and to gain some idea of the field which yet remains to be covered. There was no intention, however, to indicate what steps they should pursue in the future. The sole interest has been to reveal the situation as it presents itself through the records of the agencies, both public and private, which have been opened to us, with the hope that this broader picture might throw some light upon the particular problems with which each agency is attempting to deal.

The Scope

In order to limit the inquiry to suitable proportions it was thought best to take the births out of wedlock for a selected year as the basis of study and then to proceed with the description of the care which had been accorded these illegitimate children and their parents by the agencies operating for that purpose within the bounds of Greater New York. The year 1930 was chosen as most suitable for the purpose in mind. Its recency renders a description of the work done at this time of immediate practical importance, and the records of this year were sufficiently complete at the time the study was begun, in the summer of 1931, to make the data easily available.

The Sources

Statistics as to the illegitimate family compiled from the birth certificates were supplied by the New York City Department of Health. In addition to information obtained from this source, direct recourse to the social agencies having to do with the illegitimate family was had by means of two schedules prepared for that purpose. The first of these schedules, designed to secure information from the agency as to the nature and extent of its work with the illegitimate family, was filled in by a member of the study staff from information supplied by an executive of the agency during a conference arranged with this end in view. The second of the schedules, framed to elicit information regarding the members of the illegitimate family itself (the illegitimate infant, the unmarried mother, and the father) and the services rendered to them, was made out in some cases by a member of the agency staff from its records and its first-hand knowledge of the family, and in other cases by a member of the study staff from the records of the agency. Copies of these schedules are given in Appendix 1.

Value and Limitations of this Study

The value of the information secured as a result of the activities of the study staff lies in the picture which it presents of the characteristics of the illegitimate family in New York City in 1930 and of the care which was being provided for the members of these families. Its aim is to bring out the larger outlines of the situation rather than to go into the refinements of technique in rendering services of various kinds.

Complete and accurate information in the form of records on any point raised was not available, however. The registration of illegitimate births, doubtless incomplete in New York City, as in every other part of the registration area of the United States, does, nevertheless, furnish the most reliable, in fact, the only basis currently available for an acquaintance with the number and the parentage of children born out of wedlock, and these figures have been utilized for the year under consideration. Similarly, the records of the social agencies have been found to vary greatly, in relation to the special purposes of the agency, and in the nature and the completeness of the information given. In some cases the agency specialized in the supervision and occupational placement of the unmarried mother and had very complete information as to the latter's social and occupational history. In other cases, where legal proceedings to establish paternity were considered of prime importance, more complete information regarding the social and financial status of the father was obtained as a basis for judicial decision. In still other cases, as, for example, the hospitals giving maternity care to unmarried mothers, more complete information was given as to the mother's medical history and the physical condition of her child. Even allowing, however, for the special purposes for which the information was obtained, there remained among agencies serving the same function in the care of the illegitimate family a wide difference in the completeness of the information furnished. For example, some social service departments of hospitals included in their records not only facts as to the medical history of the unmarried mother and her child, but full information as to her social history and the disposition made of the child; while records of other hospital social service departments gave no facts as to the social history of the illegitimate family, and even omitted such primary information as the sex and color of the child and the statement of the exact date of his birth.

Presenting the most complete information were the case work agencies which concentrate their efforts almost exclusively upon the care of the illegitimate family and which have a considerable number of such clients. Records from these agencies not infrequently contained information as to the members of the illegitimate family and their social history far more abundant in scope than could be examined and analyzed for the purposes of this study. Even here, however, the nature of the information recorded varied according to the purpose of the agency. If the agency existed primarily for the placement of children in foster homes with a view to adoption, more complete information as to the heredity of the child and the position of his foster parents in life was secured; while in the case of agencies whose policy it is to keep the mother and her child together, attention had been centered upon obtaining information regarding the mother's social and occupational history in order to determine the probability of her success in earning a livelihood for herself and the child.

In this fact lies the weakness of this study, or any other study based upon the records of this group of social agencies: there had been no common agreement as to the facts necessary to be included in the records of all agencies having to do with the care of the illegitimate family. This inadequacy of data has made it impossible to generalize even with regard to the group under consideration, and all statements made in the pages which follow as to the members of the illegitimate family and the care which they receive must be strictly construed as applying only to the group for which information regarding the item in question was contained in the records.

The limitations of the schedule method of obtaining information regarding the activities of social case work agencies have been fully admitted. It is evident that much of that personal relationship of social case worker to clients which determines so largely the outcome of the effort in behalf of any particular illegitimate family does not lend itself to tabulation and statistical measurement. It should be borne in mind, however, that the present study does not aim to measure or evaluate these more personal and intangible aspects of the case work endeavor, but has limited itself, insofar as the nature of the material permitted, to those aspects of the study of the illegitimate family which do lend themselves to measurement of a statistical nature or to the method of objective description. A point has also been made of noting the questions that different groups of social workers and others raised in connection with the treatment accorded these young women, the fathers of their children, and the babies themselves.

II

THE SOCIAL SIGNIFICANCE OF THE ILLEGITIMATE FAMILY

AN illegitimate family, defined for the purposes of this study, consists of the parents who have not married each other, and their natural offspring. Use of the term should not be taken to imply that such a group constitutes a generally recognized unit insofar as social and economic usages are concerned, for in the majority of cases which come to the attention of social agencies the parents are not living together and are not coöperating in the care and maintenance of their child. It happens, however, that the welfare of the different members of the illegitimate family is so interrelated by natural and legal ties that they must be considered as more or less of a unit in any constructive plan of social action, and it is for this reason that the term is employed in the pages which follow.

Before entering into a description of the general aspects of the problem of illegitimacy as it was found to exist in New York City in 1930, it may be well to consider briefly the particular traits of the illegitimate family which render it a source of special concern to social and governmental agencies and to all others interested in human welfare.

Infant and Maternal Mortality

A series of studies conducted by the United States Children's Bureau has revealed the fact that the infant mortality rate in five cities which had been selected for special study was in some cases more than three times as high for infants born out of wedlock as for infants of legitimate birth. This excess of deaths among illegitimate infants was found to be associated with the early separation of mother and child, and knowledge of this causal relation has led to the enactment in some states of special legislation. In Maryland, in 1916, a statute was passed which provided that no child under six months of age should be separated from his mother for placement in a foster home or in an institution, except under conditions expressly laid down by the statute, among them the approval of persons capable of making a decision about the wisdom of such a separation as it would affect the infant's health. The effects of this legislation were revealed by a special study of conditions in Baltimore in 1921, in which it was found that mortality among infants born out of wedlock was reduced more than 50 percent between 1915 and 1921, while the ratio for legitimate infants was reduced less than 20 percent in the same period.[1] Similar legislation designed to prevent the hasty separation of mother and child was passed in other states with an equally favorable outcome. In still other states where corrective measures have not yet been taken in this direction many social agencies, both public and private, have adopted the policy of discouraging the early separation of mother and child with the hope that such an attitude on their part may result in the lowering of the death rate for infants born out of wedlock.

Comparisons of maternal mortality attendant upon legitimate and illegitimate births in New York City in 1930-32 have been made in a recent study directed by Dr. Ransom S. Hooker for the Committee on Public Health Relations of the New York Academy of Medicine.[2] It is there brought out that the fraction of deaths due to preventable causes is much larger among deaths associated with illegitimate pregnancy than among those associated with legitimate pregnancy. The report further remarks that "It is not at all unexpected to find a great

[1]*Children of Illegitimate Birth and Measures for Their Protection,* United States Children's Bureau Publication 166, 1926.
[2]New York Academy of Medicine, Committee on Public Health Relations, *Maternal Mortality in New York City: a Study of All Puerperal Deaths, 1931-1932,* New York, 1933.

disparity evident between the death rates from septicaemia following legitimate and illegitimate births—1.42 and 4.27." Any
effort at the reduction of maternal mortality must inevitably
consider the services rendered to these women and girls and
must find some way to protect them from the needless hazards
that now beset many of them.

Dependency

In many cases the unmarried mother who comes to the attention of the social agencies is herself a child. Not only is she
unable to provide for the maintenance of her offspring, but
she is in need of training and reëducation before she can be
expected to assume the responsibilities of adult life. Moreover, if it becomes known in the community that she has given
birth to a child out of wedlock the unmarried mother may
have difficulty in finding employment because of this fact, or
she may be forced to accept conditions of work less advanta-
geous than what is considered normal for those of her occupational group. In addition to the direct economic handicap and
danger of dependency which she experiences there may be the
less tangible, but no less real, hardship involved in the loss of
the esteem and respect of family and friends which the unmarried mother not infrequently encounters. This may make
itself felt in a lessening of the opportunity for marriage or
even for normal social life and expression, with the consequence that her morale is so weakened that she is not willing
to make the struggle for the independent maintenance of herself and her child. Moreover, the support of the illegitimate
child by the father is difficult to obtain and is rarely adequate.
Illegitimacy, as a consequence, contributes no inconsiderable
item to the burden of child dependency which the public must
assume. In order to forestall such an outcome it has been
thought wise to give aid, protection, and moral support to the
unmarried mother all during the period of her pregnancy and

of her readjustment to social life after the birth of her child; and for such a purpose the maintenance of special social agencies has been necessary.

At the beginning of the year 1930, the foundlings and children born out of wedlock who were under the care of institutions for dependent children in New York State constituted 9.1 percent of the total population of these institutions, a proportion of the total several times what the illegitimate birth rate in this State might lead one to expect.[3] Moreover, consideration of all data available for the study of the illegitimate family in New York City in 1930 reveals the fact that its members have recourse for aid, protection, and advice to social agencies of many different types with so much greater frequency than do the members of the legitimate family as to justify the belief that the existence of the illegitimate family in the population constitutes a community problem of sufficient dimensions, at least, to warrant special study. It will be the purpose of Parts Two and Three of this report to present further facts bearing upon this position.

The Legal Protection of the Illegitimate Child

Most of the recent legislation enacted to define the status of the illegitimate family has had as its primary object the protection of the interests of the illegitimate child, and as its secondary object the protection of society by so fixing the responsibility for the maintenance of the illegitimate child upon his parents that he will not be in danger of becoming a public charge.[4] In earlier periods the objective was almost solely the

[3]*The Sixty-Fourth Annual Report of the State Board of Social Welfare,* State of New York, 1930. Although it is not known what proportion of foundlings are of illegitimate birth it seems safe to assume that it is high.

[4]A digest of the laws of the state of New York applicable to New York City was prepared for incorporation in this study by Carl A. Heisterman of the United States Children's Bureau, which serves as a center for authentic information on all legislation relating to children throughout the United States and its possessions. This digest is given in Appendix 2.

immediate protection of the tax payer. Growing emphasis has been placed on the idea that the child's interest shall be considered of first importance. This attitude has found expression among other ways in legislation designed to protect the child born out of wedlock from having the fact of his illegitimate birth become generally known.

In 1925, a New York law entitled "An Act to Amend the General Construction Law in Relation to the Meaning of the Words 'Illegitimate Child' " stipulated (Sec. 138, "General Provisions"):

In all records, certificates or other papers hereafter made or executed, other than birth records and certificates or records of judicial proceedings in which the question of birth out of wedlock is at issue, requiring a declaration by or notice to the mother of a child born out of wedlock or otherwise requiring a reference to the relation of a mother to such a child, it shall be sufficient for all purposes to refer to the mother as the parent having the sole custody of the child, and no explicit reference shall be made to illegitimacy.[5]

This measure to protect the child born out of wedlock from the stigma attaching to the circumstances of his birth is a new indication of the general recognition of the significance of childhood as the time when the future adult's health, happiness, and usefulness are largely determined, and of the right of every child to conditions favorable to his normal development.

The Establishment of Paternity

There is a growing belief that it is socially desirable and good public policy to require parents to assume their natural responsibilities insofar as they are able so to do. It is explicitly stated in the legislation defining the status of the illegitimate family in New York City that: "The parents of a natural child are liable for its support."[6] In case the child has been

[5]Laws of New York, 1925, ch. 515; Supp. 1925, ch. 23, Sec. 59, General Construction Law. Also United States Children's Bureau Chart No. 16.
[6]Laws of New York, 1929, Article III-B, Section 35-b, "Obligations of parents; liability for support and education," p. 955.

abandoned by his parents or in case it becomes impossible to
establish his parentage, the responsibility for his support in
this city is assumed by the municipality.

A natural child is defined as

a child who is either begotten and born (*a*) out of lawful matrimony, (*b*) while the husband of its mother was separate from her
for a whole year previous to its birth, (*c*) during the separation of
its mother from her husband pursuant to a judgment of a competent
court; or who is begotten at a time when the husband is impotent.

In order that the parental responsibility in these several circumstances may be clearly fixed by the court, it becomes necessary to establish paternity by legal procedure.

Proceedings to establish paternity may be instituted during
the pregnancy of the mother or after the birth of the child
until it is two years of age. Later, proceedings may not be
instituted by the mother unless paternity has been acknowledged by the father in writing or by the furnishing of support.
However, the Department of Public Welfare may bring suit
in behalf of any child under the age of sixteen who is or is
liable to become a public charge. The birth of the child in
another place than New York City is considered no bar to the
institution of proceedings for his support if either the father
or the mother resides or is found in New York City.

If paternity is established the father may be required by the
court to furnish security that the money ordered by the court
for the support of the child will be paid. In case the father
defaults on the payments which the court has ordered to be
made, he may be sentenced to the workhouse. His obligation
to support his illegitimate child remains unimpaired after his
release from prison, however, and in case of further default he
may again be sentenced by the court to a term in the workhouse. If circumstances warrant, the father may be placed on
probation, in case he is unable to give security for his obligation to support his child.

A paternity case originates when a mother files with the

Department of Public Welfare a complaint demanding support for her natural child. The Department serves as a representative of the public in seeing that the responsibilities of putative fathers are defined and discharged. The Court of Special Sessions has exclusive jurisdiction in proceedings to establish paternity in New York City. The court may in its discretion issue either a warrant or a summons to secure the attendance of the putative father at the hearing. It is the practice to hold a preliminary hearing from which the public *may* be excluded.[7] The trial is by the court of three judges without jury, and the court has a continuing jurisdiction with power to modify its order at any subsequent time.

The mother may by these proceedings recover the expenses of her confinement and previous care from the father of her child in case the court so orders. With respect to her illegitimate child, in accordance with the state law, she stands in order to inherit his property if he has no legal descendants. On the other hand, she is obligated by the law to name the father of her child in order that proceedings may be undertaken to protect the rights of the child with regard to his father, and she is herself obligated to support and educate her child to the extent of her ability; she is also held liable for funeral expenses in case of his death.[8]

In order to prevent a hasty or ill-advised compromise between the illegitimate parents as to the future of their child, provision is made that any agreement entered into on behalf of the mother and child for their support shall be binding only when the court has approved such an agreement as making

[7]Because of practical difficulties connected with court procedure the public has not always been excluded from such hearings. Social workers urge the need of further measures to effect this end and to safeguard those chiefly concerned, from unnecessary embarrassment and exposure.

[8]United States Children's Bureau Chart No. 16, 1929, "Analysis and Tabular Summary of State Laws Relating to Illegitimacy in the United States in Effect January 1, 1928, and the Text of Selected Laws."

adequate provision for their welfare. The Department of Public Welfare must, moreover, be given notice and an opportunity to be heard in the matter before such a decision can be made by the court.[9]

The Abandonment of Children

The close relationship between illegitimacy and the abandonment, even exposure, of infants has long been a subject of social concern. The abandonment of a child by his parents is by law a felony in New York State.[10] A parent or other person charged with the care or custody for nurture or education of a child under the age of sixteen years who abandons the child in destitute circumstances and wilfully omits to furnish necessary and proper food, clothing, or shelter for such child is guilty of felony, punishable by imprisonment for not more than two years, or by a fine not to exceed one thousand dollars or by both. This law as it applies to unmarried mothers may be modified in its effects—at the discretion of the court—by the suspension of sentence and the placing of the unmarried mother on probation.

A previous conviction of felony or misdemeanor shall not prevent the court from suspending sentence upon a conviction under this section, or from arbitrarily fixing the limit if imprisonment or fine, in case imprisonment or fine is imposed upon conviction herein.[11]

The effectiveness of legal measures defining the rights and responsibilities of the members of the illegitimate family depends in large measure upon the coöperation and assistance

[9]*Laws of New York*, Article III-B, Section 35-c, "Agreement or compromise," p. 955.
[10]*The Consolidated Laws of New York*, annotated and compiled by William M. McKinney, Book 39, "Penal Law," Article 44, Section 480, "Abandonment of children," p. 43.
[11]*Ibid.*

of social agencies, both public and private, in the enforcement of these laws and in their sympathetic and socially intelligent interpretation with regard to the persons most concerned by them. The work of the New York City agencies in this regard will be described in subsequent chapters of this report.

III

ILLEGITIMACY IN TEN AMERICAN CITIES

ILLEGITIMACY rates in the United States vary greatly from one locality to another, and from one social group to another in the same locality. Statistics of illegitimacy, however, can hardly be said to offer a reliable index of the nature and extent of the problem created by the birth of children out of wedlock. Definitions of illegitimacy vary from one locality to another and differences in the degree of accuracy with which illegitimate births are recorded are generally known to be great. Even though the statistics were known to be accurate and comparable for the groups under consideration the nature of the problem for those most concerned might not yet be evident because of the variance in the social attitude toward illegitimate parenthood in the different groups concerned.

Some idea of the varying extent to which the problem of illegitimacy presents itself in American cities may be derived, however, from Table 1, compiled from statistics furnished by the Division of Vital Statistics of the United States Bureau of the Census, showing the registered illegitimate births in ten selected cities of the United States for the year 1930.

It will be noted that the number of white illegitimate births per thousand total white births varies from 9.9 in New York City to 41.7 in Richmond, Virginia. This width of range in the rates is difficult to explain by means of any of the facts known to us. Very high rates may be in part accounted for by the fact that a city is the site of hospitals or maternity homes where young women from other localities are received for care. Since births are not allocated by the Bureau of the Census to the residence of the mother but to the locality where the birth actually occurs, a sizable difference in the illegitimate birth rate may be the result of the location of these institutions

TABLE 1

Births Registered as Illegitimate in Ten Selected Cities ^a *of the*
United States, White and Negro Population, 1930

CITY	TOTAL NUMBER OF ILLEGITIMATE BIRTHS		NUMBER OF ILLEGITIMATE BIRTHS PER 1,000 TOTAL BIRTHS	
	WHITE	NEGRO	WHITE	NEGRO
Washington, D. C.	127	562	20.1	184.0
Chicago, Ill.	1,091	405	20.5	85.5
New Orleans, La.	160	480	25.9	152.0
Baltimore, Md.	189	699	16.1	213.8
New York, N. Y.	1,140	409	9.9	56.1
Cleveland, Ohio	368	124	22.5	81.9
Philadelphia, Pa.	482	691	15.6	139.2
Salt Lake City, Utah . . .	36	1	10.4	29.4
Richmond, Va.	99	250	41.7	207.6
Seattle, Wash.	109	8	21.8	29.6

^aThe cities were selected from among the cities of 100,000 population or more because of the contrasting social conditions represented. A complete list of these cities with population of 100,000 or more and their illegitimacy rates are given in Appendix 4.

within the limits of a given municipality. The official illegitimacy rate may also be affected by the fact that the facilities
for anonymity and the concealment of the fact of illegitimacy
vary from one city to another in accordance with the legal
requirements as to the reporting of illegitimate births and the
practice of both public and private agencies in this regard.
Actual contact with the problem reveals the fact that the possibilities of concealment vary from one community to another,
and there can be no doubt that this fact plays its part in the
determining of the recorded illegitimacy rate in a given locality.[1] In the absence of more complete proof, however, the

[1]In the next chapter, the requirements for the registration of information
bearing on illegitimacy in New York City are further discussed.

marked differences in the statistics of illegitimacy of the ten selected cities must be assumed to be indicative to some extent at least of an actual difference in illegitimacy rates. These differences in rate could be explained only by an intensive study of the intricate interplay of economic and social forces in each locality under consideration.

The figures do, however, suggest that New York City is not a concentration point for births of this type and that both its white and its colored groups are characterized by low rates for cases of such a nature that they are publicly recorded.

The Negro Rate

The number of officially registered Negro illegitimate births per thousand total Negro births varied from 29.4 in Salt Lake City to 213.8 in Baltimore. In every one of the ten selected cities and in the greater number of those given in Appendix 4 the number of Negro illegitimate births was proportionately higher than the number of white illegitimate births in the same city.

But the proportion of Negro illegitimate births in some cities for which the rates were given was lower than the proportion of white illegitimate births in other cities. For example, the proportion of Negro illegitimate births in Seattle and Salt Lake City was lower than the proportion of white illegitimate births in Baltimore and in Richmond. Other examples of the same relationship between Negro illegitimacy rates in some cities and the higher white illegitimacy rates in other cities can be established by a glance at the figures given in the appendix. An explanation of this fact suggests itself in the environmental factors influencing the two races in the different urban centers. It is generally admitted that working and living conditions are more favorable to Negroes in communities where they form a smaller proportion of the total population than in places where their numbers are relatively larger. These more favorable economic and social conditions are reflected in the illegitimacy rate which appears in this and in other studies to be lower in communities where Negroes enjoy more favorable opportunities in work and education. In other words, the Negro illegitimacy rate appears to be susceptible to the same environmental influences as the white illegitimacy rate, and when these environmental factors are favorable to the Negro the proportion of registered illegitimate births is less.

Even in cities where the proportion of Negro illegitimate births is high, as in Richmond and Baltimore, it should be noted that the demoralization of personal and family life among Negroes is probably not as great as the figures might, at first glance, seem to indicate. In the first place, the percentage of error due to reporting illegitimate births as legitimate is probably greater in the case of the white than in the case of the Negro population, and the disparity in rates is probably not as great as appears from the official figures. This would seem to follow logically from the fact that the social penalties attached to illegitimacy are greater in the one case than in the other, and hence arouse a greater desire for concealment, and also from the greater facilities for secrecy and concealment which exist in the case of the white population. Perhaps because of this situation the Negro unmarried mother is said to assume more unquestioningly than does the white unmarried mother the responsibility for her child born out of wedlock, and the members of her family are more likely to come to her aid than the relatives of the white unmarried mother. Consequently, greater respect for the natural tie between mother and child is observed on the part of the Negroes: it is said to be unusual to find a Negro unmarried mother who is willing to be separated from her child. The death rate of Negro illegitimate infants is therefore less in relation to the death rate of Negro legitimate infants than is the white illegitimate infant death rate in relation to the death rate of white legitimate infants.[2] In other words, the handicap of illegitimacy as measured by the infant mortality rates is less in the case of the Negro than of the white child.

The historical factor in the higher rate of illegitimacy among Negroes should not be overlooked. The observance of a strict monogamy, so long the goal among the white population, is at best imperfectly realized at the present moment, after many centuries of effort; while for the Negro population a strictly monogamous form of family life has been possible only since the emancipation from slavery seventy years ago. It is also the case that Negroes are less likely, because of their unprivileged position in the social and economic order, to be familiar with measures which would limit the number of births out of wedlock, and it is possible that the illegitimate birth rate of Negroes is more nearly an index of irregular relationships than is the illegitimate birth rate among the white population. It cannot be assumed, therefore, until all other factors have been equalized, that the factor of race plays any important part in producing a difference in illegitimacy rates between the white and Negro populations.

The Low Rate in New York City

The relatively low illegitimacy rate in New York City, the lowest in the group of ten cities if the white illegitimacy rate alone is considered, demands further consideration. In view of the vast population of the city, of its sex and marriage ratios, of the complexity of the national and social groups involved, with their differing customs and attitudes, of the known problems of housing and occupation, the complete explanation of this minimum rate of illegitimacy appears well

[2]*Infant Mortality in Baltimore*, United States Children's Bureau Publication No. 119, 1923; *The Welfare of Infants of Illegitimate Birth in Baltimore*, United States Children's Bureau Publication No. 144, 1925.

nigh impossible even when differences in the accuracy of recording are allowed for. The consideration which follows of the illegitimacy statistics for New York City over a period of nine years is intended to offer some possible partial explanation of the relatively small number of registered illegitimate births in this city.

IV

TEN YEARS OF ILLEGITIMACY IN
NEW YORK CITY

As was pointed out in the preceding chapter, the New York City illegitimacy rate derived from official statistics appears low when compared with the illegitimacy rates in other large cities of the United States. A partial explanation of the apparent difference may be found in the requirements as to registration of births and the greater insistence in some localities upon accuracy in the information contained in the birth certificate than is found in this city. Statistics of illegitimacy in New York City, moreover, are available only since the year 1922. This fact may indicate that the system of registration of illegitimate births has been less perfected by practice in this city than in certain other centers where there has been a longer period in which such information has been required and recorded.

It will be readily noted, too, from the statistical tables given in this and the preceding chapter that the number of illegitimate births in New York City in 1930 differs noticeably, but not widely, according to whether the information was furnished by the New York City Department of Health or the Division of Vital Statistics of the United States Bureau of the Census. This discrepancy arises from the differences in interpretation put upon the data given in the birth certificate records of infants born in New York in 1930. It should be borne in mind that on certificates filed in New York City no specific mention of the fact of illegitimacy is made, unless the reporting physician volunteers the information, as he sometimes does, by writing "out of wedlock" on the return. Statistics of illegitimacy are therefore possible only when there is a considerable amount of interpretation of the information as to the child's parentage given in the birth certificate. If the parents of the child have not the same name, and if other recorded facts seem to indicate that they do not form a legally constituted family, or if there is no information with regard to the father on the birth certificate, it is assumed that the birth in question is illegitimate, and it is so regarded for statistical purposes. It can be seen, though, that such a method of inference may give rise to a difference of opinion as to the proper interpretation of the facts given in the record, and that discrepancies in the statistics furnished by the different statistical bureaus making tabulation from the same set of birth records are almost inevitable. It should be borne in mind, too, that the New York City Department of Health makes its tabulations of births according to the date on which they are reported, while the United States Division of Vital Statistics tabulates the births according to the actual date of the birth as given in the birth certificate. This variation in method may offer further aid in explaining the divergence in results.

While it is certain, as will later be demonstrated, that the official figures understate the volume of illegitimacy in the city, it should be pointed out, however, that certain other related indices of social welfare: namely, the recorded juvenile delinquency rate and the infant mortality rate, are also relatively low for New York City.[1] These differences which are consistent with each other are, however, difficult to explain in view of the complexity of the social and racial groupings and the many adverse conditions of life in this vast urban area.

In spite of their limitations, a consideration of the official illegitimacy rates in New York City over the period of ten years for which they were available may be of some interest in an attempt to understand the situation (Table 2).

It will be seen that during the eight years preceding 1930

[1]City of New York, Department of Health, *Annual Report*, 1929; *Juvenile Court Statistics*, 1930, United States Children's Bureau Publication No. 212.

TABLE 2

Total Births and Births Registered as Illegitimate in
New York City, Each Year, 1922-31[a]

YEAR	TOTAL BIRTHS	BIRTHS PER 1,000 POPULATION	ILLEGITIMATE BIRTHS	ILLEGITIMATE BIRTHS PER 1,000 BIRTHS
1922	135,809	21.84	1,296	9.5
1923	135,183	21.29	1,209	8.9
1924	136,884	21.05	1,317	9.6
1925	134,924	20.37	1,238	9.2
1926	131,569	19.46	1,153	8.8
1927	134,784	19.59	1,340	9.9
1928	132,453	18.84	1,374	10.4
1929	130,130	18.20	1,390	10.7
1930	128,511	17.64	1,470	11.4
1931	116,621	16.31	1,406	12.0

[a]Table compiled from statistics furnished by the Health Department of New York City.

there was a marked decline in the birth rate in New York City, and a slow decline in the absolute number of births registered. In 1922 there were 21.84 births per thousand of the population, and in 1930 there were only 17.64 births per thousand of the total population. This decline in the general birth rate was accompanied by a slightly perceptible but irregular increase in the ratio of illegitimate births to legitimate births, and an absolute increase in their number. In 1922 there were 9.5 illegitimate births per thousand total births, and in 1930 there were 11.4 illegitimate births per thousand total births. This increase in the ratio of illegitimate births to legitimate births does not indicate that the illegitimate birth rate had in itself increased greatly. As a matter of fact, during the years from 1922 to 1930 the illegitimate birth rate increased at only a very slightly greater rate than did the total population; but it does seem to be a significant fact that the illegitimate birth rate did not decline but even increased slightly at a time when the legitimate birth rate was declining with noticeable rapidity.

It should be further noted that the number of Negroes in the city's population increased from 152,467 in 1920 to 327,706 in 1930, and that the proportion of Negroes in the population increased from 2.7 percent in 1920 to 4.7 in 1930. This increase in the number and proportion of a social group in which the illegitimacy rate is relatively high may have had some discernible effect upon the number and proportion of births out of wedlock, although figures showing the ratio between white and Negro illegitimate births during this period are not available. At any rate, the failure of the illegitimate birth rate to decline during the period when the legitimate birth rate was declining indicates that the problem of the care of the illegitimate family by social agencies in New York City has not diminished but rather increased in relative importance during the years from 1922 to 1930.

It is important, too, to bear in mind that the official statistics almost certainly understate the real exent of illegitimacy in New York City. Evidence of this fact was had from the reports of social agencies received in the course of this survey. Statistical tables compiled from these reports and showing the number of illegitimate infants of which they had knowledge as having been born in New York City in 1930 will be presented and discussed at length in Part Three. But it seems well to indicate at this point that the number of illegitimate births for 1930 as compiled from these social agency records, is actually higher than was indicated by either the New York City Department of Health or the United States Bureau of the Census. From the records of individual illegitimate families furnished by the coöperating social agencies, it was found that specific information with regard to 1,610 illegitimate infants born in New York City in 1930 was on file with these agencies. From other organizations which could not furnish us all the information required by our schedule for individual illegitimate families we were able nevertheless to gain information as to their knowledge of 207 more illegitimate infants born in this city in 1930. The total number of 1,817 illegitimate births of which we thus gained direct knowledge from the records of social agencies must itself be considered an understatement as to the real extent of illegitimacy, according to the belief of social workers having direct contact with the illegitimate families. It is the opinion of many of these social workers, especially of the hospital social service workers, that even their records are inadequate in this respect because of the tendency of unmarried mothers to pose as married women until such time as their need for aid in the care and support of the child obliges them to reveal the true nature of their marital status to the agency to which they turn for help. Since this need for help may not make itself felt until several months after the birth of the child, it is evident that all of the illegitimate families having an infant born in 1930 may not have come to agencies' attention by the time that this survey was begun in the summer of 1931. It is probable, too, of course, that there were illegitimate families who so arranged their affairs that they had no need of an appeal to a social agency, and whose illegitimacy was not, therefore, registered in any records to which we had access. It should be remembered, too, that a few of the hospitals and social agencies having contact with the illegitimate family were unable to supply the statistical information asked for by this survey, and that the illegitimate families with which they may have had contact were not, therefore, included in our count. Confirmation of the belief that there were additional cases known to these agencies came from one Brooklyn agency, which was unable to furnish schedules regarding individual illegitimate families at the time that the study was made, but was able at a later date to furnish certain identifying items regarding such families. It was then learned that it had dealt with ninety-nine children known to have been born in New York City in 1930. Of these, thirty-nine had been born in institutions that did furnish schedules for this study. But of these a positive identification could be made for only eighteen. Of the sixty others born elsewhere in the city, only seven could be identified as having had contacts with agencies furnishing schedules. There is the possibility that seventy-one of these children were not counted in this census, and the probability that fifty-three of them were not so counted. This item and others of a similar nature which came to light in the course of the study gave certainty to the belief that by no means all of the illegitimate families having a child born in New York City came to the attention of this study through the agency records that could be used.

The extent of the difference between the official statistics and those compiled from social agency records can be seen from the summary (Table 3) of the different figures which we were able to obtain as to the extent of illegitimate births in New York City in 1930.

TABLE 3

*Number of Recorded Illegitimate Births in
New York City in 1930*

SOURCE	NUMBER RECORDED
United States Bureau of the Census	1,549
New York City Department of Health	1,470
New York City Social Agencies	1,817

It will be seen that this conservative figure of 1,817 derived from social agency records indicates a number of illegitimate births approximately 23.6 percent higher than the official statistics from the Health Department.

The fact that the official statistics do not include a large percentage of illegitimate births which occur does not mean that these births are not recorded at all. For only a negligible number of illegitimate births which were recorded by agencies furnishing data for this study occurred elsewhere than in hospitals which presumably report all births to the Department of Health. What does seem to have occurred is that an appreciable number of illegitimate births were either reported so as to appear or were assumed to be legitimate, and were so counted in the official statistics. Evidence to show that some hospitals report illegitimate births as legitimate was actually obtained, and such practices may be held to account in a measure for the difficulties presented by the statistics.

The value of all measures looking to the protection of the members of the illegitimate family from exposure and social stigma can readily be understood and appreciated. It can be seen, too, that such an effort to protect themselves on the part of the illegitimate parents renders the gathering and the recording of accurate information difficult. It should be recalled, however, that the studies conducted in other localities previously referred to have demonstrated the fact that the death rate among infants of illegitimate birth is much higher than the death rate among legitimate infants. It is also known that the care accorded some of those who survive is far from that which a child needs. In the interest of protecting the lives of these illegitimate infants, subject to such hazards, one might well ask whether some scheme could not be devised which would, while protecting all members of the illegitimate family from the inconvenience and embarrassment of having their legal status generally known, at the same time furnish a more adequate record to serve as the basis for special measures of protection of infant and child life. The practice reported of the omission of the illegitimate infants from the usual health follow-up during the first months of their lives, on the ground of wishing to avoid embarrassment to their mothers, operates further to deprive them of the protection of which they are especially in need, and raises the question of whether the incompatibility of protecting the infant's life with protecting the social status of the infant's mother is as real as it seems at first view.

A further conclusion that impresses itself upon the mind as these figures are reviewed is that even when there is allowance for a considerable expansion in the number of illegitimate births beyond the number officially reported, the rate for the city remains relatively low when compared with other large cities. It seems to indicate that conditions have not operated to produce a social problem of this nature disproportionate in size to that created by other groups requiring special aid and protection, and that the problem is one that is of distinctly manageable proportions.

Part Two

THE CARE OF THE ILLEGITIMATE FAMILY BY NEW YORK CITY SOCIAL AGENCIES

V

METHOD OF THE SURVEY OF
SOCIAL AGENCIES

IT is the purpose of this section of the report to enumerate the New York City social agencies which render service to the illegitimate family and to describe the type of care that they give. The description is based upon information received from eighty-seven different agencies and recorded on the agency schedule given in Appendix 1. The list of these agencies also appears in Appendix 5. Because of the widely varying programs of these agencies it was not possible to secure data with respect to all the many items of the schedule, and for this reason it was considered advisable in some instances for the staff members to adapt the form to the work of the agency by the omission of questions and by the addition of other items of more pertinent information not required by the schedule. In the case of forty-five agencies or departments of agencies there is further information recorded on individual case schedules.

Even so, it was not possible in all cases to secure a statistical statement as to the extent of the different types of services rendered by a given agency. In same cases the records and reports contained no items comparable to those required by our schedule and the data which had been chosen for recording had not been classified in such a way as to make reports comparable with those of other agencies. For this reason the statistical method of presentation has been infrequently resorted to in discussing the results obtained by the use of the agency schedule. The lack of congruity among the records and reports of the different agencies would have rendered any attempt at the assembling of the data on a statistical basis totally misleading, so the method of general description, illustrated by instances from the work of particular agencies, has been followed, in an attempt to give some idea of the kinds and the extent of the services rendered by New York social agencies to the illegitimate family.

Even the classification of the eighty-seven coöperating agencies on a functional basis was rendered difficult by the fact that some agencies have functions which would make it possible to classify them under several different headings. Some maternity homes, for example, serve also as hospitals, and in some few instances maternity homes or hospitals regularly engage in the work of child placement. An attempt at classification nevertheless has been made; when overlapping of functions has occurred, this has been indicated in the description.

The inclusion of an agency in this study does not imply that it is devoted exclusively to the care of the illegitimate family in New York City, but it does presuppose that the agency in question has had some contact with this problem, and that some aspect of service related to it is regarded as constituting an integral part of the agency's program. In this sense, for example, the social service departments of hospitals, both public and private, were considered as agencies forming the proper subject matter of this study, even though their contact with the illegitimate family was in many cases of a slight and cursory nature, and though in many instances the number of cases dealt with was very small.

Allowing for the duplication of functions and services above referred to, it may be of some interest to present at this point a general view of the number of those illegitimate families with children born in 1930 receiving some form of service or attention from the various types of agencies functioning for that purpose in New York City. According to data furnished by the forty-five hospitals and agencies that reported on individual cases, it was found that the largest number of such cases was known to the social service departments of hospitals: 949 to the social service departments of city hospitals, and 470 to the social service departments of private hospitals; and that 903 had received help from the homes for mothers and babies; 659 from the case work agencies specializing in the care of the illegitimate family; 480 from the child placement societies; 126 from the preventive and protective agencies; and 69 cases from the agencies and institutions of correction. Other agencies had smaller numbers of cases.

It should be noted that the total of the above enumeration is larger than the total number of illegitimate families mentioned in other sections of this report. This is due to the fact that some illegitimate families have received help from more than one agency, and so appear more than once in the service statistics. This distribution of cases is set forth as representative only of those agencies furnishing service data in the study.

The largest number of cases for any single grouping of agencies is that for the medical and health agencies, and a description of their work follows in Chapter VI.

VI

MEDICAL AND HEALTH AGENCIES

The City Hospitals

THE social service departments of the twelve city hospitals giving maternity care were visited to ascertain the nature and extent of the social services rendered to unmarried mothers and their infants. It was found that a number equivalent to about one-half of the unmarried mothers about whom we had schedule information included within this study had received maternity care in city hospitals and had been known to the social service departments of these institutions.

The data available for the study of this group of 949 unmarried mothers varied so much in nature and extent from one social service department to another that it was found difficult to arrive at any large number of conclusions for the year under consideration (1930). There was, among these institutions under the direction of the New York City Department of Hospitals, no general agreement at this time as to the items necessary to be included in the unmarried mother records, and the information actually secured showed a wide range of variation depending largely upon the judgment of the director of social service of each institution as to what facts it was necessary and desirable to have in order to deal effectively with the group under consideration. It is true, too, that to some extent this variability in the records can be explained by the difference in the social and racial groups within the separate areas in which these hospitals are situated. The records of one hospital social service department, however, contained no information as to the race or color of the unmarried mother or the decision made as to the future of the child. On the other hand, some service departments, such as that of Lincoln Hospital, had a complete family and social history of every unmarried mother coming to the attention of the department, together with a record of the care of the child during the first months of his life after leaving the hospital.

The emphasis placed upon the various items contained in the records and the care with which they were recorded varied also as between the different institutions. The records at Harlem Hospital, for example, gave particular attention to the question of whether or not the unmarried mother had attended a clinic before the birth of the child and to the physical condition of the mother and child upon leaving the hospital. Certain items in the social history had received special attention by other social service departments. Kings County Hospital, for example, gave special emphasis to information with regard to the putative father of the child and the attitude of the family of the unmarried mother toward her care and support, with a view to determining the plan for her future care. In the social service department of the Metropolitan Hospital the records had been arranged especially to show what plan had been made for the unmarried mother before her departure from the hospital.

The closeness with which the social service departments of the different city hospitals worked with the social agencies specializing in the care of the illegitimate family depended somewhat upon the history and equipment of each separate department. In some of the more recently organized departments, such as Morrisania, for example, all cases of young women giving birth to a child out of wedlock were referred immediately to an agency of the young woman's religious group specializing in the care of the illegitimate family. Other social service departments of longer history and more established traditions undertook, themselves, to handle questions arising out of illegitimate parenthood and to make plans for the future of the mother and her child. In such departments only those cases involving legal questions or other situations requiring a long period of investigation were referred to specialized agencies. Some departments expressed a marked reluctance to refer cases to private agencies because of their disapproval of the elaborate technique of case work investigation employed by these agencies and the belief that these procedures resulted in definite harm to the client both personally and in her standing in the community. Rather than resort to the help of a social agency, some departments preferred, therefore, to rely more largely upon the family of the client to make adjustments to the situation and to accept the unmarried mother and her child into the family; or, failing that, to make provision for them without any recourse to a social agency for advice and direction.

The emphasis upon the desirability of keeping the unmarried mother and her child together varied from one hospital social service department to another, according to the opinion of the social service worker as to the relative value of the different elements involved in the situation. In some hospitals the separation of mother and child was more readily agreed to than in others. One director of social service believed that there was a grave moral danger in allowing a young unmarried mother of low earning power to keep her child because of the high cost of his care during the first few years of his life, and the heavy demands thus made upon the young woman's financial resources. This social service director held, therefore, to the idea that the early separation of mother and child, and the placement of the latter for adoption, might prove in a large number of cases the wiser course to pursue. Other departments which were more reluctant to agree to a separation of mother and child did, nevertheless, regard the high cost of boarding care for infants as a most difficult element in the whole situation of adjusting the mother and child to community life, leading in many cases to discouragement on the part of the young woman and a decision to surrender the child after a few months of hardship and futile struggle to meet her obligations. One social worker of twenty years' experience was of the belief that the unmarried mother's struggle to support her child in the face of inadequate earnings and other obstacles had resulted, in no inconsiderable number of cases, in serious emotional strain and moral disorder.

The problem of the young woman who is a non-resident of New York City giving birth to an illegitimate child in a city hospital presents difficulties of considerable complexity to the social service departments. If such a young woman is unable to meet the cost to non-residents of maternity care in a city institution it becomes necessary for the fact to be reported to the State Board of Social Welfare in order that the latter may arrange for the removal of the young woman to her place of legal residence. Pending such action the young woman may be cared for at the institution where she has given birth to her child. The social service worker, in the meantime, may communicate with the family or friends of the young woman and arrange, when possible, to have her placed under the supervision of some social agency at the place of her legal residence. Some of these non-resident young women included in the study had come to the city only a short time before the birth of the child with the hope of concealing their situation from family and friends. Still others had come to the city to work and had found themselves in difficulties before they had legally established themselves as residents of New York City.

One director of social service complained that the situation was complicated, in the area served by her hospital, by the practice which certain families had of inserting advertisements for domestic help in the newspapers of rural or semi-rural districts. Young women coming to the city in response to such appeals had come to the attention of the social service department at this hospital during the time when they were receiving maternity care at the hospital, and their removal to the place of their legal residence had had to be arranged. The settlement of these cases, as well as of others where the young women were engaged in domestic service, was sometimes complicated by the interference of the employer, who wished to obtain the return of the young woman to her place of employment. In some instances an arrangement had been reached between the employer and the young woman to the effect that the latter should be continued in her occupation until the birth of the child, with the understanding that the young woman should return to her situation as soon thereafter as possible. Such an agreement involved in many cases the promise of the separation of mother and child or the promise on the part of the employer that she would use all her influence with the hospital to secure through the proper authorities the commitment of the child soon after his birth. Such intervention by the employer was in many cases a serious hindrance to any plan for the adjustment of the unmarried mother to the situation when separation from her child seemed inadvisable.

All directors of social service insisted that their records furnish evidence that the official birth statistics give but an incomplete picture of the real extent of illegitimacy. Some unmarried mothers register as married women and the deception may not be detected at once. That this is true is attested by the fact that a not inconsiderable number of supposedly married women return to the hospital some time after their dismissal to ask advice regarding the care or placement of the infant because they have found the matter of his support too difficult to arrange. That this may explain to some extent the low rate of illegitimacy as a whole in New York City is evident.

On the whole it may be said, then, that the records of the social service departments of the hospitals under the supervision of the New York City Department of Hospitals showed such a wide diversity of method and treatment, and even of policy, with reference to the unmarried mother that few generalizations as to the type of care given can be made. If the city is to have a program, there is an outstanding need for some common system of record keeping and for the definition of some few policies of a general nature to determine the main lines of action to be taken.

Private Hospitals

Twenty-seven private hospitals giving maternity care in New York City were visited during the course of the survey in order to ascertain the amount and the types of services rendered unmarried mothers by the social service departments of these institutions. A total of 470 cases had been known to these departments. Most of them reported very few cases, but a few had considerable numbers; the largest number reported from one institution was 166 such cases in 1930.

A variety of responses to the points raised by our questionnaire was received. Some private hospitals do not receive unmarried mothers for care if it is known that they are unmarried. This limitation on admission is not intended as a discrimination against the unmarried mother, but is due to the fact that these hospitals recognize that they are not prepared to render certain special types of services which the unmarried mother would in many instances require, and judge therefore that it is more expedient to refer them elsewhere. The far greater number of private hospitals receive unmarried mothers for maternity care on the same basis that they receive the married mother. When this attitude prevails the case of the unmarried mother receives the same medical care and attention as that of the married mother, and no special notice is taken of her personal and family relationship unless she specifically requests it. In cases in which she makes no such request, she is not referred to the social service department, and there is, of course, no social record of her case.

If an unmarried mother, however, is unable to pay her expenses, or if she manifests anxiety as to her ability to care for her child upon leaving the hospital, she may be referred by some member of the medical staff to the social service department. In some hospitals a reduction of the fee ordinarily charged can be arranged by the social service department if the circumstances seem to call for it; but unless the unmarried mother is referred by a member of the medical staff for some specific service, the social service department has no knowledge of her presence in the hospital or of what arrangements she may make for the care of her child upon leaving. Instances were found of members of the medical staff who attempted to aid their patients in questions of a social nature, and gave advice as to the placement of a child, boarding homes, opportunities for employment, and other matters of a similar importance. In other institutions the medical staff appeared to give whole-hearted coöperation to the social service department, manifesting an entire willingness to leave to the latter those matters coming logically within their province.

The types of services rendered to unmarried mothers by the social service departments in the private hospitals varied as greatly as did the services rendered by the public hospitals. In the case of some departments the usual procedure was to refer the young woman immediately to an agency of her particular religious group specializing in the care of the illegitimate family. Other hospital social service departments attempted to handle for themselves all questions growing out of the situation of illegitimate parenthood, giving advice as to the separation of mother and child, the adjustment of family relationships, and other matters connected with each individual case. Still other hospital social departments, which were not equipped for dealing with the unmarried mothers on a case work basis, did, nevertheless, attempt to render some service by supplying when needed, as a means of meeting temporarily a need for relief, clothes for the mother and infant, or money in small sums. In many cases where such services were rendered by the hospital social service department, the aid given was considered sufficient, and the young woman was not referred to a case work agency unless she asked explicitly to be so referred.

Two or three social service departments in private hospitals were found in which the staffs were unaware, because of their newness to the work, of existing facilities for the care of unmarried mothers by specialized agencies. They were attempting, under great difficulties, to deal with the cases.

It was observed that in some instances the reference of a young woman to a social agency for help was not decided upon until she was on the point of leaving the hospital with her child. At the time when friends or relatives called for her she was furnished with a card bearing the name and address of an agency to which she might later turn if in need of assistance. A check-up of the records reveals the fact that a large percentage of these young women did not avail themselves of the information furnished them. It is not known whether their disappearance from the scene was due to their failure to understand the steps necessary to be taken, or to their success in making, with the aid of family and friends, a satisfactory adjustment of their personal relationships, or whether they had made some highly unsatisfactory arrangement. No agency, either public or private, knew what arrangements had been made for the care of the child in such cases, or whether his health and legal rights had been properly safeguarded. Other hospital social service departments adopted the more practical policy of arranging a meeting between a representative of the agency and the young woman, while the latter was still a patient in the hospital, in order that there might be no failure to understand what types of assistance were available for her in making plans for her own future and that of her child.

Records varied greatly as to the amount and accuracy of the

information they contained. In a few of the hospitals where the department of social service had developed its work to a high standard of service and efficiency, complete records were regarded as of fundamental importance in any sincere attempt to be of aid to the illegitimate family, and much attention was given to the kind and amount of information which they should contain. In the case of other hospitals where the activities of the social service departments were limited to such matters as deciding the cost of care, the giving of small sums for relief, the presentation of Christmas baskets, friendly visits in the ward and similar work, the keeping of records was considered of no importance. One director of social service declared that she considered records unnecessary to good work and their requirement an unfair imposition upon busy people. Other social service departments, while recognizing the importance of records to effective work, were nevertheless unable to keep them because of the pressure of other duties.

A number of social service departments in private hospitals gave testimony as to effective aid rendered them by auxiliary committees of women who give support and advice in connection with the work of the department. These committees, in many cases, held monthly meetings to discuss ways and means to be of service, and, aside from the substantial material aid contributed, were of value in formulating the policies of the department and in making its work understood. In some cases members were able to give some of their time to taking an active part in the program of work, and in a still larger number of cases opportunities for the employment of unmarried mothers were found through the help of the committee. Clothing for mothers and infants was provided in many cases, as well as carfare and small sums for temporary relief.

There was some evidence that unmarried mothers or their families had been exploited in making financial arrangements simply because they were not familiar with the types of service available for them. In one instance, which came to our attention through a specialized agency to which the case had been referred, a young foreign girl unfamiliar with the facilities available was led to pay a fee for her maternity care and medical attendance far above the customary payment, and, when her savings were exhausted, was referred by the institution in question to an agency, for the purpose of receiving charitable assistance. In another case cited by an agency, the father of a young unmarried mother was induced by a physician to pay a supplementary fee of one thousand dollars in order that the strictest privacy might be observed, and received in return for the fee no other service than an introduction to a specialized agency. Needless to say, such instances did not occur in carefully supervised institutions, but the possibility of their occurrence, in circumstances where there are no policies of treatment, and no person or persons whose duty it is to represent the interests of the unmarried mother and her child, is evident.

Some of the private hospitals received the young women for a period of care preceding the birth of the child, but in the greater number of cases the customary period of care was from ten to fourteen days. Care before the birth of the child was given through a clinic, as was the follow-up work after the discharge of the unmarried mother from the hospital. A return to the clinic for the examination of mother and child was said to be more difficult to obtain in the case of the unmarried than of the married mother, because of the desire for secrecy, and for this reason a special follow-up in the interest of the health of the child was found to be necessary. In some instances young women had made application to prenatal clinics in the hope of being able to have an abortion performed, and when this was found to be impossible disappeared from view. The follow-up of these cases is obviously necessary, but in the press of other duties many hospital social service departments are unable to do so, and still others consider that it is not within their province to do so.

In general, it may be said that among the private hospitals in

New York City giving service to unmarried mothers, of which a large proportion were covered by this study, there was not found any set of policies or practices which might be said to be common to the group. The social work done with the unmarried mother was seen to vary according to the attitude and wishes of the management of each individual institution, and showed a range varying all the way from a helpful and understanding case work approach to a complete indifference to the social and family situation of the unmarried mother.

Other Medical and Health Agencies

In addition to the hospitals, other health agencies offering some form of maternity service were visited. The contacts of these associations with the illegitimate family appeared to be less frequent than those of the hospitals offering maternity service, because of the nature of the problems arising out of the family and social situation. One maternity clinic offering home service stated that, while it makes no discrimination against unmarried mothers, it prefers, nevertheless, not to assume responsibility for their care, because of the difficulty of the social problems which arise. It was pointed out by the workers in charge that the unmarried mother is frequently living separated from her family and friends in a furnished room or a hotel, and that the giving of home maternity care in such cases was not to be considered. Nevertheless, the agency in question had given home service to five unmarried mothers coming within the scope of this study; whose infants, that is, were born in New York City within the year 1930. Of these unmarried mothers all were young Negro girls living at home, whose parents or relatives were willing to accept the responsibility for their care and who could therefore be reasonably classed within the group for which the agency was prepared to care. On the other hand, young women living apart from their families were referred to agencies of their particular religious group prepared to give them shelter, or at least to assume the responsibility for their supervision until such time as some permanent arrangements for the future could be made.

Another agency offering maternity care through a clinic service and confinement care in the home reported some contacts with unmarried mothers in the course of its work. These contacts, which numbered about ten during the course of the year under consideration, were largely with out-of-town young women who had come to the city for maternity care with the hope of concealment from family and friends. These young women were, more often than not, able to pay for the services for which they were asking, and were thought to need nothing more than medical care and a kindly sympathetic interest during the prenatal period. It was the policy of this agency to refer the young women to one or other of the private hospitals for maternity care without resorting to any agency specializing in the social case work with unmarried mothers. It was the belief of this health agency that the so-called "higher type" of young woman did not receive the care suitable to her needs at these agencies, and that she had little to gain from their supervision. It was, however, the practice of this agency to refer the young woman to one of the child placement societies upon her departure from the hospital, taking special precaution that the strictest possible secrecy be maintained and that the investigations be limited to the minimum.

The other health agencies visited, while reporting some contacts with illegitimate families, had not been willing, nevertheless, to assume responsibility for their family and social problems, but had consistently referred them to social agencies for the adjustment of difficulties growing out of their social situation, and had assumed for the health problems of.these families only such an interest as circumstances seemed to indicate as advisable. This unwillingness of persons specializing in health work to assume responsibility for the social problems of their clients seemed general among persons engaged in health work, although their understanding of and their attitude toward the types of social service work being offered determined very greatly the agency to which the unmarried mother applying to them for maternity care was referred. Many of the nurses in these agencies were of the opinion that an early separation of mother and child was advisable and urged upon their patients an immediate resort to a child placement agency. There were others who inclined to the opposite view and were disposed to refer their clients to agencies accustomed to follow another course in the solution of these difficulties. In making such references to social agencies there seemed to be no policy more general than the personal reaction of the person in charge of the case, or her supervisor, to determine what type of advice the young woman in question should receive.

The Element of Secrecy

A widely prevalent belief among all the hospital and health agencies visited for this study was that the strictest possible secrecy should be observed with reference to the fact of illegitimacy, in order to protect the unmarried mother from social censure. This desire to maintain secrecy at all costs seemed to lead to an unwillingness on the part of certain of these agencies to encourage or even to allow the unmarried mother to initiate proceedings to establish paternity or to put any pressure on the father to support his child. This failure to establish paternity in turn had necessitated in some cases the separation of the mother from her child, because of the heavy financial burden of his support. It is believed that this attitude precludes the building up of any humane public interest in the child or its mother. It also cuts directly across existing family ties. It leads in some instances to the separation of a young unmarried mother from her own parents and her brothers and sisters, at a time when she has the greatest need of their advice and protection.

A case which came within the scope of this study was that of a young woman, still a minor, who appealed to a hospital social service worker for protection before the birth of her child. Provision for her care was made, and, since she was unwilling that her parents be informed, they were led to believe that she had found temporary employment in another state. The forwarding of her mail from that address was arranged by the social service worker through the coöperation of a friend. The child, born in the institution, was separated from his mother soon after his birth and placed with an agency for adoption. The young woman, who had thus passed a period of several months in the same city with her parents, returned to them as though coming from her place of employment, and resumed her accustomed place in the family.

This usurpation of parental rights by the staff workers in these medical and health agencies is justified by them on the ground that the parents of the unmarried mother might be guilty of an unreasonable severity toward her, if aware of her illegitimate motherhood. The elaborate schemes to deceive parents of young unmarried mothers into which some of these staff workers enter appear to them to be a necessary part of the protection of the unmarried mother from vindictive prejudice and blame. It was admitted by some of those interviewed, however, that some parents from whom an attitude of unreasonable anger and prejudice had been expected did often, after the first shock had passed, show a disposition to protect the daughter, and this attitude of protectiveness had even extended to the illegitimate child himself.

It should be noted that an analysis of case records included in this study shows that few of those workers who had been willing to assume the responsibilities of parents by aiding the young unmarried mother to deceive her natural guardians had been able, because of their multifarious duties, carefully to fulfill the duties which they had so obligingly assumed.

This preoccupation with secrecy as the most important element in the situation is sometimes accompanied, too, by the separation of the illegitimate child from his mother so soon after birth as to endanger his life. This early separation often leads, as some of those workers themselves attest, to profound sorrow and regret on the part of the unmarried mother and in some cases to emotional disturbances of such a nature as to require special care. It is said to be not altogether unusual for the unmarried mother, having surrendered her child in the period of anxiety, fear, and physical depletion immediately following his birth, to return later, when her physical and social and economic condition has improved, in a frantic but futile attempt to reclaim him.

The emphasis upon secrecy insisted upon by these agencies has not infrequently led to the undoing of the work of one agency by another, as cases coming within the scope of this study clearly show. A long series of investigations and efforts at constructive case work on the part of one agency were nullified by another which accepted the case without the knowledge that the first agency has been interested. One young unmarried mother, who had had her fare to New York City from another state paid by the agency to which the hospital had referred her, which had in mind the surrender of her child for adoption, refused upon her arrival to give up the child. Instead, she made application for the surrender of her child to another agency, while at the same time making appeal to still a third agency for help in keeping her child with her. It was evident, too, from our study of cases, that important items as to heredity, financial condition, and family situation which were known to one agency were neglected by another in making a final decision on the case, simply because the second agency had been so intent upon maintaining secrecy that it had not been willing to consult with the first agency having to do with the case.

It is generally agreed that much of the secrecy surrounding

the illegitimate family at the present time must be maintained. It is often asked, however, whether this need for secrecy should be construed in such a way as to deprive the natural guardians of the young unmarried mother, who presumably are as interested as she is in protection from gossip and publicity, of all opportunity to sustain and advise her at this important crisis in her life. The question also arises: might not the confidential exchange of information between agencies having to do with the unmarried mother lead to more effective work, without in any way exposing the members of the illegitimate family to any danger of having their situation become generally known?

Child Placement by Hospitals

In several instances the social service departments of hospitals and other health agencies stated that they placed children born in their hospitals for adoption. One hospital social service department had placed six children for adoption in 1930, and several other departments stated that they had placed one, two, or three children for adoption in that year. In all we had knowledge that seventeen children coming within the scope of this study had been placed by medical and health agencies in family homes with a view to adoption. In almost every instance the worker responsible for the placement had been careful to warn the parties to the proceeding to secure legal counsel in order that the formalities of the law might be duly observed.

Records of the parentage of the child to be placed for adoption and of the economic and social status of the foster parents in such cases were scant or altogether lacking. One social service worker who had placed two children for adoption during 1930 declared that she had kept no records whatsoever of the cases and that not even her associates in the work of the department knew what steps had been taken. It was the belief of this worker that all such matters as adoption should be regarded as strictly confidential, and that no follow-up work was necessary, if proper care had been taken in the beginning to see to it that the foster parents were suitable guardians for the infant to be placed in their charge.

It was evident that this work of child placement by unauthorized persons was taking place because of the total ignorance of the legal limitations upon such a proceeding and that the persons engaging in the work had had no end in view but to render service. This view was confirmed by the fact that other social service workers, who were aware of these legal limitations and who refused absolutely to place children for adoption, did nevertheless state that they received some requests for infants by persons uninformed as to the steps necessary to be taken in order to obtain a child for adoption. It was stated that persons wishing to adopt a child would not infrequently make appeal directly to the hospital social service departments or to some member of the medical staff. Such requests when made to a physician were sometimes transmitted to the social service workers in the hope that the latter might be able to render service.

Separations of mother and child in the case of placements by hospital workers were made early, most frequently upon the dismissal of the unmarried mother from the hospital at the end of a ten-day period. Because of the pressure of work in the social service departments, there had apparently been little or no occasion to follow up the case to ascertain how the child was faring in the foster home or what adjustment to social life the unmarried mother had been able to make.

The Recommendation of Cases to Specialized Agencies

Those who believe that the high death rate among infants born out of wedlock, the many instances of inadequate care accorded those who survive, and the mental and physical strain on the mothers make it imperative that special measures should be taken to safeguard the welfare of the mothers and children urge that social workers in hospitals should in all cases refer unmarried mothers and their children to agencies that can advise and direct them during the period when they are readjusting themselves to community life. Hospital and health workers were found to differ greatly in their views as to the desirability of this step. Some hold any "interference" by another social agency to be undesirable and unjustifiable in the cases where the unmarried mother declares herself to be capable of managing her own affairs. Others who admit that some supervision is desirable, in the interest of protecting the life of the child, declare that they refer an unmarried mother to a social agency only as a last resort. On the whole, therefore, it should be said that hospital social service records reveal diverse practices with regard to the recommendation of unmarried mothers to private social agencies: some hospital social service departments refer their cases; some refer only the more difficult cases; and some departments attempt to handle for themselves all the cases of unmarried mothers coming to their attention, except those where some legal point involved demands the reference of the case to another agency.

This failure to refer any cases on the part of some may be due, to a great extent, to the failure of the specialized agencies as a group or groups to arrive at any agreement as to fundamental principles in the course of action to be followed. Some agencies, for example, make the separation of the child from its mother at an early age an easy matter; others urge that the mother and child should be kept together for at least a minimum period. Some agencies believe that the closest secrecy should be observed in safeguarding the interests of the unmarried mother and that she should even be aided, if necessary, in deceiving her own parents; other agencies believe that the parents of the young woman should be informed and invited to coöperate in making plans for her future. This lack of agreement as to general principles to be followed is puzzling to staff workers in hospitals and health agencies, and leads to a general distrust of the specialized agencies.

The question of the amount of investigation necessary before determining a course of action in a particular case also arouses much discussion. Some agencies that have elaborated the case work approach hold that a thorough investigation of the young woman's family and social situation is necessary in order to determine what factors may have contributed to her illegitimate parenthood and are likely to affect her chances of success in adjusting herself to the requirements of the future. Other workers hold that these investigations should be limited to a minimum in order not to compromise the standing of the young woman in the community and make her readjustment to normal social life more difficult. These latter hold that even when investigations are conducted with all care and prudence there nevertheless results for the young woman much difficulty and embarrassment; that the elaborateness of the case work method is unnecessary in view of present conditions; and that a simpler adjustment to community life is possible when the necessary material aid is given without an elaborate course of investigation and diagnosis of causes.

Whatever may be the merits of the contrary views, it is evident that the failure of the agencies to understand each other and to agree upon at least a few general principles of action is hindering their effective coöperation. Such coöperation is of first importance in protecting the interests of a group of persons whose chances for survival and normal development are hindered by the very circumstances of their birth. As a consequence, a large group of young women leave the hospitals after the birth of an illegitimate child; and no further knowledge is had as to whether the child survives his infancy and what his subsequent history may be. The importance of this fact will be realized when it is called to mind that the first contact of the majority of unmarried mothers is with a health agency, usually the maternity department of a hospital, and that if these hospitals fail to refer them to specialized social agencies the chances of their seeking such help at a later period are greatly diminished.

VII

THE HOMES FOR MOTHERS AND BABIES

Twelve institutions, in New York City and the vicinity, classified as homes for mothers and infants, were visited. In all these were found mothers who had given birth to a child out of wedlock in New York City in the year 1930, and for that reason they were included in the study. Although the records were in many cases incomplete, we were able nevertheless to obtain some information as to 903 young women, subjects of this study, who had received care in these institutions for periods varying from two or three days to two years. Among these 903 unmarried mothers were a number who had also received some help from hospital social service departments, from specialized case work agencies, and from other agencies in the city offering help to the illegitimate family. Because of the brevity of the records we were not able to find out in every case through what agencies these young women had found their way to the homes, but in the greater number of cases where there was record of this point the recommendations had been from the social service departments of hospitals. This indicates, as do other facts in the study, that the young women had usually made their first appeal for help to medical and health agencies. While in some of these institutions the records contained a full account of the social, occupational, and medical history, in other cases references to such points were omitted altogether, and even such facts as the date of entry and departure of the young woman had not been noted. For example, in one home, records were limited to such entries as: "July 16. Mary Jones received with infant. Very untidy. Bad temper. Left." In such cases the institution had apparently limited its program to providing care and supervision for the young woman while she was in residence, leaving all questions of occupational and social adjustment to the referring agency.

The variations in type of program of these homes for mothers and babies can best be seen, perhaps, from the length of time which the unmarried mother is allowed or is expected to remain. Some of the institutions are avowedly "shelters" in type; that is, they offer to the unmarried mother or to the expectant mother who is in need of emergency care for a few days a place to stay while she arranges a more permanent program under the direction of a social work agency. These shelters as a rule attempt nothing more than the temporary physical care of the young women who come to them, although there was evidence in every case to show that the workers in charge took care to see to it that the few young women who were not already under the direction of a social agency were referred to those best able to give them the care of which they had need. Still other homes, which offer care of a more prolonged nature, were nevertheless willing to receive for a period of short duration those unmarried mothers for whom the agencies had need of a temporary shelter while more permanent arrangements were being made.

Although it is evident that the work of shelters is limited in scope and quality, the necessity for their maintenance was insisted upon by the social agencies expressing an opinion on the subject. It was pointed out that young women not infrequently appeal for help at the moment when their resources are exhausted and when they have need of immediate assistance. Many such cases can be arranged for in a more satisfactory way after the lapse of a few days, when family relationships have been adjusted or when a suitable boarding home for the young woman has been found. Pending such arrangements, however, the providing of shelter for an unmarried mother, with or without her child, seems generally recognized as forming an essential part of the present system of protection and care.

Such temporary shelter, however, while recognized as a necessary part of the program of care for some unmarried mothers, is not the end for which most of these institutions have been established. Most of them are committed to a program of care and reëducation for unmarried mothers extending over a period of time more or less prolonged. One institution, for example, refuses to accept an unmarried mother for care if she will not sign an agreement to remain for a period of one year. Another institution caring for unmarried mothers requires a minimum period of residence of three months. Still another institution requires a period of residence of three months unless the young woman is able to pay a stipulated sum for her care.

In more than one instance it was found that young women who were not able to meet the expense of their care were required to pass a longer period in the institution than those who could pay for their maintenance. The reasons for this seeming discrimination are obvious. None of these institutions have any legal hold upon the young women who come to them for care. They have not been committed to these institutions by the courts, like the unmarried mothers in correctional institutions, described in another section of this report, but they have come voluntarily to ask assistance, or else have been sent through the good offices of another agency to which they have made such application. If, therefore, the young woman resident at a home for mothers and babies is not content with the treatment which she is receiving, she is technically at liberty to depart. If, however, she is in destitute circumstances when she makes appeal for help, and if she has no money with which to meet the situation, she may be required, as a condition of her admission, to sign an agreement to remain in the institution for a given period of care and to reimburse the institution for the expense of her care by services rendered during that time. Even in cases where the unmarried mother is not required to work in the institution to repay the cost of her care, she may nevertheless be required to sign an agreement to remain for a stated period and to abide by the regulations. It is obviously easier to require this prolonged residence from the young woman who cannot meet her expenses than from the young woman who is in a more independent position financially, and over whom, therefore, the institution is without power to exercise compulsion. One case was cited in the making of this survey of an expectant mother who presented herself for free care at a maternity home, but, upon learning that her acceptance would entail a sojourn of three months, refused to remain. She returned after a few days with the fee ordinarily required for care in such cases, but firmly refused to come to terms with the director of the home until it was understood that no compulsion would be exercised to induce her to remain longer than the exigencies of her physical state required.

The problem of the young woman who can pay for her care is not of frequent occurrence, however, for such young women do not as a rule present themselves for care at these institutions demanding a prolonged residence. The most frequently occurring case is that of the young woman without resources and in need of immediate help, unable or unwilling to receive help from relatives and friends, and amenable, therefore, to whatever terms the institution may ask of her.

It is believed by the institutions which require a prolonged period of residence that such a course is necessary to any satisfactory adjustment of the questions growing out of illegitimate parenthood and to the rendering of effective service. It is pointed out in the first case that the physical welfare of the infant requires that he not be separated from his mother during the early months of his life. When the mother is in destitute circumstances, a continued period of residence in an institution is regarded as a practical method of assuring that she will keep her child with her during the nursing period. Requiring several months' stay in the institution by mother and child is one of the methods suggested for lowering the mortality rate of illegitimate babies. It is pointed out in justification of the residence requirement that the unmarried mother who is without financial resources would almost certainly be obliged to seek employment upon leaving the institution, and that this would involve, in the majority of cases, separation from her child, with consequent lessening of his chances of survival. It is believed, too, that the unmarried mother who has been under financial strain should be relieved of such preoccupations during a reasonably prolonged period, while she recovers her physical strength and has the quiet and leisure in which to decide upon the course of action which she wishes to pursue with reference to her child.

It has often been pointed out by those connected with maternity homes that young unmarried mothers who at first were eager to surrender their infants for adoption find themselves, after a few weeks' association with the child, of a contrary opinion and grateful to those who have made such a period of reflection possible. These workers have seen instances when a hasty decision as to the separation of mother and child has resulted in much unhappiness for the young woman and fruitless efforts on her part to recover possession of the child. Moreover, it is said, in further justification of the residence requirement, that the successful readjustment of the unmarried mother to normal social life requires a period of preparation continuing for weeks or even months, and presupposes such preliminary steps as the adjustment of family relations, the finding of suitable employment for the mother, the legal establishment of the paternity of the child, and other important moves requiring that shelter and maintenance be provided for the mother and child.

Those who, on the other hand, are less inclined to regard the detention of an unmarried mother in a maternity home for a period of three or four months as a prerequisite to good care point to disadvantages connected with such a procedure. Many

social agencies are disinclined to make use of the homes for
mothers and babies requiring a long period of care, because
they believe that the prolonged absence of a young woman
from the contacts of normal family or social life may be detrimental rather than helpful to her chances for a successful readjustment. It is further stated that the withdrawal from family
and social ties of these young women involves their segregation
and close association during the period when they are under
the care of the institution, and that these conditions permit the
exchange of confidences and the forming of new and dubious
friendships, comparable to those formed in institutions of correction, with effects for the individual equally harmful. It was
suggested by some social workers that the development of
supervised boarding homes for those unmarried mothers who
are without shelter would prove a suitable substitute for institutional care, and would offer a more normal and wholesome
environment than that now afforded by institutions specializing in the care of the unmarried mother.

Many other workers in this field, who were not opposed to
the use of institutions, stated, nevertheless, that they could not
give their approval to the fixed requiremens of these institutions with regard to periods of residence on the part of unmarried mothers. They pointed out, in support of this view, that a
period of three or four months' residence in an institution
might be desirable in the case of some young women, but might
also be distinctly harmful and undesirable in the case of others.
These social workers, while recognizing the need filled by these
institutions in the program of care for the unmarried mother,
insisted nevertheless that the lead of some of the more progressive institutions, which have attempted to adjust the length of
the period of residence of the unmarried mother to her particular case, rather than to require a stated period of residence
of all those coming to the institution, might be followed. It
should be pointed out that some of the institutions criticized

have already rendered their requirements of residence more flexible to meet the need of their clientèle, and that in some instances no rigid requirement as to length of residence is enforced.

There is a tendency in certain organizations, however, to detain the younger unmarried mothers for the more prolonged period of care and reëducation, while the "shelter" facilities of only a few days' duration are offered to the second offenders and to the older women who are presumably less capable of profiting by the educational facilities of the institutions requiring a longer period of residence. For example, the Shelter for Jewish Women (since discontinued) was found to devote itself to the service of the older and more experienced women of this group, while the young unmarried mothers were sent to Lakeview, where the most adequate and modern facilities for the study, the care, and the reëducation of the unmarried mother exist. In other sectarian groups, a tendency to a like specialization in the care of the unmarried mother begins to be manifest in the increased emphasis on the case work approach and the need for individualized treatment.

Much comment was received upon the program of reëducation which is offered by these institutions. At the above-mentioned Lakeview Home, the usual grade and vocational subjects are taught by teachers assigned by the Board of Education, and credit may be obtained upon a continuation school basis. In addition to this course, special subjects, such as child care, the domestic sciences and arts, stenography, typing, and office work, are taught. Not all of the other institutions manifested such breadth of outlook, and the training of the unmarried mothers who were detained in some of them was limited to practice in laundry work and household duties, with the formal school subjects omitted altogether. In one institution, which required a relatively long period of residence of young unmarried mothers, no training except religious instruction and practice in housework and child care was offered. Some few instances were found where it appeared that the work requirements of the unmarried mothers were graduated to the needs of the institution rather than to the individual needs and abilities of the unmarried mothers. In these institutions, as a consequence, results detrimental to the mental and physical health of the inmates could be noted.

In addition to the program of formal education, the general atmosphere and surroundings of the institutions in which the young women receive care was admitted to be of the utmost importance in determining the value of their residence there. In some of the more progressive institutions efforts were made to maintain a congenial home atmosphere with as little evidence of constraint and institutional discipline as was consistent with the proper maintenance of the home. In one instance a well-chosen collection of books suitable to the needs and tastes of the young women was at their disposal, as well as a radio, a victrola, and a piano for use during the evening recrea tion. The young women were allowed some liberty in the choice of their leisure-time activities, and a general atmosphere of freedom and contentment prevailed. The program of activities of each young woman was carefully prepared after a consultation between the director of the home and the house physician, in order that the health, both mental and physical, of the young woman might be properly safeguarded. On the other hand, an institution of similar aim and purpose conducted under different auspices appeared to have overlooked almost altogether the recreational needs of those coming under its care. The young women concerned were kept busy at manual employment according to their strength throughout the entire course of the day, and the only diversion from their round of employment was the period of religious instruction under some member of the staff. The few books and magazines which existed in the home were exclusively of a religious nature. The

receiving by the young women of visitors, even of social workers with whom they had had previous acquaintance, was discouraged, and every effort was apparently made so to insulate
the inmates from all outside contacts that the system of instruction and discipline fostered by the institution would operate
unobstructed. It was on the basis of such practices that some of
the more vigorous protests against the maternity homes were
voiced by those social workers who had been dissatisfied with
their use. It was the contention of these workers that it was
detrimental to the mental health of this group of young wom-
en, who had in many cases been accustomed to a life of great
personal liberty and freedom from restraint, to subject them
suddenly to a régime of discipline and routine during the
period when they appeared to have need of the greatest personal consideration and the comfort and support of their
friends.

The use of the religious influence as a means of reëducation
and character training was generally recognized. The fact that
most of the institutions for the care of the unmarried mother
have been established and conducted under religious auspices
of a sectarian nature is sufficient to explain this. In general an
effort was made to respect the traditional religious affiliations
of the young women, but one or two instances came to light in
which such considerations were disregarded, and efforts were
made to effect a new alignment of religious interests in spite of
repeated protests from the young women concerned. Such a
procedure, however, seemed not to be a part of the general
policy of these institutions, but a result of the particular prejudices of those in immediate authority over the young women.
Complaints were made by many social workers that aside
from questions of the particular affiliations of the unmarried
mothers under the care of these institutions, there had been in
some cases a forcing of the religious interest without due regard
to their disposition and state of mind. It was complained, too,

that this constraint in the field of religion had been accompanied in some institutions by a neglect of the natural and normal recreational needs of those who had been obliged to seek shelter there.

The relation of homes for mothers and babies to other agencies having to do with the illegitimate family appeared not to be clearly delineated, except in the case of those sectarian societies in which all of the social work agencies were well coördinated under a single control. In such cases the functions of the various agencies having to do with the unmarried mother were defined, and the coördination of these agencies under a single direction assured a harmonious and profitable division of labor. When agencies outside of these coördinated groups are obliged to make use of institutions for unmarried mothers conducted under other auspices than their own, they have evidently found it difficult to work out a satisfactory basis of understanding. For example, as was mentioned above, some of the institutions caring for the unmarried mother are reluctant to admit representatives of another agency for conferences with the young women, because of a fear that such an influence from the outside might lessen the control which they believe the institution must have over its inmates. The question might also arise, and there was evidence from the reading of many case records that it does arise in many instances, as to whose direction a young unmarried mother should follow, if she has been referred for care by a case work agency to an institution operating under different auspices and if there should develop a difference of opinion between the two organizations as to the wisest course to pursue.

There was the case, for example, of a young woman referred by a hospital social service department to a case work agency. After a thorough investigation, and a number of conferences between client and worker, it was decided between them that the young woman should keep the custody of her child, and that she should go for a short time to an institution where she could receive care with her child while more permanent plans for her future were being made by this case work agency. The young woman, however, while under the care of the institution where she had been sent, was so moved by the insistence of those under whose immediate authority she was that she began to take steps for the surrender of her child at the same time that the agency which had sent her there was proceeding with the original plan. The difficulty of arriving at any consistent course of procedure under such circumstances appears to be great. The need for the acceptance of a plan of coöperation between the agencies not conducted under the same auspices is, therefore, evident.

It was the general consensus of opinion among social workers interviewed on the subject that homes for mothers and their infants should have no connection with adoption societies, either directly through the management or through the board of directors in such a way that the policy of the one would be affected by the needs and necessities of the other. Such comments were occasioned by complaints against a maternity home where it was said that influence had been brought to bear upon the inmates, by members of the management who were also connected with an adoption society, to surrender their infants for adoption. It was argued by those who commented upon the situation that the desirability of placing infants in childless homes applying for infants to adopt should not be allowed to enter into the decision as to whether a particular mother should give up her child for adoption; and that this disinterested decision was rendered more difficult by any overlapping of management between the maternity homes and the adoption societies.

Many social workers interviewed in the course of this survey gave voice to the opinion that there should be larger facilities for the care of the illegitimate child in institutions which permit the mother to return to him in the evening after her hours of work: that is, an extension of the same type of facilities formerly offered by the Washington Square Home. In order to ascertain whether or not there was a demand for this type of care a number of day nurseries were visited to see whether unmarried mothers were availing themselves of the services offered by these institutions, and whether or not the type of care offered by the day nursery might be regarded as a suitable substitute for the type of care which these social workers believed to be in demand. It was found after a survey of nine day nurseries that unmarried mothers were indeed making some use of the facilities offered. The number of illegitimate children in proportion to the total number of children cared for was in every case small, but there was ample evidence that this type of care had been resorted to by some unmarried mothers who were making their adjustments to community life unaided. Social workers connected with the day nurseries, however, were of the opinion that the care of the illegitimate by the day nursery offers so many difficulties as to render its general use inadvisable. It was pointed out that the unmarried mother, if she lives separated from her family, is not likely to have a place suitably equipped for the care of her child when she takes him home in the evening after her day's work, and that because of this situation the health of the child is likely to be neglected. It was also pointed out that such a method of care puts an unusual strain upon the unmarried mother, because she is burdened with the care of her child every evening after her return from work, and cannot, through use of the day nursery, so easily arrange for an occasional free evening as she might were she able to live at an institution with her child. Nor is she as likely to be as free to make such an arrangement through family or friends as is the married mother who uses the nursery.

A number of agencies suggested the necessity of providing certain specialized institutions for a type of care of unmarried mothers whose need it is hard to meet at the present time.

There was general complaint that it is difficult to make provision for the venereally diseased unmarried mother who is in need of institutional care. Many of the shelters and the homes for mothers and babies cannot, because of their limited facilities, accept for care those mothers who are venereally diseased. Moreover, some of these young women need reëducation and vocational training as well as medical care, and should be receiving these services at the same time. The supervision of this class of mothers in the community is hardly desirable, because of the hazard to community health while the disease is in an infectious stage, and also because of the difficult task of securing regular attendance by the unmarried mother at a clinic for the treatment of her condition. Social workers who had had experience in dealing with this situation stated that only too frequently the unmarried mother disappears from view after the birth of her child and refuses to continue the treatments of which she does not realize the importance to her health. The need of further institutional facilities for the care of the venereally diseased unmarried mothers, so that they can, during the period when they are undergoing medical treatment, be prepared, educationally and vocationally, to resume their places in community life, was emphasized as one of the more acute community problems in this field.

Unfortunately the results of the Wassermann Tests had not always been entered on the social service records available to us. In spite of this omission in so many cases there were nevertheless seventy-five cases of young unmarried mothers suffering from venereal disease, who were not, therefore, eligible for residence in any of the institutions which we have described. Statements from hospital social service workers, who were not able to furnish definite statistics, but who had worked directly with this group of young women, indicate that the prevalence of this disease would be revealed as much more widespread if the records had been accurately kept and that its treatment demands special attention from those interested in community health.[1]

Other suggestions were made as to the necessity of providing a home with a program of education and activities adapted to the needs of unmarried mothers from clerical and professional pursuits who require institutional care because they lack the financial resources for making independent arrangements. It was thought that the program of activities of some of the long-existing homes for mothers and babies had been based on the need of the group from which the greatest number of unmarried mothers come, that is, unskilled domestic servants; and that unmarried mothers from more skilled occupational pursuits have difficulty in finding a home suited to their particular needs. These young women, no less than the domestic servant, are often under the necessity of seeking shelter away from family and friends during the months immediately preceding and following the birth of the child, and social workers have suggested that the provision for meeting these needs is at the present time far from sufficient.

All of the agencies answering the inquiry agreed that the facilities for caring for the Negro unmarried mother are far from meeting the need. More work of the excellent character of that of the Katy Ferguson Home was believed to be urgently needed, and, since many of the existing homes for mothers and babies are unable to receive colored girls, there is evidently need of expanding the existing accommodations for them or of providing additional facilities. Considering the overcrowding in Negro families in this city at the present, and the low

[1]Since these paragraphs were originally written, one institution, Inwood House, has revised its program to provide service of this kind. It had 43 unmarried mothers in care in December, 1933.

economic level in which the family life of a large number must be maintained, it seems obvious that many unmarried Negro mothers with their children would derive benefit from shelter and care away from their families until they are able to become self-supporting once more. Of the 434 Negro unmarried mothers of which we had schedule information, only 83 had received care in the types of homes described in this section, and it is evident that the chief burden of the support of those not so sheltered had been assumed by their families and friends.

VIII

THE FAMILY WELFARE AND THE
PROTECTIVE AGENCIES

THE family welfare societies in New York City do not as a rule consider it to be a part of their special function to deal with cases of illegitimate parenthood. When encountered, such cases are referred for counsel by most of the societies questioned on the subject to agencies specializing in their care. But a survey of the records for the year 1930 reveals the fact that a number of the family welfare societies visited for the purposes of this study had nevertheless had to deal with unmarried mothers whose infants were born in New York City in 1930. These mothers had had some connection with the problem of dependency, which had brought them to the agencies' attention. Occasionally the unmarried mothers were found in families which for other reasons were clients of these family welfare societies. Sometimes family groups which were supposedly constituted in a legal manner were found to be illegitimate after they had come under the agency's care. The treatment of such cases of illegitimate parenthood was decided upon an individual basis, but it was found that it was the practice to refer the unmarried mothers, when they were young and in need of intensive care, to the specialized agencies able to give this care. The proportion of such cases of illegitimate parenthood to the total number of cases handled by the family welfare societies was very small, and their care constituted no considerable burden of work.[1] The actual number of illegitimate families within the scope of this study which had been accepted for case

[1] Among the family welfare agencies reporting some work with unmarried mothers whose infants were born in New York City in 1930 were the Association for Improving the Condition of the Poor, the Charity Organization Society, and the Brooklyn Bureau of Charities.

study and treatment by one family welfare society was seventeen; another society of similar method and aim had nine cases; while a third society had only one case.

Foremost among those dealing with the care of the illegitimate family in New York City were the agencies specializing in protective work for young women. The work of the correctional agencies devoting themselves to the care of young women committed to them by the courts is described in another section, but the agencies dealing primarily with the unmarried mothers who come to them voluntarily for advice and aid must now be considered. From the agencies of this type furnishing data, knowledge was had of 659 cases which had received some care from them.

As a rule, the agencies specializing in the case work supervision of young unmarried mothers not in institutions are of more recent origin than the institutions, which were pioneers in this field of protective work. The fact that they exist at all is due to a changed social attitude of people generally from that of the decades which saw the establishment of institutions for "homeless and hopeless women in the County of Kings" and for "friendless women." At that time it would have been all but impossible to arrange for other than institutional care for these young women, and the growth of special establishments for the purpose was a logical response to the type of problem then existent. It should be further noted, also, that the supervision of unmarried mothers in the community began as an extension of the work of institutions and as a means of aiding these young women in their first steps of readjustment to community life. Later, when the notion of preventive work had gained a foothold, new organizations sprang up to develop the new method, and the work of supervising the unmarried mothers in the community came to parallel the care given by the institutions. This work is believed to fill a need in the care of unmarried mothers analagous in some respects to the work of probation and parole in the case of women prisoners and other delinquents whose conduct has brought them into conflict with the law.

While some few of the agencies coming within this category consider themselves prepared to deal with unmarried mothers of all creeds and racial groups, there is a well-marked tendency within recent years for this work of supervising the unmarried mother in the community to be concentrated in the hands of the main religious groups of the city's population. This tendency to draw within sectarian lines, always existent, has become more pronounced within recent years with the development of inclusive and well-rounded programs of social welfare work by some of the various religious bodies. For example, one case work agency which has for a long time occupied a prominent place in protective work for young women, and which is avowedly non-sectarian in aim and spirit, has reported a relative decrease in the number of unmarried mothers coming under its care within the last decade, and has attributed this decline to the fact that young women who would formerly have availed themselves of its services are now being cared for by agencies of their own religious allegiance who are prepared to render equally effective service in this field. This tendency finds social justification in the belief that the program of re-education and readjustment to social conditions is more effectively accomplished under the tutelage of that group with which the young woman's ideals and outlook on life have originally been formed, and which can, therefore, add to the usual methods for social rehabilitation that of a religious motivation and sanction.

The method of all these societies[2] in dealing with young

2Among the agencies consulted with regard to this division of the study were: the State Charities Aid Association Department of Mothers and Babies; the Church Mission of Help, New York; the Church Mission of Help, Brooklyn; the Jewish Board of Guardians; and the Guild of the Infant Savior, which has both a shelter and a case work service.

women who have given birth to a child out of wedlock is that of the usual case work procedure. An investigation is conducted·into the personal, family, and social history of the young woman in order to ascertain, if possible, the factors contributing to her unconventional behavior, and to lay the basis for a plan of procedure for her future care and protection. Arrangements are made for the correction of physical defects, if any; for the securing of shelter and medical care for mother and child; and for vocational advice and placement of the mother when this may seem advisable. In all of the societies studied, an attempt at case work approach and planning is made, but the degree to which this can be realized depends of course upon the number of staff members available for the work and the number of cases coming to their attention. Obviously a society having 196 unmarried mothers coming under its care in 1930 could give less time and attention to planning for their care than could a society having 36 unmarried mothers in 1930, when the number of social workers available for the work was approximately equal in the two organizations. In the former case, where the burden of work for each member of the staff is much heavier, the amount of investigation and individual planning and supervision which can be attempted is small, although the need for such work is realized and, insofar as possible, achieved.

The number of illegitimate families coming within the scope of the study under the care of these specialized agencies was in one case 196, in another 144, in another 23, in another 14, and in still another 11. Other agencies having fewer cases were also included in the study. In each case the total number of illegitimate families under actual supervision during the year was larger than our figures show, since we have included for study only those illegitimate families having a child born in 1930, and all of these societies had under their care at the time this study was made some families who had had children born previous to that year, as well as some who had had illegitimate infants born subsequent to that year.

All of the societies questioned on this point reported that they are able to give a certain amount of material aid in the form of temporary relief whenever the unmarried mother is without financial resources. Board for the unmarried mother and her child may be paid temporarily, and clothes may be furnished for the mother and child until such time as the mother is able to provide them through her own efforts. In a few instances agencies reported that they had been able to offer special scholarships and opportunities for vocational training to young women in need of such assistance and capable of profiting by such an educational investment. Of still greater importance is the fact that these agencies assume the duty of making such an adjustment between the unmarried mother and members of her family that the young woman may not be deprived of their aid and moral support in her efforts to maintain herself and her child.

Because of the emphasis on the case work approach and individual treatment within the last few years, none of these agencies questioned has a fixed or rigid policy as to what course of action shall be followed with reference to the keeping of mother and child together. It is true that some societies, because of their traditions and the direction which has been given to the work by their founders, lean to one or the other school of thought as to the advisability of the separation of mother and child, even though they admit that a decision in any particular case must be determined by the circumstances most pertinent to the individuals concerned. There does persist, however, a strong belief and tradition that the natural tie between mother and child should be respected, and its strengthening encouraged, except in cases where individual and social factors render this attitude inadvisable. In fact, the societies which have specialized in the supervision of unmar-

ried mothers in the community have insisted, even more than
have agencies of other types, that there should enter into the
decision as to the separation of mother and child no other consideration than the welfare of these two in the community life,
and that such considerations as the well-meaning wish to supply childless couples with children for adoption should be
given no weight in this important decision. These societies
believe that the number of such couples wishing to adopt children, and their material circumstances, should not become a
factor in determining the separation of a child from its natural
guardians; and that such a separation should be resorted to
only when the interest of mother and child, apart from all
other considerations, makes such a step seem necessary. This
attitude is in marked contrast with that of the workers in some
of the medical and other types of agencies, who are almost as
much interested in finding a baby for a couple wishing to
secure a child, as they are in aiding the unmarried mother.

It has been pointed out in a preceding section that the ability of protective agencies dealing with unmarried mothers to
render service depends upon the understanding which other
agencies, primarily the hospitals and the health agencies, have
of their work, and upon the willingness of these institutions
to refer young women to them. Since a large percentage of the
young women included in our group made their initial appeal for help to a hospital or other health agency, it is evident
that the point of contact between the protective agency and
the unmarried mother must in many instances be through the
hospital social service workers, if contact is to be made at all.
As was indicated in the section above referred to, it is the belief
of some that these societies have developed a too elaborate system of investigation and analysis for the problem of illegitimate parenthood as it presents itself under modern conditions,
and that in their zeal to understand all of the conditions entering into the client's beliefs and reactions, they have overlooked

certain important factors of unfavorable community opinion and censure which may be aroused by such investigation and which may render any permanent adjustment to community life exceedingly difficult. It is not within the province of this study to indicate the degree of truth in this contention of the health and medical workers, but it seems pertinent to indicate that such a belief on their part sharply limits the number of their recommendations of cases to specialized social agencies, and thus in a very material way limits the field of usefulness of these agencies.

In addition to the agencies actually engaged in protective work involving the care of the unmarried mother, there were agencies[3] both public and private which were able to do some protective work with girls and young women whose family and social environment was such that they were regarded as in danger of becoming delinquent. These agencies, because of the extent of their contacts with girls and young women of the less privileged groups, often encountered the problems of illegitimate parenthood among those who came to their attention for care. In general, it was found to be the policy of these agencies to refer such cases as came to their attention to the agencies specializing in their care; but in some cases, when the contact of the agency in question with the case had extended over a long period of time and when the members of the staff were thoroughly familiar with all of the factors involved in the situation, the agency had attempted to handle directly the problem growing out of illegitimate parenthood. In all, we learned of 126 cases cared for by these agencies. One public department, recently established, which had had contact with forty unmarried mothers coming within the scope of this study, had re-

[3]Among the agencies consulted with reference to this section were the New York Society for the Prevention of Cruelty to Children; the Brooklyn Society for the Prevention of Cruelty to Children; the New York Crime Prevention Bureau; and the Queens Children's Society.

ferred these young women to specialized agencies for the unmarried mother in accordance with their particular religious
affiliation. In making these contacts, this agency, because of its
extensive work in the field of the prevention of delinquency,
had been able to contribute substantially to the solution of the
problems of these young women by the completeness of the
information that it was able to furnish regarding their social
background and by the discriminating nature of its choice in
the reference of cases to the specialized agencies. Other agencies engaged in protective work with children occasionally
encountered cases of illegitimate parenthood. These cases were
often characterized by the extreme youth of the principals,
and not infrequently involved legal proceedings of a criminal
nature which these societies were prepared to prosecute. One
society had rendered services to forty-six unmarried mothers
coming within the scope of this study; another, above referred
to, had had forty such cases under its care; and still another
had had thirty under its supervision. Other societies having
smaller numbers of cases, which had not been accepted for prolonged care, but which had been referred to other agencies
after a preliminary investigation had been made, were also
included in the study. Nevertheless, for the solution of the
social problems growing out of these cases they were frequently
referred to the specialized agencies, although the special nature
of the legal proceedings involved usually required that the
original agency continue to maintain a close and active interest
in the case.

The hearty coöperation of these children's protective societies and the case working agencies would seem to be of especial
importance, because these are almost always cases in which the
unmarried mother is extremely young and in which the case
work approach, and a prolonged period of supervision and
reëducation, would be particularly necessary and particularly
promising in results. This coöperation, however, seemed not

always easy to effect, because of the highly specialized nature of the work of the societies involved, and because of the lack of any generally defined basis of coöperation which all agencies involved were willing to accept. The need for such a basis of coöperation was, however, generally admitted, although the difficulties in the way were equally evident.

IX
THE AGENCIES AND INSTITUTIONS
FOR DELINQUENTS

A NUMBER of unmarried mothers coming within the scope of this study were found to have received care in institutions of correction or from agencies specializing in the care of delinquent young women. In all, six organizations for delinquents that give some care, either institutional or advisory, to unmarried mothers were visited.[1] All of these agencies receive for care some unmarried mothers from the area of Greater New York, and all of them had had under their supervision some of the cases selected for inclusion within the scope of this study, namely, the unmarried mothers whose children were born within the area of Greater New York between January 1 and December 31, 1930. In all, sixty-nine such cases were found.

Unmarried mothers in institutions of correction, or under the supervision of agencies dealing primarily with delinquents, offer problems of care somewhat different from those presented by unmarried mothers under the care of medical and case work societies. Young women of the first mentioned group have in general committed some offense which has brought them into conflict with the law, and which, in the opinion of the court, has necessitated their detention or supervision for a period of time. This additional evidence of a low adaptive power to social conditions growing out of early unfavorable environment or personal traits renders the problem of the reëducation of this group of young women and their readjustment to social conditions more difficult than in the case of the unmarried mothers whose illegitimate parenthood constitutes the chief

[1] The New York State Reformatory for Women, the New York State Training School for Girls, the Correction Hospital of the New York City Department of Correction, Inwood House, the Wayside Home School for Girls, the Women's Prison Association of New York, and Isaac T. Hopper Home.

difficulty in the way of their readaptation to social life. Moreover, the care of the unmarried mother is an institution existing primarily for the care and reëducation of delinquent
women and girls committed by the courts necessitaties a modification in the customary routine of life and the development
of specialized programs of care, thus creating an additional
problem for the institution's management. In all of the institutions visited during the course of this inquiry, the unmarried
mothers constituted only a small minority of the total group
under care, but somewhat elaborate adaptations in institu-
ional regulations were necessary in order to meet their need
and to see to it that their infants received proper attention. For
example, all of the institutions caring for delinquent young
women arrange that births take place outside the institution
in the most conveniently accessible hospital. This rule operates
to obtain the best medical care for the unmarried mother, and
also to prevent the possible stigma to the child of having his
birth occur in an institution for delinquents. In all of the institutions except Correction Hospital it is arranged for the
unmarried mother to keep her child with her and to give him
her personal care during the nursing period. At Correction
Hospital it is not expedient, because of the nature of the institution and the large number of prisoners there, to have the
mother keep her child with her, but arrangements are made
through the social service department to have the mother
nurse her child for a short period at least at the hospital to
which she has been sent for maternity care. If the prison sentence of the mother then necessitates her retention for a more
or less prolonged period, it becomes necessary to separate her
child from her and to arrange for his care elsewhere.

In one institution able to care for twenty-five delinquent
young women there were only three unmarried mothers whose
infants were born in 1930; in another institution having a
capacity for five hundred young women there were in 1930

only twenty-four unmarried mothers whose infants were born in 1930; while still another agency having slightly less than four hundred women under its supervision in 1930 had only two cases of unmarried mothers whose infants were born in that year. In these institutions where young women were cared for with their infants, however, the practice of arranging for their detention in a separate part of the institution was usually followed, in order that the routine of life might be so modified in their favor as to safeguard the health of both mother and infant. In one case it appeared that the eagerness of those in authority to return the young women to the regular routine of the institution had resulted in the separation of the mother from her child earlier in the nursing period than is usually considered safe for the baby; but in the other institutions no such tendency was observed. The difficulties of administration occasioned by the necessity of making arrangements for the care of a small number of unmarried mothers in each of several different institutions for delinquents caused the query to be raised by some social workers as to whether it would not be more expedient to segregate these cases in one or two institutions, thus abolishing the necessity for the special adaptations in several institutions. This, however, raises the question of the offenses for which the young women have been committed by the courts, and of the legal possibility of making a classification of offenders on the basis of illegitimate parenthood alone.

Records of unmarried mothers in some of the institutions included in the survey reveal the fact that a not inconsiderable number of women delinquents who have not received maternity care within the institution have, nevertheless, borne an illegitimate child prior to their admission, from whom they have been previously separated. This circumstance indicates that illegitimate parenthood among delinquent young women has been of more frequent occurrence than the small proportions of unmarried mothers with infants among the total population of the institution at a given time might seem to indicate. There have been instances in which the cause of the unmarried mother's appearance before the court has been her abandonment of her child or her failure to provide for it. In cases of this nature, however, the young woman is usually put on probation unless there is some other record of delinquency. Aside from maternity care these institutions are often called upon to give prolonged medical care to those young women who are venereally diseased and to those who have become addicted to the use of drugs. In such cases, this care is provided by the institution itself either within its own walls or by coöperation with outside medical agencies, the restoration of the young women to normal physical health being considered an essential part of the program of these institutions.

Along with the change in the attitude of society toward the delinquent, and with the increased emphasis upon reëducation instead of punishment, the programs of institutions for delinquent young women have undergone marked modifications. For example, the Wayside Home School for Girls[2] takes pains to emphasize that it is "not a reformatory or a prison to which criminals are consigned for punishment, but a school where girls or young women committed by the courts may be trained for useful careers." The programs of other institutions have shown corresponding changes, and the young women detained there have been regarded as subjects for special treatment and reëducation rather than as objects for punishment. This change in attitude would seem to apply to the unmarried mother with special justice, even when her record has not been otherwise flawless, because of the necessity of protecting her child; and this consideration has secured for her many exceptions to the regular institutional routine. Even so, the problem of her adjustment to normal community life remains far more complex than that of the young woman who

[2]The Wayside Home School for Girls, Inc., *Annual Report for 1929 and 1930.*

has been spared the necessity of undergoing the restrictions of a period of enforced detention and isolation.

If the unmarried mother has had a long career of delinquency, or if she shows marked instability of character while under observation in the institution, it may become necessary for arrangements to be made for the separate care of her infant after her departure from the institution. In some cases the undesirable traits of character or heredity manifested by the unmarried mother may affect the availability of her infant for adoption. and the alternative to leaving him under his mother's care may be institutionalization or at best placement in a supervised boarding home. The fact of an unmarried mother's being committed to an institution for delinquents does not, of course, preclude the possibility of her child being considered a subject suitable for adoption, if traits of character and conduct manifested by the mother encourage the belief that her child would have a reasonable chance to succeed in a well-selected foster home. One institution visited reports that it does successful placement of some infants for adoption through its social service worker, and that the results of the experiment would seem to justify its continuance. The other agencies consulted report, however, that they refer their unmarried mothers to the regular child-placing agencies in case the separation of mother and child seems advisable at the time they leave the custody of the institution.

A general view of the information furnished by all the agencies for delinquents included within the scope of this study reveals the fact that the majority of unmarried mothers of this group, as in the group at large, wish to keep their infants with them, and that they are able through the help of social service workers and others to arrange for their care and support. Tables given in another section of this report will show the number and proportion of unmarried mothers in this group who have kept their infants in their own custody and the number and proportion of those who have surrendered their children for adoption or for institutional care. The supervision of mother and child is provided or arranged through the parole officers, so that the institution continues its interest in their welfare until such time as their successful adjustment to society seems reasonably assured. The number and proportion of successful readjustments were difficult to ascertain from the data available. Indications are, however, that the number of successful adjustments varied somewhat with the character of the inmates selected for care by a given institution. Institutions specializing, for example, in the care of the younger and more hopeful types seem to attain, as might be expected, a larger measure of success than those to whose care is entrusted the older and more hardened offender. In each instance, however, the chances of successful adjustment by the unmarried mother have been increased by the fact that the program of education and training adds to the chances of success in the economic struggle, and thus makes more practicable the support of the child by the unmarried mother. The educational program in one institution includes courses in homemaking and child care, as well as in beauty culture, salesmanship, stenography, millinery, and other subjects. One institution reports that it has had unusual success in placing young women who have followed its course in salesmanship. The general consensus of opinion with regard to the possibility of placing unmarried mothers was that there was no marked prejudice against them when the demand for their services was on a purely economic basis, and that they were regarded as successful in their work in about the same proportion as were the other young women delinquents receiving care in these institutions.

The practice with regard to the parole of unmarried mothers from the institutions for delinquents varied according to the history and policy of each institution. One institution releases unmarried mothers on parole to a social work representative of the religious group to which the young woman belongs. Another institution employs its own parole officers, but works in coöperation with the representatives of the young woman's religious group. All of the institutions concerned provide for the religious training and instruction of the inmates, the unmarried mothers receiving, of course, the same training as the others. The Women's Prison Association, while not affording facilities for institutional care in the usual sense of the term, does offer facilities for temporary shelter of unmarried young women delinquents. Because of the nature of its work with women delinquents just leaving prison, few unmarried mothers with young children are encountered, but when this occurs the case is usually referred to some agency specializing in their care.

X

THE CHILD PLACEMENT SOCIETIES

THIS study cannot enter into a discussion of the general problems connected with the placement of dependent children in foster family homes. Visits were made, however, to a number of agencies engaged in such placement, in order to ascertain what contact these societies might have had with the young women who had given birth to children out of wedlock in New York City in 1930. All but one of the societies visited were found to be in accord with the purposes of the survey, and, with this one exception, they all agreed to furnish statistical data as to the number of children included within the scope of this study who had come to their attention for care. From the statistics furnished us, we secured knowledge of 480 children and their mothers who had received some service from these agencies.

The contact of the child placing agencies with the unmarried mother differs in many essentials from that of the case work agency specializing in the care of the illegitimate family. For the unmarried mother who comes to the child placement society is usually one who has made a definite decision to relinquish the custody of her child and whose wish it is that the society act as intermediary for her in placing the child in a family home where he may be considered for adoption. Since the separation of the mother from her child is to be permanent, the major interest of the society for child placement is in the child himself, in the selection of a foster home for him, and in his successful adjustment to it. Although this centering of interest in the child does not preclude on the part of these agencies a continued sympathetic interest in the unmarried mother herself, it does nevertheless connote a point of view markedly different from that of the agency which has as the main feature of its program the social rehabilitation of the unmarried mother. Several child placement societies, however, reported that they did consider it a part of their responsibility to aid the unmarried mother to a successful readjustment to social life. One society was accustomed to refer the unmarried mother to another agency capable of finding employment for her. Another society had made some attempt through members of the board to find situations for the young women whose infants had been accepted for adoption. Still another society, through its psychologist, continued a sympathetic interest in the young woman after the placement of her child, offering aid and advice when necessary. In a number of cases, it was reported that some financial aid had been given to the mother during the time when she was seeking employment.

This difference in point of view between the child placement societies and those specializing in the care of the unmarried mother may be the cause of a divergence in policy as to the separation of the unmarried mother from her child and a difference of opinion as to the time at which the separation should occur. It has been pointed out in a preceding section that the most progressive agencies specializing in the care of the unmarried mother are opposed to the early separation of mother and child because of the high death rate among infants attendant upon such separations. These agencies insist also that a decision as to the separation of a mother from her child should be delayed for a period of a few months, until the mother has returned to normal health of body and mind, and is, therefore, in a position to make an unhurried and well-considered decision.

The point of view of the adoption societies with reference to the early separation of mother and child was in most cases markedly different from the point of view of the case work agencies. One agency visited in the course of our inquiry accepts for care children from a few days of age up to the age at which it would be difficult to place them for adoption. In speaking of their policy the worker in charge was inclined to justify the admittedly dangerous course of early separation of the child from the mother on the ground that the child of the unmarried mother is an exception to the general rule, and that even if the agency should refuse to accept the infant during the early weeks of its life, this policy would by no means prevent such separation. It was the belief of this agency that the keeping of the child by the mother during the early months of the nursing period could not legitimately be insisted upon by case work agencies, when the aid given to such a course by these agencies is at present so inadequate and so unsatisfactory. It was pointed out, furthermore, that even if the unmarried mother retains the custody of her child during the first few months of his life, such a course does not ordinarily imply that she gives him her personal attention during this time, because of the lack in facilities above referred to; but that more probably than not she leaves him for care in the least expensive boarding home for infants available to her, where he receives care less likely to result in his survival than if he were under the direct supervision of the child placement agency. This agency contends, therefore, that the policy of encouraging the mother to keep the custody of her child during the first few months of his life is without social value unless adequate and satisfactory facilities, either public or private, are provided for the mother so that she can actually remain with her child during the nursing period.

It was the conviction of this agency, and also of some others interviewed on the subject, that the usual lot of the illegitimate child whose mother has kept him is that of a succession of changes from one cheap boarding home to another during the early formative years of his life, with consequences disastrous to health and to character growth. It is because of these circumstances, they declare, that they cling to the policy of accepting the infant at as early an age as possible, with the hope of providing for him a stable and wholesome environment in a good foster home during the early years of his life.

The demand for infants suitable for adoption by homes eligible both from a material and educational point of view may, it was frankly admitted by more than one agency, have some influence upon the policy of the agency with reference to accepting infants for adoption. One agency which had placed about forty infants for adoption in 1930 stated that the number of acceptable homes demanding infants for adoption was about ten times as large as the number of suitable infants available for adoption. That eagerness to meet this demand for infants, coming from childless couples having homes of good material and social standards, may have much influence on the policy of the child placing agencies with reference to accepting children for adoption can readily be understood. The desire to satisfy the demand for infants made upon them by such homes had caused agencies, in one or two instances, to take active steps to procure infants. It was found that one agency had made numerous inquiries at hospitals with reference to the infants of unmarried mothers who might wish to surrender them; and similar inquiries as to the availability of such infants for adoption had even been sent to other states.

Some unmarried mothers were referred to the child placement societies by the hospital social service workers and the health agencies immediately upon the dismissal of the mother from the hospital. In these cases the decision as to the separation of the infant from his mother had been made during the ten-day period after the birth of her child, during which the mother remained in the hospital. Some social workers who did not believe that this period was long enough to allow the mother to recover health of mind and body sufficient to make a decision of such great importance to herself and the child justified an immediate decision to surrender the child on the ground that, even if the mother should wish to keep her child with her, economic conditions would make it impossible for her to provide suitable home and educational opportunities. An early separation seemed to them preferable, therefore, not only in the interest of the child, but also in the interest of preventing the formation by the unmarried mother of a strong emotional attachment for her infant, and her consequent unhappiness when the burden of his support necessitated his surrender for adoption. It was for this reason that some unmarried mothers were referred promptly to the child placement societies upon their departure from the hospitals.

Some agencies, in accepting these children referred from hospitals, neglected to avail themselves of information in possession of the social service departments of the hospitals as to the heredity and physical condition of the child, when this information might have had an important bearing upon the decision as to the placement of the child. One instance was cited of an unmarried mother who had given to an adoption society a false name and correspondingly inaccurate information as to her parentage and social condition. On the basis of this misinformation the child had been placed in a family, when the real facts as to the circumstances were well known to the hospital social service worker and might have been had for the asking. One hospital social worker complained that a child placement society had asked that infants of unmarried mothers be referred to it, but had been unwilling to guarantee that the infants so obtained would be placed in homes of the religious affiliation of the parents.

It was evident, too, that the opinion of some workers in charge of maternity homes as to the advisability of an unmarried mother keeping the custody of her child had an important bearing upon the recommendation of this young woman to child placement societies or to the protective societies. Some agencies specializing in the care of unmarried mothers complained that their clients had been urged to surrender their infants for adoption when they had been sent only for temporary shelter to one of the maternity homes, and that this home had made it a practice to refer young women to a child placement society with which it maintained close relations.

One agency for child placement had been so anxious to make placements that it was willing to accept for placement younger children of large families whose parents were unable, because of poverty or unemployment, to care for their families unaided —a policy that differs from that of the more progressive agencies working in this field, which refuse to deal with such cases, but refer them promptly to the family welfare society in order that some provision may be made to keep the family together. It has long been a tenet of good child care service that no child of a legally constituted family should be separated from his parents for reasons of sheer economic distress, and good agencies refuse to consider such a separation as a way out of family difficulties. This agency observed good practices neither for legitimate nor for illegitimate children.

In every child placing society some attempt is made to learn the facts of most importance in the heredity of the child; the best agencies working in this field regard such an inquiry as a necessary protection to the families applying to them for infants to adopt. There was evidence in some societies, however, that this inquiry into heredity was of an extremely perfunctory nature. Information as to the father was often lacking, even in careful agencies, either because the mother was unwilling to supply the data or because she knew little of the man.

One agency, committed to very thorough work in determining the heredity of the child before offering him for adoption, had made it a practice to request an interview with the father as well as with the unmarried mother, in order to secure the main facts as to the parentage as completely and as accurately as possible. This agency, because of its fortunate method of approach, was able to secure a large measure of coöperation from the unmarried fathers, and the records in this regard were correspondingly complete. It was even possible, in a number of cases, to obtain from the father of the illegitimate infant a voluntary agreement to pay the board of the child during the period preceding his placement for adoption; and the worker in charge of this division of work in the society reported on the part of the unmarried fathers an interest in the welfare of their progeny which compared quite favorably with that manifested by the unmarried mothers. It should be noted, however, that on the whole the success of the greater number of societies in securing the coöperation of the unmarried fathers has not been so marked. In some cases this failure would seem to be due to the methods employed to secure such coöperation, and in other cases to a lack of interest on the part of the society.[1]

It can readily be seen, too, that the work of the staff members of a child placing society in securing accurate information with regard to the heredity of the child on the paternal side would be limited. Their interest in securing this information appeared to be limited because they were not under the necessity of securing support for the child by establishing paternity; and also because of the fact that families wishing to adopt infants are usually eager that all facts connected with the birth of these infants be carefully safeguarded. Many of these societies had abandoned this effort altogether, except insofar as the unmarried mother could or would provide information. Since there is no generally accepted agreement as to the minimum

[1]While little actual follow-up work to discover the extent of the later interest of the natural father in his child has been done it may be interesting to recall that in the Pennsylvania study of adoptions conducted by Dr. Neva R. Deardorff it was found that of the 60 illegitimate children adopted by relatives, 7 of these had been adopted by the natural father. See Commission Appointed to Study and Revise the Statutes Relating to Children, *Report to the General Assembly*, 1925.

of information about the heredity of a child to be obtained
before a society should be willing to accept him for adoption,
it is evident that the opinion and beliefs of those in immediate
charge of the work would influence largely the society's practice in this regard.

The frequency with which adopted children return to make
anxious inquiry as to their real parentage has led some societies
to prepare a summary of the heredity and the circumstances
surrounding the surrender of each adopted child in such a
form as to be available to him if he seeks such information
when he becomes of age. Other societies, however, suppress
such information as completely as possible, and insist that all
information regarding the heredity of the child and his surrender be guarded with the utmost possible secrecy if indeed
they have it at all. It was in part this desire to adhere to the
strictest possible secrecy which had led, in some instances, to a
neglect to make inquiry, from those able to give pertinent
information, into the heredity of the child and to the attempt
to justify ignorance regarding the elements in the situation
dealt with. Still other societies, while agreeing that all due
secrecy should be observed to protect the standing of the unmarried mother and her child, insist that the interests of both,
to say nothing of the interests of the prospective foster parents,
require that there should be available, for those entitled to
know, a statement as complete as possible of the heredity and
social circumstances of the infant and both his parents. The
societies of long experience in this field know of cases where
problems involving inheritances, or family relationships of
great and sometimes tragic importance, have remained without possibility of solution because the agencies chiefly responsible have failed in their duty of keeping complete and accurate records or of informing themselves originally regarding
the nature of the case.

Statistics as to the number of illegitimate children born in

New York City in 1930 who had been accepted by these societies for adoption placement had not in all cases been kept in a form to render them available for the purpose of this report. One society, however, reported the acceptance of one hundred such cases; another, that of forty-three cases; still another, twenty such acceptances; and other societies reported still fewer cases. These figures do not include, of course, the children offered for adoption privately, of whom we have reason to believe the number was by no means negligible, nor those offered for adoption by persons not authorized to place children for adoption.

The State Charities Law of New York requires that every case of a child being accepted for care away from its own family must be reported immediately to the State Department of Social Welfare, and that a report on every change in the child's status, including its final discharge from care, must be filed with the Department. The data about each child include information as to its place of birth, age, and legitimacy. From these reports it is possible to see the number of children born out of wedlock who come into foster care, the types of care employed, and the final disposition made of these cases.

Thus far, however, the Department has not tabulated or published in any detail the facts reported on children in foster care. A recent report on the *Volume, Distribution, and Cost of Child Dependency in New York State for 1931* does not show any classifications of the children under care according to the marital status of their parents. It is hoped that the new Division of Research will begin shortly to make such analyses of the material on file with the Department.

XI

THE AGENCIES IN RELATION TO EACH
OTHER AND TO THE CITY

WORK with the illegitimate family in New York City is carried on by a large number of agencies both public and private, of which we have had direct knowledge of eighty-seven in the course of this study. These agencies perform services of a widely varying nature and operate from diverse points of view, sometimes in harmony with other agencies working in the same field, sometimes in ignorance of them, and sometimes in opposition to them. There were apparent to us no general principles or policies which were commonly accepted by those working in this field, nor did there appear any evidence of a working agreement among them as to how their services should be made available to persons having need of them. As a consequence there seemed to be considerable overlapping and duplication of services in some cases; and in other cases wasted effort of another nature, the nullification of the work of one agency by the work of another proceeding from different principles.

There was evidence, too, that some illegitimate families were receiving intensive supervision and care over long periods, while others with a need equally great had failed to come in contact with any agency which would give them the advice and supervision which they required. Nevertheless there was found a growing coördination of work within sectarian lines, and the elimination of wasted effort by the organization under one direction of all work for illegitimate families of the same religious faith. This trend toward unification had not, however, extended to all of the main religious groupings of the city's population, nor had it achieved its maximum of efficiency among those which had attempted it. It was found, too, that certain agencies doing a highly specialized type of work had failed so to relate their work to that of other agencies as to render the greatest possible service.

It was evident that some agencies working in this field were operating, because of their inexperience or their lack of knowledge, on principles generally regarded by all schools of social thought as contrary to the best interests of the individual and society, and that these agencies had not been restrained by any force of public opinion operating upon them or by any legal authority presumably exercising supervision over them. As a consequence, certain members of illegitimate families had not been protected in the rights which were legally theirs, because they had not been properly advised of them by those to whom they had appealed for counsel. In other cases, the welfare of one member of an illegitimate family had been needlessly sacrificed to the welfare of another, simply because the agency operating in the case had so centered its efforts upon the amelioration of the lot of one particular member of the family that it had failed to see the question of the essential human rights involved in the case of the other persons who were parties to the proceedings.

The tendency of social agencies at work in this field to emphasize the welfare or duties of one or another member of the illegitimate family to the exclusion of the other members may explain to some extent the overlapping of work and the lack of understanding between these agencies. The agencies placing the chief emphasis upon the welfare of the child would have of necessity a point of view different from those placing the chief emphasis upon the rehabilitation of the unmarried mother. The need for some agreement upon common principles is evident here. There seemed existent a tendency for many agencies to leave the unmarried father altogether out of account, and those who did give some attention to this member of the illegitimate family did so mainly in the interest of securing support for the mother and child. Among the more progressive workers in this field, however, there was a disposition to place a greater emphasis upon securing the voluntary coöperation of the unmarried father, and their efforts, as has been previously related, were crowned with a considerable degree of success. Other agencies which were willing that legal proceedings be instituted for the establishment of paternity were nevertheless not in the habit of making an appeal for voluntary coöperation to unmarried fathers, because of their belief that no coöperation could be secured except by legal compulsion.

In addition to the lack of coördination among agencies, it seemed significant in the study that with approximately 1,800 illegitimate families in which births occurred in 1930, there were engaged in their care 87 different agencies. It is true, as has been pointed out in the preceding sections, that not all of these agencies devote themselves exclusively to this form of social endeavor, for to many of them the care of the illegitimate family is incidental to some larger program of social action which they have undertaken. However, the fact of having so large a number of organizations occupied with the adjustment of the difficult and complex problems growing out of illegitimate parenthood appeared to render any general agreement as to principles and policies extremely difficult, and to explain to a great extent the duplication of service referred to. It was pointed out by workers with long experience in the care of the illegitimate family that the volume of work of certain of the specialized agencies in this field, and their tendency to utilize the experience of others in the development of the case work technique, has enabled them to base their policies upon a rounded and adequate experience in this work. It was likewise indicated that other agencies attempting less intensive work with illegitimate families and dealing only with a few cases are without a sufficient experience upon which to base their general principles of work, and that, in such instances, the personal opinion and prejudices of the worker in immediate charge are likely to be the determining factors in the course of action pursued.

As has been pointed out, the largest number of cases come in contact with the medical and health agencies. Second in importance are the homes for mothers and babies, and next, those dealt with by the agencies specializing in the care of the illegitimate family. The other groups of agencies had dealt with smaller numbers of cases.

In Part Three, the specific services rendered to the individual members of the illegitimate families will be described. The characteristics and aspects of the social situation of these persons which render economic independence difficult and which lead to an appeal for help to social agencies of one type or the other will serve further to make clear the type of assistance rendered.

Part Three

THE ILLEGITIMATE FAMILY AND ITS MEMBERS

XII

THE ILLEGITIMATE FAMILY AS A GROUP

In addition to securing information regarding the social agencies which render service to the illegitimate family in New York City, an attempt has been made to describe the illegitimate family itself, as it is portrayed in the records of the agencies and institutions devoted to its care. It was believed that some general knowledge of the personal characteristics and of the social standing of those who have become parents without the benefit of social and legal sanction might indicate ways in which the attempt to be of service to them could be rendered more fruitful and lasting. It seemed reasonable to believe, too, that the work of protecting young persons from the handicap of illegitimate parenthood might be furthered by a better understanding of those who have already become parents out of wedlock, and of those circumstances in their environment which might be regarded as, in a sense, contributing to their unconventional conduct.

It was for these reasons that the individual case schedule (given in the Appendix 1) was prepared and submitted to the agencies. It will be noted that a great number of items of information were requested in the schedule. The limitations imposed upon the study by the difference in the nature of the records of the coöperating agencies have been discussed in the Preface. The same fact will be amply illustrated in the deficiencies of the statistical tables which follow in this section.

It would be well to bear in mind, too, that the information actually recorded by the agencies was in the greater number of instances given by the unmarried mother herself, in a personal interview with the social worker. In the case of some agencies this information had been supplemented and checked by a social investigation, or by interviews with other relatives of the illegitimate child; but such investigations had not always been made, and the record, in such cases, contained nothing more than the statements of the unmarried mother as to her social history and her needs at the time. Particularly was this true of the information furnished by the New York City Department of Health, which compiled special tables from the birth records of illegitimate infants born in New York City in 1930.[1] It can be readily seen that information supplied from this source could hardly have been checked by social investigation, because of the very nature of the circumstances under which it was obtained. It should be recalled that the birth certificate is filled in by the attending physician or by the institutional staff, and returned to the Department of Health within ten days after the birth of the child. In the case of the illegitimate child, the information contained on the certificate would of necessity be, in most cases, that which was supplied by the mother herself, while she was still under the care of a physician or in the institution. In the case of some of the social agencies, however, more ample opportunity for verification had existed, and it is not surprising that the information gleaned from such sources should differ in some particulars from the data compiled from the birth certificates. Illustrations of these differences will be given in the succeeding chapters.

As has already been stated, some items of information were obtained from the social agencies regarding 1,817 illegitimate families having an infant born in New York City in 1930. Of this number, agencies were able to furnish schedule information regarding 1,610. Of these schedules eleven were so incomplete as to prevent their inclusion in the study, leaving 1,599 schedules of illegitimate families to form the basis of our tabulations.

[1] The Health Department maintains a policy of refusing access to these birth records, even for purposes of scientific study.

The question of the duplication of cases arose because some illegitimate families had received help from two or more agencies. The difficulties of eliminating duplicate records were increased somewhat by the fact that some agencies had not been willing to furnish names and addresses of the illegitimate parents, and by the fact that in the case of other agencies, which did furnish such names and addresses, these had been incorrectly given by the illegitimate parents and no effort had been made to correct the record. After a preliminary consideration of these difficulties, it was asked that certain groups of the sectarian agencies effect an inter-agency clearing of duplicates, and by this process the number of doubtful cases which remained to be considered was less than a hundred.[2]

The difficulties of detecting duplicates in this group of cases at first appeared to be great, but they were gradually resolved as the study of the material contained in the records progressed. It will be noted from a glance at the individual case schedule that sixty-seven different items of information were required. While not all of these items were available in all cases, the comparison of records on the basis of the items recorded brought out fairly clearly the cases of similarity. Of great help also was the fact that the records of the agencies usually stated by which other agency the case had been referred to them and also to which agency they had referred the family for further treatment, so that overlapping in these cases was fairly clearly indicated. It happened also that the date of birth of the child and the hospital in which he had been born were usually indicated, and this fact was of assistance in detecting duplication between hospital social service departments and other agencies. In some cases, where a coincidence in certain items of information between two records was accompanied by a discrepancy in

[2]For the 1,599 illegitimate families, a single schedule was secured for 895, two schedules for 478, three for 159, four for 59 and five or more for 8 such families. Thus, over 1,000 records were identified as duplicates.

others, an effort was made to identify the cases by a return visit to the agencies concerned, a rereading of the records, and a personal interview with the worker in charge of the case. By employing a combination of these methods in cases not readily identified, a decision was reached in each case and the overlapping of agency records eliminated. This was a difficult and time-consuming process.

It should be noted, incidentally, that the process of identifying, counting, and studying the illegitimate births in this city would be greatly simplified if the Health Department and the agencies, including the hospitals, that serve such cases, would consent to pool all of the data in their possession bearing on them. It would then be possible to construct one unduplicated file which would be as nearly complete as the information on record would permit. The illegitimate births inferred to be legitimate by the Health Department and not later discovered by social agencies would, of course, remain as a source of error in the figures.

A discussion of the personal history and characteristics of the different members of the illegitimate family, based upon the records of the social agencies and upon the data compiled by the Department of Health from the birth certificates of infants born in New York City in 1930, and thought to be illegitimate, follows.

XIII

THE UNMARRIED MOTHERS

The term *unmarried mother* has frequently occurred in the course of this discussion of the illegitimate family. Such a designation is common among the social agencies for the mother of an illegitimate child, and for that reason it has been employed in the study. It should be noted, however, that not all of the women who have given birth to a child out of wedlock are single women. Some women who were married, but not to the father of the child, and still others, widowed or divorced or separated from their husbands, who had given birth to an illegitimate child, were included within the classification of unmarried mothers. The term designates, therefore, the mother of an illegitimate child, and it is so employed in the pages which follow.

If the information contained in the records of social agencies is more abundant for the unmarried mother than for any other member of the illegitimate family, it should be remembered that many of these organizations were established for meeting the problems connected with her care, and that their records are framed with the view to aid this endeavor. It will be observed, too, that it is usually the unmarried mother's application for aid which brings the illegitimate family to the attention of the agency, and that information regarding her characteristics and needs is the first to be recorded. Agencies specializing in the care of children usually receive illegitimate children along with a larger group of legitimate children, and do not, therefore, shape their records to show the particular needs and characteristics of the illegitimate family. As will be shown in a section which follows, information regarding unmarried fathers is limited in scope, because some agencies dealing with the problems of the illegitimate family ignore their existence and others consider their participation in the affairs of their illegitimate families of such slight importance that they make little or no effort to secure information regarding them.

Following is the information regarding the unmarried mothers which we were able to secure from the New York City Department of Health on the one hand, and from the records of New York City's social agencies on the other. In all cases in which the data from the Health Department have been set forth, they are so labeled. All of the other data have been derived from social agency records.

Legal Residence

In any inquiry of this type there is need to know at once in how far the problem described is indigenous to the community and in how far it is created by the introduction of persons coming directly from other places.

Inquiry was made as to what percent of the unmarried mothers coming under the care of New York City social agencies were legal residents of the city. Table 4 shows the results of the inquiry.

TABLE 4

Unmarried Mothers Classified by Residence

RESIDENCE	NUMBER	PERCENT
Total	1,421	100.0
Resident	1,101	77.5
Non-resident	320	22.5

Data on legal residence were not available on 178 of the 1,599 cases used in this study. While it is true that it is possible, within the year necessary to acquire legal residence, for the young woman to conceive as well as bear the child, such a rapid sequence of events is not characteristic of all the non-resident cases here studied. Some of them were found to be young women who had homes elsewhere and who had come to New York City to have their babies.

A little less than one-fourth of all the unmarried mothers for whom such information was given were non-residents. The problem of the care of non-resident young women in the maternity divisions of public hospitals has already been discussed in Part Two. Their care by private agencies presents fewer complexities, however, and the decision as to whether or not the young woman should be returned to the place of her legal residence was usually based upon the consideration of her personal and family situation.

A slightly larger percentage of white than of Negro unmarried mothers fell in the class of non-residents, as Table 5 shows.

The fact that the white unmarried mother is more likely to be cut off from her family and her social group by the discovery of her illegitimate parenthood is probably one reason for the slightly greater number of non-residents among the white group. The fear of discovery and the possession of more adequate economic resources for seeking concealment in the city were generally given by social workers as explanations of the difference in the proportion of non-residents in the two racial groups. Considering the circumstances of the two groups, the similarity seems more significant than the difference.

There was almost exactly the same proportion of non-residents among the native and the foreign groups. Some of the foreign born young women, as it is later pointed out, had left the father of the child in the country of their origin, and had come to this country in order to escape the censure of their families and friends. Other foreign born young women, however, had established a legal residence elsewhere in this country, and had come to the city for maternity care for the same reasons which had impelled the native born young women to come for such care. Statistics furnished by the Health Department show the number of 1930 births of illegitimate infants

TABLE 5

Unmarried Mothers Classified by Residence, Color, and Nativity

| | TOTAL | | WHITE | | | | | | NEGRO | | | | | |
| | | | TOTAL | | NATIVE BORN | | FOREIGN BORN | | TOTAL | | NATIVE BORN | | FOREIGN BORN[a] |
RESIDENCE	No.	Percent	No.	Percent	No.	Percent	No.	Percent	No.	Percent	No.	Percent	No.
Total	1,381[b]	100.0	980	100.0	716	100.0	264	100.0	401	100.0	374	100.0	27
Resident	1,068	77.3	745	76.0	545	76.1	200	75.8	323	80.5	296	79.1	27
Non-resident	313	22.7	235	24.0	171	23.9	64	24.2	78	19.5	78	20.9	...

[a]Percentage not computed, base less than 100.

[b]From this table 218 cases of the 1,599 studied were excluded because one or more of the items needed were not recorded.

of non-resident mothers as 133. As might have been expected, the largest number of such births, 118, occurred in Manhattan, a fact doubtless to be attributed to the greater facilities for maternity care as well as to the greater facilities for anonymity. It may be of some interest to note, also, that of the 133 non-resident unmarried mothers whose residence was noted in the Health Department statistics, 128 were white and only 5 were colored.

Attention should be called to the fact that of the unmarried mothers whose residence was reported in the Health Department statistics, only 9 percent were non-resident; while among those whose residence was noted by social agencies the proportion of non-residents was 22.7 percent. Moreover, it is puzzling to find that the social agencies discovered 320 non-resident women and girls in a group of 1,421 cases, while only 133 unmarried mothers are noted as definitely non-resident in the Health Department statistics of 1,470 cases. Eighty-one of the non-resident unmarried mothers, as reported by the Health Department, were from New York State, 22 were from New Jersey, 8 were from Pennsylvania, 7 from Connecticut, 6 from Massachusetts, and smaller numbers had come from other states. Of the non-resident cases reported by agencies, 53 were from New York State, 17 from New Jersey, 8 from Pennsylvania, 8 from Connecticut, and 11 from Massachusetts. Although the agencies reported 320 cases as non-resident, places of residence were given for only 114 cases. The others were noted simply as non-resident. It is possible that in some of these latter cases it would have been difficult to have assigned a definite place as the legal residence of the unmarried mother. Girls who had been wandering about for a few years, girls who refused to give their home addresses other than that they were not in New York City, the differences in the persons comprehended within the two groups—all of these circumstances give rise to the marked differences between the two sets of figures here presented, and indicate the need for the better coördination of information on this problem.

There is no way at present to learn the extent to which unmarried mothers who are New York City residents seek aid in other places. It is, therefore, practically impossible to make an illegitimacy rate corrected for residence. It is, however, probable that if such correction could be made, New York City's rate would be lower than it now is, since it seems unlikely that the number of New York City cases seeking maternity care outside the city equals or is larger than the number of non-resident cases recorded in this city.

Marital Status

Since the social situation presented by the birth of an illegitimate child to a woman who is or has been married differs considerably from that of the mother who has never been married, it is well to see in how far these mothers of illegitimate children conform to the usual idea of an unmarried mother.

The marital status of 1,538 unmarried mothers for whom such information is given is shown in Table 6.

TABLE 6

Unmarried Mothers Classified by Marital Status

MARITAL STATUS	NUMBER	PERCENT
Total	1,538	100.0
Single	1,416	92.1
Married	52	3.4
Divorced	12	0.8
Separated	37	2.4
Widowed	21	1.3

A little less than 8 percent of the unmarried mothers were or had been married, while the remaining 92 percent of them were reported to be single.

Although our observations are valid only for the groups for which we have information as to marital status, it may be worth noting that illegitimate parenthood represented a departure from legal family ties less frequently in the case of the young women than in the case of the unmarried fathers, of whom 29.6 percent were or had been married.

Comparison of white and Negro unmarried mothers as to marital status (Table 7) reveals the fact that a higher percentage of the white group were married. In partial explanation of this fact it will be shown that more of the white group are found in the later age groups.

A discussion as to the relation between the marital status of the mother and the plans possible for the future of the child is presented in a later chapter. The fact that all of the unmarried mothers referred to in the above classification had appealed to social agencies for help indicates that unaided they had not found it possible to settle the difficulties growing out of their situation. A study of individual records revealed, furthermore, that this inability to remain independent of social agency help had in some cases grown out of the fact that the young woman concerned was or had been married, and that the family complications thus introduced had been of moment in the decision to appeal for outside help. Widows and women separated from their husbands in some cases had found their own relatives unwilling to aid them in the care of an illegitimate child, and they were thus forced to seek agency assistance. In the case of the married women still living with their husbands, the illegitimate child was in a few cases accepted in the home. But in the others his care had to be arranged in an institution or foster home.

Age

Information as to the age of the unmarried mother was more generally given in the social agency records than any

TABLE 7

Unmarried Mothers Classified by Marital Status, Color, and Nativity

MARITAL STATUS	TOTAL		WHITE							NEGRO						
	No.	Percent	TOTAL		NATIVE BORN		FOREIGN BORN		TOTAL		NATIVE BORN		FOREIGN BORN[a]	
			No.	Percent	No.	Percent	No.	Percent	No.	Percent	No.	Percent	No.
Total . . .	1,467[b]	100.0	1,042	100.0	764	100.0	278	100.0	425	100.0	395	100.0	30
Single . .	1,349	92.0	949	91.1	693	90.7	256	92.1	400	94.1	373	94.4	27
Married . .	50	3.4	42	4.0	30	3.9	12	4.3	8	1.9	6	1.5	2
Divorced . .	10	0.7	7	0.7	6	0.8	1	0.4	3	0.7	3	0.8	. . .
Separated . .	37	2.5	28	2.7	24	3.1	4	1.4	9	2.1	9	2.3	. . .
Widowed . .	21	1.4	16	1.5	11	1.5	5	1.8	5	1.2	4	1.0	1

[a]Percentage not computed, base less than 100.

[b]From this table 132 cases of the 1,599 studied were excluded because one or more of the items needed were not recorded.

other item of information concerning her, except religion. This care to record her age was evidently based upon the practical consideration that virtually every move made upon the behalf of the unmarried mother is conditioned by her age. Her age, for example, determines the nature of the legal proceedings which are to be instituted against the unmarried father; her age influences also the type of maternity home to which she may be sent and how long she can remain there; and her age is considered of first importance also in the type of treatment and aid which the unmarried mother is to receive if she is placed under the care of a case work agency. Out of a total of 1,599 records, the age of the unmarried mother was recorded in 1,562 cases.

The distribution in age groups is shown in Table 8.

TABLE 8

Unmarried Mothers Classified by Age

Age	Number	Percent
Total	1,562	100.0
Under 16	77	4.9
16–19	583	37.3
20–24	615	39.4
25–29	190	12.2
30–34	67	4.3
35–39	23	1.5
40 and over	7	0.4

It will be noted that there were 77 unmarried mothers under 16 years of age, or 4.9 percent of the total number about which we had information. Among them were one unmarried mother 11 years of age and one unmarried mother of 14 who gave birth to her second illegitimate child in 1930. In the age group 16 to 19 years of age there were 583 unmarried mothers, or 37.3 percent of the total, or an average of 146 for each year within the span. Under 20 years of age there were, therefore, 42.2 percent of the total number of unmarried mothers. In the age group 20 to 24 years of age, there was an average of 127 for each year in the span; and after 25 years of age the proportion of unmarried mothers in the later age groups were progressively less. There were seven unmarried mothers over 40 years of age. If the age table of unmarried mothers is compared with that of the unmarried fathers, it will be observed that a higher proportion of the latter were in the later age groups.

Further analysis of the figures as to age reveals that the Negro unmarried mothers were more frequently found in the lower age groups than the white unmarried mothers (Table 9).

It will be observed that of the Negro unmarried mothers 47 percent of those whose ages were known were from sixteen to nineteen years of age, while 8.7 percent were under sixteen years of age, making a total of 55.7 percent under twenty years of age. Of the white unmarried mothers only 36.1 percent were under twenty years of age. As has been indicated in Part Two, this large number of Negro unmarried mothers in the younger age groups, and the limited facilities existing for their care, have evoked from many social workers a decided insistence that social measures be undertaken to meet their special needs.

A comparison of age groupings of native and foreign born unmarried mothers reveals the fact that a considerably higher proportion of the latter were in the older age groups. This fact is very probably due to the recent restrictions upon immigration, and the fact that there are proportionately fewer young women among the foreign born group than formerly. It may also be influenced by differing conceptions of extra-marital relationships among some of the foreign born groups.

Table 10 reveals the age distribution of unmarried mothers as given in the Health Department statistics.

While the numbers in the above table are different from

TABLE 9

Unmarried Mothers Classified by Age, Color, and Nativity

AGE GROUP	TOTAL		WHITE						NEGRO					
			TOTAL		NATIVE BORN		FOREIGN BORN		TOTAL		NATIVE BORN		FOREIGN BORN[a]	
	No.	Percent	No.	Percent	No.	Percent	No.	Percent	No.	Percent	No.	Percent	No.	
Total	1,490[b]	100.0	1,067	100.0	780	100.0	287	100.0	423	100.0	394	100.0	29	
Under 16	74	5.0	37	3.5	33	4.2	4	1.4	37	8.7	36	9.1	1	
16–19	547	36.7	348	32.6	293	37.6	55	19.2	199	47.0	193	49.0	6	
20–24	590	39.6	456	42.7	333	42.7	123	42.9	134	31.7	124	31.5	10	
25–29	185	12.4	153	14.3	75	9.6	78	27.2	32	7.6	23	5.8	9	
30–34	65	4.4	50	4.7	33	4.2	17	5.9	15	3.6	13	3.3	2	
35–39	22	1.5	16	1.5	9	1.2	7	2.4	6	1.4	5	1.3	1	
40 and over	7	0.4	7	0.7	4	0.5	3	1.0	...	...	...	...	...	

[a] Percentage not computed, base less than 100.
[b] From this table 109 cases of the 1,599 studied were excluded because one or more of the items needed were not recorded.

TABLE 10

Unmarried Mothers Classified by Age and Color
(Health Department Data)

AGE	TOTAL	WHITE	NEGRO
Total	1,470	1,091	379
14 or under	26	15	11
15–19	612	407	205
20–24	580	464	116
25–29	161	132	29
30–34	52	40	12
35–39	29	25	4
40 and over	10	8	2

those given in the social agency statistics, it will be noted that the two sets of figures agree in having a high percentage of the cases in the age groups under twenty-five.[1] Because of the difference in age groupings used, the Health Department statistics bring out more clearly than do the social agency statistics the extreme youth of some of those who have become mothers out of wedlock.

Race and Nativity

The facts of race and nativity of the mothers of illegitimate children are of value from two points of view. Since social attitudes toward illegitimacy vary somewhat among cultural and racial groups, it is important to see the cases classified according to these backgrounds. It is unfortunately impossible to make this analysis properly from existing records. Neither birth certificates nor agency records have the data regarding

[1]Some difference is also due to the fact that the mother may have had a birthday between the time of the filing of the birth of her child and of her application to a social agency. This would not, however, account for the excess of births to women 35 years of age and over, reported by the Health Department in a total series less than that of the agencies. It is possible that the agencies did not know all of these older women.

the birthplace of the mothers' parents requisite to the classification of these mothers into their proper cultural groups. It would be highly revealing to know, for instance, whether the native born were of recent immigrant stock or of the older native families. It has long been known that foreign born persons themselves do not get into behavior difficulties in unusual proportions, but it has been thought that the children of foreign born persons are often confused and uncertain as to the standards of conduct expected of them.[2]

The 1,470 birth certificates classified by the Health Department as referring to illegitimate infants born in New York City in 1930 are theoretically the most complete picture available to us of the illegitimate children born in New York City in 1930. They yielded the information as to the nativity and color of the mothers which is summarized in Table 11.

TABLE 11

Mothers of Illegitimate Infants Born in New York City, 1930,
Classified by Color and Nativity
(Health Department Data)

| | | NATIVITY | |
COLOR	TOTAL	NATIVE BORN	FOREIGN BORN
Total	1,470	1,119	351
White	1,091	773	318
Negro	379	346	33

Before commenting on these figures it may be well to see how the data from the Health Department compare with those from the agency records. These appear in Table 12.

It will be seen from these two tables that though forty-nine more cases are in the agency group than are in the Health

[2]It is pointed out by Professor Edith Abbott of the University of Chicago that there are no good data on which to base conclusions regarding the prevalence of crime among the native born of foreign parentage.

TABLE 12

Mothers of Illegitimate Infants Born in New York City, 1930,
Classified by Color and Nativity
(Social Agency Data)

| | | NATIVITY | |
COLOR	TOTAL	NATIVE BORN	FOREIGN BORN
Total	1,519ᵃ	1,196	323
White	1,085	793	292
Negro	434	403	31

ᵃFrom this table 90 cases of the 1,599 studied were excluded because one or more of the items needed were not recorded.

Department total, this difference is largely accounted for by colored cases. The total number of white cases is almost the same in the two groups. The difference is, moreover, among the native born Negroes, rather than among the foreign born colored. Among the white cases there were no very significant differences between the proportions of native and of foreign born women in the two sets of data, though the agencies, even with their larger total number of cases, report twenty fewer foreign born white mothers.

Had it been possible to secure from the social agencies the data on the additional 298 births that made up the total of 1,817 which were known by them to have occurred in 1930 in the city, these proportions might have been somewhat modified.

Owing to the varying sex and age proportions within the general nativity groups in the population, it is necessary to standardize the groups chosen for comparison. In this case the race and general nativity distribution of unmarried mothers, fifteen to twenty-nine years old, have been compared with the race and nativity distribution of females fifteen to twenty-nine years in the general population.

The results appear in Table 13.

TABLE 13

Unmarried Mothers, Fifteen to Twenty-nine Years Old,
Each General Nativity Group, 1930

NATIVITY AND COLOR	TOTAL FEMALES 15-29 YEARS IN NEW YORK CITY	UNMARRIED MOTHERS 15-29 YEARS	UNMARRIED MOTHERS PER 100,000 FEMALES 15-29 YEARS
Native white	708,891	723	102.0
Foreign born white . .	250,127	259	103.5
Negro	59,827	391	653.5

It will be seen that the rates per hundred thousand females of appropriate ages among native and foreign born white females are strikingly similar. The Negro rate is between six and seven times greater than the white rate.

Since the proportion of non-resident mothers in each of the nativity groups was relatively the same, these comparisons may be regarded as fairly accurate.

Countries of Birth of the Foreign Born

Information regarding the country of birth of the foreign born unmarried mothers was given in some of the agency records and the data available has been compiled in Table 14.

It should be pointed out that the figures in Table 14 include fewer unmarried mothers of foreign birth than the Health Department figures cited previously, in which the country of origin of the foreign born unmarried mothers was not given. It should be emphasized, moreover, that no deductions as to the illegitimacy rates among these foreign born groups can be drawn from these figures, since there are available no statistics as to the age and sex distribution among these groups. A few available facts of another nature may, however, be commented upon here.

TABLE 14

Foreign Born Unmarried Mothers Classified by Country of Birth

COUNTRY OF BIRTH	TOTAL	PERCENT	WHITE	NEGRO
Total	323	100.0	292	31
British Empire	179	55.4	151	28
England	12	3.7	12	0
Scotland	14	4.4	14	0
Ireland	98	30.3	98	0
Canada	21	6.5	21	0
British West Indies	34	10.5	6	28
Norway, Sweden, and Holland	12	3.7	12	0
Germany	44	13.6	44	0
Austria, Hungary, and Switzerland . .	13	4.1	13	0
Czechoslovakia, Yugoslavia, and Greece	8	2.5	8	0
Russia, Poland, and Finland	39	12.1	39	0
Italy	17	5.3	17	0
France	6	1.9	6	0
Central and South American countries.	5	1.5	2	3

A recently published tabulation made by the U. S. Bureau of the Census of the 1930 ratios of males to females in these nationality groups shows the following: for each 100 females in New York City who were born in England, there were only 97.7 males who were born in England; the same ratio for Scotland is 97.4; Northern Ireland, 77.7; Irish Free State, 80.1; Canada (French), 93.1; Canada (other), 75.2; West Indies, 106.2; Norway, Sweden, and Holland, from 108.1 to 210.9; Germany, 104.8; Austria, Hungary, and Switzerland, 84.6 to 108.4; Czechoslovakia, Yugoslavia, and Greece, from 82.5 to 215.5; Russia, Poland, and Finland, 78.9 to 105.5; Italy, 126.7; France, 79.0; and Central and South American countries, 134.0.

Among the population of foreign born women in New York City (1,141,685), those from the British Isles numbered 181,-

810, or 15.9 percent. But this group furnished 38.4 percent of the illegitimate births to foreign born women referred to in the above table. Women born in Canada are less than two percent of the foreign born women but they furnished 6.5 percent of the births to this group of foreign born women. These percentages for women born in Germany are 10.2 and 13.6 respectively; for women born in Italy, they are 17.0 and 5.3; for the women born in Russia, Poland, and Finland, they are 29.8 and 12.1.

It seems probable that an unbalanced ratio between the sexes within a nationality group, combined with the problems of adjustment experienced by the single woman in a foreign country, is a not insignificant underlying factor in this problem.

The question may also be raised as to why some nationality groups whose illegitimacy rate is low in their own countries should contribute a disproportionate number of illegitimate births to the number of such births among the foreign born for which we have information in the agency records. For example, the Irish groups, which contributed 30.3 percent of the number of illegitimate births among the foreign born in New York City in 1930 for which we had information, had in their own country in 1928 only 4.6 percent of the total number of births illegitimate, one of the lowest illegitimacy rates in Western Europe; while the Italian and the German and other groups, which have a higher illegitimacy rate in their own countries than do the Irish, apparently contribute proportionately fewer illegitimate births in New York City.[3] The social and family conditions under which these young women come to New York City, and the occupations which they customa-

[3]The percentage of total births illegitimate was reported as follows for the countries of Western Europe with which this study is concerned: (1926) Norway, 6.54; Sweden, 14.57; Italy, 4.96; (1927) Belgium, 4.6; Denmark, 11.00; Germany, 12.00; (1928) England and Wales, 4.5; Scotland, 7.4; Ireland, 4.6. *Encyclopaedia of the Social Sciences*, VII, 579 ff.

rily enter immediately after their arrival, would be of importance in any attempt at a scientific explanation of this phenomenon. While we have no statistical data to support the affirmation, it is generally asserted that the young women among certain foreign born groups: for example, the Italians, do not customarily come to this country except as members of family groups; such circumstances would presumably give them a protection which a young woman coming alone and separated from her family group would not have. It is generally stated, too, that the foreign born Irish young women, who come more often alone and separated from their family groups, also enter into the field of domestic service in greater numbers than do young women of other nationality groups. This circumstance would be of significance in explaining the high proportion of illegitimate births among this group. At any rate, in commenting upon our figures with regard to the number of illegitimate births among the foreign born in New York City, it would seem necessary to take into account the illegitimacy rate in the countries from which these groups come. These European rates would appear to be significant not only in explaining quantitatively the rates among the foreign born in New York City, but also in understanding the attitude toward illegitimacy prevailing among the various groups of foreign born in the city and the difficulties which the unmarried mothers of these groups may be expected to meet among their own people. For example, less tolerance in cases of illegitimacy might be expected among a group such as the Irish foreign born, who have been little accustomed to the problem in their own country; while a more tolerant attitude might be expected of another foreign group among whom pre-marital sex relations have been more freely admitted.

It should be recalled, too, that our figures for the country of origin of unmarried mothers are incomplete, and that they can be in no way taken as characteristic of the groups named in the table, but as descriptive only of that small group of un-married mothers for which we have information.

If further analysis of the figures on the foreign born is attempted it will show that for the Negro group only 9 percent of the mothers were of foreign birth. In the face of the com-plaints of many agencies that the West Indian Negro contrib-utes a disproportionately large number of members to this group, these figures seem low. It should be remembered, of course, that the Negroes coming from Puerto Rico and the Virgin Islands are listed as native born, and hence are counted with the native population. But these add only twenty-three cases to this total of thirty-one West Indian Negroes. There were fifteen Negro unmarried mothers born in Puerto Rico, seven in the Virgin Islands and one in the Canal Zone.

Perhaps the most significant fact of all is that, though the rates for the Negroes may be high, and though the problems attaching to the birth of an illegitimate child to a foreign born woman may seem to present peculiar difficulties, the largest single nativity group of mothers of illegitimate children is the native born white group. These mothers exceed in number the Negro and the foreign white cases combined.

Were the social investigations and the records of agencies more complete, and were it possible to study them carefully, it probably would be possible to find out the cultural back-ground or racial stock of these women, and possible to relate more closely than can here be done the circumstances of individual cases to these cultural backgrounds. It would, for instance, be of value to know whether, as has been said, these native born women were also of the older native stock, or whether they were the children of recent immigrants, whether they were of urban or rural backgrounds, and whether they were from groups and families in which illegitimacy was accepted tolerantly or even casually. Such study would be helpful from the point of view of understanding the cultural groups in America and also from that of seeing the individual mother in her cultural setting.

A little additional light on cultural background appears in a later section on religion.

Occupation

Tabulation of the schedule replies from social agencies with regard to the occupation and nativity of unmarried mothers reveals that the distribution of 1,212 cases for which such information was given was as summarized in Table 15.

It will be observed that slightly more than one-half of the total number of unmarried mothers for whom information as to occupation was given were found to be engaged in domestic service. The significance of this figure will be realized if it is recalled that of all gainfully employed females in New York City in 1930 only 18.5 percent were engaged in domestic service. This comparison, however, like that for general nativity, should be standardized for age and other factors, before it can be made with precision. That is, only those gainfully employed women who are in the appropriate age groups should be considered as forming the population background upon which percentage might be computed. The crude comparison, however, agrees with the findings of studies of illegitimacy made elsewhere, which show a disproportionate number of unmarried mothers as having been engaged in domestic service. Since the figures given above, however, are derived from the records of social agencies, the only conclusion which we are justified in making from them is that of the cases of the rather large number of unmarried mothers coming to the attention of social agencies by their requests for assistance, 52.1 percent were engaged in domestic service.

As might have been expected, a much higher percentage of Negro than of white unmarried mothers were engaged in domestic service. A higher percentage of school girls in the

TABLE 15

Unmarried Mothers, Classified by Occupation, Color, and Nativity

OCCUPATION	TOTAL		WHITE						NEGRO				
			TOTAL		NATIVE BORN		FOREIGN BORN		TOTAL		NATIVE BORN		FOREIGN BORN[a]
	No.	Percent	No.	Percent	No.	Percent	No.	Percent	No.	Percent	No.	Percent	No.
Total	1,212[b]	100.0	878	100.0	623	100.0	255	100.0	334	100.0	304	100.0	30
Professional . .	61	5.0	52	5.9	38	6.1	14	5.5	9	2.7	7	2.3	2
Clerical	215	17.7	211	24.0	186	29.9	25	9.8	4	1.2	2	0.7	2
Domestic service.	631	52.1	386	44.0	205	32.9	181	71.0	245	73.3	227	74.7	18
Factory	196	16.2	164	18.7	134	21.5	30	11.8	32	9.6	24	7.9	8
School	87	7.2	48	5.5	45	7.2	3	1.2	39	11.7	39	12.8	...
Miscellaneous .	22	1.8	17	1.9	15	2.4	2	0.7	5	1.5	5	1.6	...

[a]Percentage not computed, base less than 100.

[b]From this table 387 cases of the 1,599 studied were excluded because one or more items needed were not recorded.

Negro group is discernible, and this fact is in harmony with what has previously been said with regard to the greater proportion of Negroes in the lower age groups of unmarried mothers. Similarly a smaller percentage of Negroes than of whites was found in clerical and professional pursuits, and this fact accords with the occupational distribution of these two racial groups of the general population.

Statistics compiled from the birth certificates of illegitimate infants born in New York City in 1930 and furnished by the Health Department reveal a different distribution of unmarried mothers in occupational classes (Table 16).

TABLE 16

Unmarried Mothers Classified by Occupation
(Health Department Data)

OCCUPATION	NUMBER	PERCENT
Total	671	100.0
Professional	57	8.5
Clerical	203	30.3
Domestic service	291	43.4
Clothing	24	3.6
Trades	17	2.5
Transportation	5	0.7
Public service	2	0.3
Miscellaneous	72	10.7

It is noteworthy that only 671 birth certificates had data on mother's occupation. On account of the divergent classifications used, only the professional, the clerical, and the domestic service groups can be compared with the figures from the agencies. There is an interesting similarity between the figures for the women in professional and clerical pursuits. The Health Department's figures on domestic service are conspicuously short, as they are in several of the other categories.

While no conclusions can be drawn from such obviously defective data, a rather arresting question arises: Does the close similarity of the figures reported by the Health Department and by the agencies on the women in professional and clerical occupations indicate that there has been relatively complete reporting of such cases? And does it also mean that practically all of these cases come to be known to agencies of some type? On a priori grounds it might seem that these would be the women who could probably employ a private physician, who might help them place their babies without resort to agencies.

Nothing short of an actual case-by-case examination and comparison[4] of the data in agencies and in the Health Department would reveal whether the professional and clerical women reported by the agencies are the same persons as those reported by the Health Department. Should that turn out to be the case the answer to the questions asked above would seem to be in the affirmative.

As has been previously mentioned, it was reported by the medical and health agencies that some unmarried mothers engaged in clerical and professional pursuits had evinced a firm resolve to avoid all contact with the specialized case work agencies, because of their fear of exposure from the investigations which these agencies customarily make. These workers reported that the young women concerned had usually very definite ideas of what plans they wished to make, and that they were fearful of intervention by agencies known to them as favoring a course of action different from that which they had planned for themselves. The varying attitudes involved in these questions have been discussed in a preceding section, and attention was called to the fact that agencies willing to

---

[4]See section on the number of children borne by these mothers for a further illustration of the need for mobilizing all of the data in birth records and agency records in the study of these cases.

waive the usual investigation procedures and accept the surrender of infants in the first weeks of life had made it possible for these young women to return to their customary pursuits within a short time after the birth of the child.

Young women less acquainted with such facilities, however, appeared to come more readily to the social agencies for assistance and advice, and were, therefore, more subject to social investigation. It is usually assumed that young women of this type are found in greater numbers in the less skilled pursuits, such as domestic service. It should be pointed out, however, that it is not only the economic factor that enters into the question of an appeal to a social agency. Some of the unmarried mothers coming to social agencies have no need of material assistance, but are bewildered and in need of direction in a difficult situation. Other young women, more familiar with the resources available and more accustomed to the independent direction of their affairs, had neither the need nor the desire to appeal for such advice, as the health and medical agencies testified. It seemed true, also, that the medical and health agencies having the first contact with these young women were more likely to refer to the specialized and the case work agencies those who appeared least capable of solving their own difficulties.

One medical worker when consulted as to her basis for recommendations to specialized agencies remarked:

I send them to an agency only if they are low-class and ignorant. I would not dream of mentioning an agency to a nice girl. She wouldn't stand for it. If a nice girl wants to give up her baby I send her to ————, where they make the least fuss about taking babies.

It is evident, however, from the information furnished from social agencies, that some young women from clerical and professional pursuits do make use of the facilities offered them by social agencies. These included, of course, the social service departments of hospitals. While it is probably true that the more ignorant and bewildered young women are the more likely to seek advice from the other types of agencies, it is evident also that these agencies offer services which have caused some young women of other groups to appeal to them.

The sixty-three young women in professional pursuits included school teachers, nurses, social workers, and others. Most of them were young in their professional careers, and very few were in highly paid work. Their appeal to social agencies was based upon their need for shelter and protection away from their families, aid in supporting the child, and planning for his care. A large proportion of this group was composed of non-residents, who had come from small towns to the city for protection and concealment.

It seems of importance to note that ninety unmarried mothers included in the tabulations from social agency records were school girls. This group includes, of course, those in the younger age group who would be in need of special care and protection.

Education

Table 17 shows the results of the attempts to classify information received from social agencies as to the educational attainments of unmarried mothers coming under their care. It is correlated with general nativity. It should be pointed out that in order to be placed within a particular educational category of the table it was necessary only that the girl or woman have done some work of that grade. For example, 184 unmarried mothers in the group "high school" means only that all members of this group had done some high-school work, and not that they had all finished high school.

It will be observed that in less than one-half of the total number of records of illegitimate families had any entry as to the mother's education been made. This omission of an important item of information in so many cases is to be ex-

TABLE 17

Unmarried Mothers Classified by Education, Color, and Nativity

EDUCATION	TOTAL		WHITE						NEGRO				
			TOTAL		NATIVE BORN		FOREIGN BORN		TOTAL		NATIVE BORN		FOREIGN BORN[a]
	No.	Percent	No.	Percent	No.	Percent	No.	Percent	No.	Percent	No.	Percent	No.
Total	666[b]	100.0	555	100.0	396	100.0	159	100.0	111	100.0	102	100.0	9
Elementary school First to fourth grades	49	7.3	38	6.8	20	5.1	18	11.3	11	9.9	11	10.8	...
Seventh to eighth grades	367	55.1	303	54.6	192	48.5	111	69.8	64	57.7	56	54.9	8
High school	183	27.5	154	27.7	133	33.6	21	13.2	29	26.1	28	27.5	1
Normal school	7	1.1	6	1.1	6	1.5	...	...	1	0.9	1	1.0	...
College	15	2.3	12	2.2	10	2.5	2	1.3	3	2.7	3	2.9	...
Professional school	45	6.7	42	7.6	35	8.8	7	4.4	3	2.7	3	2.9	...

[a] Percentage not computed, base less than 100.
[b] From this table 933 cases of the 1,599 studied were excluded because one or more of the items needed were not recorded.

plained by the fact that many of the records used in this study were those of medical and health agencies, which recognized no need of making an inquiry as to education of the mother in order to perform the specific function for which they regard themselves as responsible.

The outstanding fact here is that more than 60 percent of the total group about which we had information had never gone beyond the eighth grade at school. Contrary to a belief, prevalent among some social agencies, that unmarried mothers now come largely from the "better educated" classes, it is found that only a little over 10 percent of the group for which data are available had any training beyond high school. A comparison of the educational attainments and the occupational status of these women, reveals that about the same actual number had higher education as were reported to be following professional occupations; the number of those in clerical occupations is about like the number who had gone to high school. Whatever the educational attainment of those not reported, it seems that a high proportion of them had not achieved an occupation which is dependent in large degree on education and special training.

Comparison of the educational attainments of white and Negro unmarried mothers of our group reveals the fact that a larger proportion of the Negro mothers than of the white had never gone beyond the eighth grade in school, and that fewer of the Negroes had received college or professional school training. The differences are not striking, however. If the education of the unmarried mothers about whom we have data is compared with that of the very few unmarried fathers reported, fewer proportionately of the former than of the latter are found in the upper educational groups.

Comparison of the native born unmarried mothers with the foreign born unmarried mothers as to educational attainment reveals a marked difference in favor of the former.

An attempt was made with regard to sixty-seven unmarried mothers, who had received some training beyond high school, to determine whether their philosophy as to the validity of our existing matrimonial institutions had entered into the determination of their illegitimate parenthood. Insofar as the study of the case records relating to the young women permitted any deductions in this regard, no such relationship was revealed. Not only was this the case, but it was clear that these young women who had expressed themselves with regard to their illegitimate parenthood looked upon it as a regrettable misfortune; and that while many of them were prepared to meet the situation courageously, there were not among their number any, whose records came to light in this study, who attempted to justify their situation as desirable in the light of existing social conditions.

Information as to the educational attainments of unmarried mothers had been secured most consistently and accurately by those agencies interested in the vocational adjustment of these young women after the birth of the child; the information in Table 17 relates particularly to the young women who had asked for such vocational counsel. It should be pointed out that the group of young women several times referred to, who had been able to pay for their care in private hospitals, had not been the subject of a social inquiry, and no record as to their schooling was, therefore, available, though in many cases their occupation was recorded. Such a distribution in educational groups as we have presented must accordingly be regarded as describing only that part of our group for which the information was specifically recorded, and is not a basis for generalization.

Religious and Cultural Connections

The care of the unmarried mother and her child has been one of the types of social work which has been a concern of

TABLE 18

Unmarried Mothers Classified by Religion, Color, and Nativity

RELIGION	TOTAL		WHITE						NEGRO				
			TOTAL		NATIVE BORN		FOREIGN BORN		TOTAL		NATIVE BORN		FOREIGN BORN[a]
	No.	Percent	No.	Percent	No.	Percent	No.	Percent	No.	Percent	No.	Percent	No.
Total	1,495[b]	100.0	1,068	100.0	781	100.0	287	100.0	427	100.0	396	100.0	31
Protestant . .	713	47.7	325	30.4	262	33.5	63	21.9	388	90.9	365	92.2	23
Catholic . . .	597	39.9	559	52.4	394	50.5	165	57.5	38	8.9	30	7.6	8
Jewish	185	12.4	184	17.2	125	16.0	59	20.6	1	0.2	1	0.2	...

[a]Percentage not computed, base less than 100.
[b]From this table 104 cases of the 1,599 studied were excluded because one or more items needed were not recorded.

organized religious groups for a long time. It is, therefore, of some value to know the religious preferences of these young women, together with their cultural connections and occupational status.

Religious affiliation was the best reported item of information on the individual case schedule. Of the total of 1,599 cases studied, data on religion was available on 1,565 of them. Of these 745 were reported to be Protestants, 631 were Catholic, and 189 were Jewish. Table 18 shows the classification of the data furnished by social agencies as to the religious affiliations and nativity of the unmarried mothers.

Estimates as to the 1930 distribution of New York City's total population into the main religious bodies were as shown in Table 19.

TABLE 19

Estimate of the Religious Composition of the Total Population of New York City, 1930[a]

RELIGION	NUMBER	PERCENT
Total	6,930,446	100.0
Roman Catholic	2,365,247	34.1
Protestant	2,556,595	36.9
Eastern Orthodox	116,544	1.7
Jewish	1,876,545	27.1
Unclassified	15,515	0.2

[a]Walter Laidlaw. *Population of the City of New York, 1890-1930*, Cities Census Committee, Inc., 1932.

If the distribution of the total number of unmarried mothers of this study into the three religious groupings is compared with the distribution of the city's total population in these groupings, it will be observed that the Protestant and Catholic groups contributed more, and the Jewish group less, than the expected proportion to the total number of illegitimate births.

It should be indicated, however, that such an attempt at comparison has little significance, because the age and sex distribution in these religious groupings are not known. In order to be significant the comparison should include the number of young women fifteen to twenty-nine years of age in these religious groups in New York City in 1930 for consideration with the number of unmarried mothers fifteen to twenty-nine years of age at this time. Since the statistical basis for such a comparison is lacking the above figures are stated for what they may be worth.

The Cities Census Committee has estimated the Negroes to be more than 90 percent Protestant in faith.[5] Among the Negro unmarried mothers the proportion of Protestants is a little higher. A few were Catholic. One Negro unmarried mother had declared herself to be of the Jewish faith. Among the native white women, the Protestants furnished about one-third, the Catholics about one-half, and the Jewish group about one-sixth of the total.

Since occupation and religious affiliation are such important factors in the types of care which an unmarried mother receives and in the plans which can be developed for her, it seemed desirable to correlate these two items of information. This has been done in Table 20.

As is shown here, the proportion of unmarried mothers engaged in domestic service remains large for both Protestant and Catholic groups, even after the occupational data for the Negro unmarried mother is presented separately. Of the white Protestant group (native and foreign born) 48 percent were engaged in domestic service, and of the white Catholic group (native and foreign born) 50.6 percent were engaged in domestic service. The proportion of Negro unmarried mothers in domestic service is, as was to have been expected, higher in

[5] Walter Laidlaw, *Population of the City of New York, 1890-1930*, Cities Census Committee, Inc., 1932, p. 274.

TABLE 20

Unmarried Mothers Classified by Occupation, Religion, and Color

| OCCUPATION | TOTAL | | PROTESTANT | | | | CATHOLIC | | | | JEWISH | |
| | | | WHITE | | NEGRO | | WHITE | | NEGRO[a] | | | |
	No.	Percent	No.	Percent	No.	Percent	No.	Percent	No.	Percent	No.	Percent
Total	1,185[b]	100.0	256	100.0	287	100.0	477	100.0	30	100.0	135	100.0
Professional . . .	60	5.1	18	7.0	7	2.5	23	4.8	1	4.8	11	8.1
Clerical	212	17.9	64	25.0	1	0.3	91	19.1	2	19.1	54	40.0
Domestic	614	51.8	123	48.1	217	75.6	239	50.1	20	50.1	15	11.1
Factory	192	16.2	28	10.9	23	8.0	93	19.5	5	19.5	43	31.9
School	85	7.2	17	6.6	34	11.8	26	5.5	2	5.5	6	4.4
Miscellaneous . .	22	1.8	6	2.4	5	1.8	5	1.0	. . .	1.0	6	4.5

[a]Percentage not computed, base less than 100.

[b]From this table 414 cases of the 1,599 studied were excluded because one or more items needed were not recorded.

both the Protestant and Catholic groups than the same proportion for white unmarried mothers. But only 11.1 percent of the Jewish unmarried mothers had been engaged in domestic service.

As has already been stated, studies of illegitimacy, made in this country, and in certain European countries as well, have revealed a proportion of unmarried mothers engaged in domestic service greatly in excess of the proportion in this type of occupation of all gainfully employed females.[6] It is not generally believed that the occupational factor alone is sufficient to explain behavior resulting in illegitimate parenthood, although certain conditions connected with domestic service may be regarded as unfavorable to normal social and recreational outlets for the young women engaged in it. It is rather that the occupational status of these young women seems to serve as one index of the generally low social and economic level at which they live. This occupation, together with its associated conditions, such as less favorable educational advantages, generally lower wages, and certain traditional prejudices and unfavorable attitudes with regard to this branch of gainful occupation for women, may select and influence types of girls and women who are already more exposed to this kind of misfortune than are those in other occupations. It should be pointed out, too, that many of these young women are separated from their family and social groups because of the circumstances of their employment, and that they lack, therefore, the protection and guidance which such associations normally give. However complex the causes, the fact remains that the incidence of illegitimacy is high among young women engaged in domestic service, and this would appear to lead to the expectation that any social or racial group having a high percentage of its gainfully employed women in domestic service would

[6]*Illegitimacy as a Child Welfare Problem*, Parts I and II, United States Children's Bureau Publications 66 and 75; 1920, 1921.

have a relatively high proportion of illegitimate births.[7] This observation seems to be sustained by the results of this study.

However difficult may be deductions as to the relation between occupational status (as indicative of social and economic conditions) and the prevalence of illegitimacy in a particular group, it should be noted, as a matter of practical importance, that the type of care provided by any one sectarian group will be influenced somewhat by the occupational status of the young women coming to its attention. This has indeed proved to be the case, as will be recalled from the description of these facilities given in Part Two, where it was shown, for example, in the case of the methods employed by the Jewish agencies in caring for the unmarried mothers, very few of whom were domestic servants. Within the three sectarian groups there was observed a tendency for specialization of agencies in order to care for one group or other of unmarried mothers roughly corresponding with the occupational groupings represented by our classification. This tendency to specialization was regarded by social workers as a necessary response to the varying needs of young women coming from the different occupational classes, and it seemed to be the consensus of opinion among them that such specialization should be encouraged. As has been intimated at various places throughout this discussion, criticism of social agencies caring for unmarried mothers has often reverted to the fact that the methods of care and reëducation adopted originally for one occupational group have evidently been applied without much discrimination to unmarried mothers of another occupational group, thus provoking resentment and criticism not only from the young women themselves, but from coöperating agencies as well. Social workers aware of this problem were insistent in their demand for increased specialization of separate agencies or for

[7]See Appendix 5 for detailed table on unmarried mothers classified by occupation, color, nativity, and religion.

increased specialization within the agencies which would allow for more individual consideration in investigation and in treatment.

Health

Considerations as to the mother's health had been of importance in deciding what plans were to be made for her and her child, and agency records generally included a statement of some nature with regard to this item. An unmarried mother who was not in good health, for example, would not ordinarily be recommended for a position at housework with her child. Furthermore, if she were found to be suffering from an hereditary ailment or from a disease which might possibly affect the health of her child, this would influence the decision of an adoption agency as to whether or not the child would be accepted for placement.

Of a total of 1,599 illegitimate family records, 994 contained some statement as to the health of the unmarried mother. A classification of these replies was difficult because of their vagueness. Statements were sometimes made that the unmarried mother was in "poor" health, but no specification was made as to the nature of her ailment. A category was therefore devised to include those who were in "poor" health but the nature of whose malady was not stated. When more specific information was given this was classified, as shown in Table 21.

It will be observed that 83.7 percent of the total number of unmarried mothers for whom health information was given were stated to be in "good" health. The statements as to health in some agencies were based upon the results of a physical examination, but in other agencies the entry as to the health of the unmarried mother had apparently been based upon her statement as to her own health, or the social worker's impression of her client's health. In cases where there had been an overlapping of work, where an unmarried mother had received

TABLE 21

Unmarried Mothers Classified by Condition of Health, Color, and Nativity

CONDITION OF HEALTH	TOTAL		WHITE						NEGRO				
			TOTAL		NATIVE BORN		FOREIGN BORN		TOTAL		NATIVE BORN		FOREIGN BORN[a]
	No.	Percent	No.	Percent	No.	Percent	No.	Percent	No.	Percent	No.	Percent	No.
Total	994[b]	100.0	752	100.0	525	100.0	227	100.0	242	100.0	224	100.0	18
Good	832	83.7	638	84.8	439	83.6	199	87.7	194	80.2	179	79.9	15
Poor	66	6.6	56	7.4	39	7.4	17	7.5	10	4.1	8	3.6	2
Venereal disease	74	7.5	38	5.1	31	5.9	7	3.1	36	14.9	35	15.7	1
Epilepsy	4	0.4	3	0.4	3	0.6	...	...	1	0.4	1	0.4	...
Mental disease	16	1.6	16	2.1	12	2.3	4	1.7	...	...	...	...	...
Physical deformity	2	0.2	1	0.2	1	0.2	...	...	1	0.4	1	0.4	...

[a] Percentage not computed, base less than 100.

[b] From this table 605 cases of the 1,599 studied were excluded because the items needed were not recorded.

help from several different agencies, she had sometimes undergone as many physical examinations; while other unmarried mothers of whom we had record had apparently not undergone a physical examination at all, at the time that the record had been made. As has been indicated in a previous section, the maternity homes studied were found to be strict in insisting upon a Wassermann test before applicants were admitted.

Of the total number of unmarried mothers considered in the above table, 16.3 percent were said not to be in "good" health. The fact that about one-sixth of all the unmarried mothers about whom health information was given were not in good health explains the urgent necessity of institutional care in some cases, and the necessity for giving temporary relief and free medical care in others.

Of those not in good health, 6.6 percent were said to be in "poor" health, and a further 7.5 percent were said to be suffering from a venereal disease. Social workers interviewed on the subject, however, insisted this was an understatement of the prevalence of this disease among unmarried mothers, and the evidence given in support of their contention has been given in Part Two. The age classification of our group, however, and the fact that relatively few of the unmarried mothers had any long history of sex delinquency, should also be borne in mind in attempting to explain why the incidence of venereal disease among them appeared to be lower than in some institutions for delinquent women.

As might be expected from the general social and economic conditions under which the two races live, a higher percentage of white than of Negro unmarried mothers was found to be in good health. The incidence of venereal disease, also, was higher among the Negro than among the white unmarried mothers. Although the figures in any category are small, and are not, therefore, to be regarded as of any great weight statistically, it may be interesting to note that the sixteen cases of "mental disease" were all among the white unmarried mothers, while no such cases were reported among the Negro unmarried mothers. Whether this fact is to be explained in terms of the greater facilities for the examination of the white group in this respect, we are not prepared to state.

Consideration of the health of unmarried mothers with reference to their nativity reveals the fact that a larger percentage of the foreign born white than of the native born unmarried mothers was in "good" health, and that the incidence of venereal disease was higher among the native born than among the foreign born. Again it should be insisted that the considerable number of cases in which health was not reported would invalidate any general conclusion which might be made for the group as a whole, and our statements must be strictly construed as applying only to that group for which the information was given.

The Number of Children They Have Had

Table 22 was compiled from the birth certificates by the Health Department to show the total number of children borne by the girls and women who gave birth to a child out of wedlock in New York City in 1930.

TABLE 22

Illegitimate Births in New York City, 1930, Classified by Color of Mother and Order of Birth (Health Department Data)

ORDER OF BIRTH	NUMBER OF MOTHERS		
	TOTAL	WHITE	NEGRO
Total	1,470	1,091	379
First child	1,270	963	307
Second child	145	98	47
Third child	24	14	10
Fourth child	13	5	8
Fifth child	5	5	. . .
Sixth child	7	4	3
Seventh or over	6	2	4

It will be observed that 200 out of a total of 1,470 women giving birth to an illegitimate child in 1930 had previously given birth to at least one child; that is, a little more than 13 percent of all the mothers had had a child previously. We have no means of knowing the legal status of the children born to these mothers before 1930, but it is possible that some of them were legitimate. Among the agency records there were 118 mothers who had been married at some time prior to the birth of the child considered in this study.[8] Moreover, it was found, through a perusal of the records of social agencies, that in some cases where more than one illegitimate child had been born to parents, the latter were living together and constituted in most respects a normal family group, except for the fact that no legal marriage had been entered into. These illegitimate families, however, were not stable, self-sustaining units, and it was largely because of this fact that they had come to the attention of the family welfare societies.

It will be noticed from the above table that the number of instances of unmarried mothers with several children is small; only thirteen had had four children; five had had five children; seven had had six children; and six had had seven or more children. It should not be inferred, however, that the children were all children of the same father, for no such information was given in the records.

It will be observed, also, that the proportion of Negro illegitimate mothers having more than one child was slightly higher than the proportion of white illegitimate mothers having more than one child—11.7 percent of the white mothers,

[8] Owing to the inaccessibility of the birth records, as well as to the attitude of some private agencies, it was impossible to coördinate the bodies of fact on individual cases on record at the Health Department and at the agencies and institutions, and therefore to secure the benefit of knowledge based on all recorded materials. The situation here illustrates the need, if this problem is to be thoroughly studied, of securing data in such a way that all the available facts pertaining to a given case can be assembled and analysed.

but 19 percent of the Negro mothers, had had more than one child. In this connection it may be well to recall the age groupings of the unmarried mothers previously given. It will be noted that a larger proportion of the Negro unmarried mothers is found in the lower age groups; this fact suggests the possibility of an average number of children for women of this group larger than that for the white mothers.

As between the native born and the foreign born unmarried mothers there was no significant difference between the proportions having more than one child.

The Health Department was able to supply statistics not only as to the number of children previously born to the women of our group but also the number of *children living* of these women. From Table 23 it can be seen that the two hundred mothers who had previously had children had borne a total of at least 523 children.[9] Of these at least 75 had died. Thus there had been a mortality rate of 145, or about one-seventh. While this is not comparable to the standardized infant mortality rate, since we cannot be sure that among the children who are not living were some who were born dead and some who lived beyond the age of one year (both of which classes are excluded from the standardized rate), it does seem clear that the children of these mothers had a markedly poorer survival rate than characterizes the general population in which the infant mortality rate for 1930 was 57.2, or about one-eighteenth of the babies born.

Table 23 indicates the number of children borne by the mothers in each nativity group and the number now living.

Even though the numbers are small, they confirm what is

[9] The exact number cannot be given, because there is uncertainty as to the total number of children borne by the 6 mothers who had had 7 or more children. The 187 mothers for whom the data are precise both as to the number of children born and number living, (i.e., those who had borne from 2 to 5 children) had had a total of 439 children. Of these 65 were not living at the time the certificate for the child born in 1930, was filed.

TABLE 23

Illegitimate Births in New York City, 1930, Classified as to Number of Children Born, Number of Living Children, Color, and Nativity of Mothers

NUMBER OF CHILDREN LIVING, COLOR, AND NATIVITY OF MOTHERS

NUMBER OF CHILDREN BORN TO MOTHERS	TOTAL	TOTAL				1 CHILD LIVING			2 CHILDREN LIVING		
		Total	White Native	White Foreign	Negro Total	White Native	White Foreign	Negro Native	White Native	White Foreign	Negro Native
Total	1,470	1,091	773	318	379	698	286	320	64	22	43
One	1,270	963	685	278	307	685	278	307	...	...	...
Two	145	98	71	27	47	12	8	13	59	19	34
Three	24	14	9	5	10	...	...	...	4	2	5
Four	13	5	2	3	8	1	...	...	1	...	3
Five	5	5	3	2	...	...	...	...	...	1	...
Six	7	4	2	2	3	...	...	...	...	...	1
Seven or more	5	2	1	1	4	...	...	...	...	...	...

TABLE 23 (continued)

NUMBER OF CHILDREN LIVING, COLOR, AND NATIVITY OF MOTHERS

NUMBER OF CHILDREN BORN TO MOTHERS	TOTAL	3 CHILDREN LIVING			4 CHILDREN LIVING			5 OR MORE CHILDREN LIVING		
		White Native	White Foreign	Negro Native	White Native	White Foreign	Negro Native	White Native	White Foreign	Negro Native
Total	1,470	5	5	9	1	2	3	5	3	4
One	1,270	...	...	...	...	...	...	...	...	...
Two	145	...	...	...	...	...	...	...	...	...
Three	24	5	3	5	...	...	...	...	...	...
Four	13	...	2	3	...	1	2	...	...	...
Five	5	...	...	...	1	1	...	2	...	...
Six	7	...	...	...	...	...	1	2	2	1
Seven or more	6	...	...	1	...	...	...	1	1	3

generally remarked with regard to mortality among the race and nativity groups. On the detailed work sheets it is shown that of the 31 foreign born mothers (27 white, 4 Negro) who had had 2 children, 10 of them (8 white, 2 Negro) had only one child living; while of the 114 native born mothers (71 white, 43 Negro) who had had 2 children, 23 (12 white, 11 Negro) had only one child living. In other words, about one-third of the foreign born mothers of this group had lost a child; while of the native born mothers about one-fifth had lost a child. The same relation holds true of the unmarried mothers of the two nativity groups who had had more than two children. The available data seem to indicate that the foreign born unmarried mothers of our group who have had more than one child have been less effective in keeping their children alive than have the native born American mothers. The economic factor, as well as different customs and health practices, must have been influential here.

As might be expected, the data indicate that the Negro unmarried mothers with more than one child were as a group less successful in keeping them alive than were the white unmarried mothers. This corresponds with the statistics for all Negro infants; the mortality rates for them are much higher than for the infants of the white population. An explanation of this fact in the social and economic environment of this group has already been suggested.

All of the tables given above have been derived from data given on the birth certificates. Our attempt to derive comparable tables from the records of social agencies was not successful. While some of the agencies and institutions specializing in the care of the illegitimate family had not failed to include this item in their records, so large a proportion of the agencies had failed to include it that our figures derived from their records cannot be regarded as of any significance on this point.

How They Find Help

An attempt was made to ascertain by what means the unmarried mothers come to the attention of social agencies. It has been shown in Part Two that the majority of young women make their initial appeal for help to the *medical and health* agencies, but through whom they came to these agencies it was difficult to learn. An effort at further elucidation of the point was made in the analysis of *social agency records* themselves. Many of these records contain an item of information "by whom referred," or "source of application," or other phrase designed to indicate through what sources these young women had come to them. The classification of these items of information is shown in Table 24.

TABLE 24

Unmarried Mothers Classified by Their Mode of Application to Social Agencies

MODE OF APPLICATION	NUMBER	PERCENT
Total	1,447	100.0
In person	496	34.3
Relatives	150	10.4
Doctor	26	1.8
Clergy	43	3.0
Police	10	0.7
Agency	623	43.1
Other	99	6.8

It will be seen at once that the greatest number came to the social agencies through "another agency." Another analysis of this fact reveals that the "other agency" was frequently a medical or health agency, which confirms the observation made in Part Two. When the young woman had not come through "another agency," she had most frequently made personal application for help. How she had learned of the existence of the agency to which she had made application was revealed through a further study of the records. In some cases she had learned of the agency through a friend; in a few cases she had sought for the address through the telephone directory; in some cases she had written to the woman's page of newspapers and magazines; one girl had written to the radio station from which a talk on protective work for young women had been broadcast; and some girls had been sent to the agency by their employers, who had made inquiries as to means of helping them in their difficulties.

Of the young women who had not acted directly on their own initiative in coming to the agency, one hundred fifty, or a little over 10 percent, had been sent to the agency or had been accompanied there by relatives who had made inquiries on their behalf and had sought this means of helping them. Twenty-six young women had been sent by their physicians; forty-three had been sent by clergymen, and ten had received the address of the agency from police officials, other than the Crime Prevention Bureau, to whom they had made an appeal for help.

Further inquiry as to whether the Negro unmarried mothers came to social agencies through other channels than the white unmarried mothers reveals some apparent differences as shown in Table 25.

It will be seen from this table that a larger percentage of Negro unmarried mothers than of white unmarried mothers came to the agency through relatives. This is probably due to the fact that the Negro unmarried mothers were on the whole younger than the white unmarried mothers and revealed their condition to their relatives; probably also to the fact that the relatives of the Negro unmarried mothers are said to be more likely to make efforts on their behalf at such a time than are the relatives of the white unmarried mothers. It will be observed

TABLE 25

Unmarried Mothers Classified by Their Mode of Application to Social Agencies and by Race and Nativity

MODE OF APPLICATION	TOTAL		WHITE						NEGRO					
			TOTAL		NATIVE BORN		FOREIGN BORN		TOTAL		NATIVE BORN		FOREIGN BORN[a]	
	No.	Percent	No.	Percent	No.	Percent	No.	Percent	No.	Percent	No.	Percent	No.	
Total	1,382[b]	100.0	986	100.0	710	100.0	276	100.0	396	100.0	367	100.0	29	
In person	451	32.6	343	34.8	258	36.3	85	30.8	108	27.3	99	27.0	9	
Relatives	148	10.7	44	4.4	38	5.4	6	2.2	104	26.3	100	27.2	4	
Doctor	26	1.9	22	2.2	15	2.1	7	2.5	4	1.0	4	1.1	...	
Clergy	42	3.0	42	4.3	19	2.7	23	8.3	...	...	...	...	...	
Police	10	0.7	5	0.5	4	0.6	1	0.4	5	1.2	5	1.4	...	
Agency	608	44.0	467	47.4	326	45.9	141	51.1	141	35.6	126	34.3	15	
Other	97	7.1	63	6.4	50	7.0	13	4.7	34	8.6	33	9.0	1	

[a]Percentage not computed, base less than 100.

[b]From this table 217 cases of the 1,599 studied were excluded because one or more items needed were not recorded.

further that fewer Negro unmarried mothers than white unmarried mothers were referred by other social agencies. This will be readily understood when it is remembered that fewer agencies exist for the care of Negro unmarried mothers, and that the latter are less likely than the white unmarried mothers to have received services from more than one agency.

The channels through which the native and foreign born unmarried mothers come to the social agencies also differ somewhat, as the above table shows. That foreign unmarried mothers are less likely than native unmarried mothers to have come to an agency through the intermediary of relatives probably arises from the fact that they are less likely than the native born unmarried mothers to have relatives in this country who can make efforts in their behalf. Cases were found of nine unmarried mothers who had left the father of the child in Europe, and who had come to this country before the birth of the child in order to escape the blame and censure of relatives. Others who had been in this country several years had nevertheless no relatives to whom they could turn when they found themselves in need of assistance. The fact that the foreign born unmarried mother is living away from her relatives explains further, perhaps, why she is more frequently referred by "another social agency." If there are no relatives with whom the first agency can adjust matters, it is obvious that community resources must be used, and that the unmarried mother must often be referred to another social agency for the services of which she has need.

By far the most striking fact in this connection is that such a very large proportion of these cases are known in some way to social and health agencies. It should again be emphasized, however, that this contact with social and health agencies does not imply that the illegitimate families so known are receiving adequate treatment from a social viewpoint. In fact, as has already been pointed out, such contacts between the illegitimate families and these agencies were often of a nature extremely casual.

But even in such cursory relationships, the fact of the illegitimate status of these family groups had become so readily known as to indicate the futility of the elaborate and rigid precautions taken by the official registration authorities in refusing to collate records for a carefully guarded study of the problem. When this study was originally conceived, it was somewhat naturally assumed that when the number of cases known to agencies came to be compared with the number of births registered, there would be a larger number of registrations than of cases known to the agencies. It was thought that there might be a sizeable group of birth certificates coming from physicians' private practices and unknown to any type of organized social or health work. The reverse has proved to be the situation. While it cannot be said that every unmarried mother and her child who were registered in 1930 were known to a social or health agency, since such a statement could be made only after comparison and actual identification of individual records, it does seem more than probable that a very high proportion of these cases did find their way to agencies of some type. In other words there seems good reason to believe that few illegitimate children are born who do not come in contact with some organized form of assistance.

The almost invariable contact with social and health agencies does not insure that an intelligent, rounded, and effective service will be rendered to the unmarried mothers and their children, as was clearly shown in Part Two of this study. One of the most serious bars to better work is the belief—largely mistaken, it would seem—that secrecy is being and will be maintained in these cases. Since practically all of these cases come eventually to social agencies—some of them to more than one agency—the questions might well be raised as to why a larger proportion was not referred originally by the medical and health agencies for social study and assistance, and why more systematic plans are not made at the start to give these women and girls the help and guidance which they so often need.

Incidentally, the question arises of why, since these cases come almost invariably to be known to other agencies in the community, the Health Department should guard with such extreme secrecy the data in its possession with regard to them, and omit its usual services of follow-up of babies for fear of embarrassing their mothers. It is obvious that this is not a group of cases in which a deep secret is being successfully guarded by doctor, patient, and Health Department. As was reported earlier in this study, in at least 1,419 instances these girls and women were known to social service departments of hospitals, public and private; 903 were known to have made contacts with homes for mothers and babies; 659 with case work agencies specializing in the care of unmarried mothers; 480 with child caring agencies; 126 with preventive and correctional agencies; and 69 with agencies and institutions of correction, and some others with agencies of other types. The staff on this study arrived at the belief that, in a very high proportion of cases, a more realistic professional attitude toward them would conduce to a more systematic and intelligent service to these clients, much better working relationships among the agencies concerned, and certainly a better understanding of the nature of the problem. Some kind of original contact that would thereafter responsibly steer these cases through the intricate processes necessary for their adjustment, or make sure that another responsible agency would, seems to be the only way in which the present chaotic conditions can be reduced to some degree of order. In this connection the Scandinavian guardianship arrangements and the Minnesota plan in our own country come to mind.

XIV

THE UNMARRIED FATHERS

What Is Known of Them

IN the statistical tables which follow it will be evident that adequate information regarding unmarried fathers is conspicuously missing from the records of social agencies, both public and private. Among the 1,599 schedules secured for this study, 1,013 contained one or more items of information about the father, while 586 had no information whatever as regards him. As will be shown later, a very large proportion of the cases were unreported for each item taken separately.[1]

Several reasons for this dearth of information have already been suggested. In the greater number of cases, the information for the record of the agency was supplied by the unmarried mother. In the case of agencies considering all members of the illegitimate family in the plan of action, the information thus supplied by the unmarried mother was supplemented by some social investigation.

In many cases, however, the unmarried mother was unwilling or unable to supply information regarding the father of her child. In some cases, she stated that the name and address which the father of her child had given her during their friendship had proved to be fictitious, and that she had not been able to discover the facts of his actual identity and position in life. In other cases, the unmarried mother supplying information for the social service record had stated that her relationship to the father of her child had been of a nature extremely casual, and that she had not taken the precaution to learn his name

[1]See Appendix 2 for law relating to the filing of information on unmarried fathers on birth certificates. The prohibition against reporting his name on a birth certificate does not, of course, apply to the records of these children and their mothers made by agencies and institutions.

and address. While complete information as to the nature and duration of the friendship between the parents of the illegitimate child was not available, it was nevertheless evident from the records that no inconsiderable number of the relationships were of a casual nature, and had followed upon unsupervised gatherings of young people at dance halls, at the beaches, and in the parks. Conspicuous also were the cases of young women who had accepted invitations from young men unknown to them who had offered a ride in an automobile. In cases of this nature, it is easily seen that the difficulties of obtaining information as to the identity of the man had been insurmountable.

More important, however, than the lack of information on the part of the unmarried mother as to the identity of the father of her child was her unwillingness to impart it. It was often found that a relationship of this type, followed by the father's desertion and his refusal to assume his share of responsibility for the care of the child, had engendered a resentment and bitterness which made the unmarried mother unwilling to refer to him at all. This attitude had been encouraged by the belief of certain of the social agencies that the care of the illegitimate family did not require that cognizance be taken of the existence or of the responsibility of the unmarried father. One head of a maternity home remarked, "We ask no questions about the father. He is of no importance in the situation." Another social worker remarked, "Our policy is to help the mother to forget a disagreeable experience. Therefore we ask no questions about the father. He is of no importance in the situation." Where such beliefs prevail, it follows logically that the records of the illegitimate family contain no information as to the father of that family.

There are no good data in this country with regard to the subsequent marriage of persons whose first child was conceived before marriage. It is probable that there is a larger number of cases in which men do not desert the mother under these circumstances than of cases in which they do. Whatever ideals of honor and responsibility have led some men to assume the duties of husbands and fathers should, it would seem, be at least considered in these cases in which the birth occurred while the parents were still unmarried. It will be shown later that a considerable fraction of the fathers were ineligible to marry. The agencies' records, moreover, were often not of a character to reveal whether or not a marriage eventually took place. The fragmentary information available on this point did, however, reveal that twenty-four marriages subsequent to the births of the children had taken place. It seems unlikely that this is the total of the marriages which had been or would be contracted by the parents of the 1,599 children born out of wedlock here studied.

In his report for 1931, the Commissioner of Public Welfare reported in connection with the filiation proceedings, all of which must originate in the Department of Public Welfare and may be begun before the child is born, that

> It is the policy of this Department in its interviews with the complainant and the defendant prior to the acceptance of an agreement or the taking of court action to endeavor to effect the marriage of these persons when the facts of the particular case show that procedure to be to the best interests and welfare of all concerned.

It was reported that forty-nine marriages were thereby effected in the course of the year.

While it must be admitted that the greater number of unmarried fathers who were relegated to oblivion by the agencies entered no protest against the treatment which they received, this was not true of all of them. In one case, an unmarried father appeared at a maternity hospital where the mother was receiving care and demanded to see his illegitimate son. This permission was refused by the social worker, on the ground that the mother and father of such a child should not be allowed to communicate with each other. In another case, an unmarried father called at an institution where his illegitimate child was being cared for and was refused permission to see him because he was in arrears with his payments for the board of the child. In another instance, it was reported that the unmarried father had not been allowed to see his child because he was not furnished with a special permission card from the Department of Public Welfare.

It seemed evident from the reading of many records that the punitive attitude adopted by some agency officials was a deterrent to the development of paternal affection and responsibility. Statements from some unmarried fathers revealed their resentment that they had not been informed of their paternity until a summons to answer a court proceeding had been served upon them. Others were indignant that they had not been given the opportunity to effect a settlement without undue publicity and loss of position. Still others complained that an interview with the mother of the child had not been allowed by the agency, when the father had wished to discuss with her plans for the future of their child. That this attitude of resentment toward the agency was carried over by the unmarried father to the unmarried mother and her child, and used as a justification of his unwillingness to coöperate was also evident.

In some instances the energetic intervention of the social worker had prevented a settlement of difficulties between the young parents of an illegitimate child which might have resulted in a marriage. While all the more progressive agencies at work in this field were agreed in their belief that no attempt should be made to force or even to encourage a marriage not fully and freely desired by those most concerned, there were, nevertheless, some social workers who believed that more marriages would occur by mutual agreement between the illegitimate parents, were not obstacles set up to prevent all communication between them. At this point, it was suggested that the policy, followed by some maternity homes and social workers, of keeping the father from seeing his child and communicating with the mother under suitable conditions might prevent the settlement of their difficulties by a marriage agreeable to both. Cases were even reported where the awakening of paternal affection by the opportunity to know and visit his child had also caused the man to change his attitude toward the unmarried mother, and had induced a willingness on his part to effect some satisfactory arrangement with her. If social workers feel justified in keeping the unmarried mother with her child during the first months of its life, in order to foster the development of maternal affection, the refusal of permission to an unmarried father to see his child during the same period appears strangely illogical, when the development of paternal affection appears to be an important item also in assuring the welfare of the child.

It was evident that here, as at other points in their contact with the illegitimate family, some social workers were prone to insinuate their own beliefs and standards into the client's thinking, without due regard to the traditions and practices which had been important in forming the latter's viewpoint. For example, in the case of one unmarried mother, whose social record was available for the study, a marriage between her and the father of her child was discouraged, because in the social worker's opinion the basis of understanding between the young people was not sufficiently idealistic and intellectual in nature. Although the parents of the illegitimate child were of an age competent to marry, and were willing to marry, and although the parents of both were willing that they should be married, the social worker in charge of the case was of the opinion that the young woman was so far superior to the young man in intelligence and will-power that the marriage would not prove to be satisfactory for her. Accordingly, the unmarried mother with her child was sent away for a vacation in the country, at a distance which would discourage the attentions of the young man. Through a visit to the latter's family an effort to discourage the proposed marriage received some support, and the young man himself was advised to cease his attentions. The young woman, however, after a few months at a new place of employment secured for her, was found to have entered into a second illegitimate union with a man who apparently had no intention of marrying her, and at the time when the last entry was made in the record, the social worker had been obliged to make plans for the reëntry of the young woman into a maternity home pending the birth of a second child.

While social workers were generally agreed that high ideals of marriage should be inculcated, it was emphasized also that the stressing of an ideal above that usually achieved by most marriages at a given social level might operate to prevent some marriages of illegitimate parents which would have a fair chance to succeed.

As has previously been remarked, some agencies manifested a disposition to make a case work approach to the unmarried father as well as to the unmarried mother, with results showing a considerable measure of success. It was said by one social worker that unmarried fathers manifest some of the same evidences of fright at the revelation of their illegitimate parenthood as the unmarried mothers. The fact that the unmarried mother is less able to run away from the situation, it was pointed out, does not preclude her desire to do so, and many records show evidence that the first reaction of the unmarried mother to her child was the desire to escape from it. The unmarried father, it was said, experiences also the desire for escape from the situation, and, since he can run away, often does. It was regarded by some of the agencies as the task of the social worker to reassure the unmarried father after his first reaction of fear and induce him (if he can be found), to assume some measure of his responsibility. One social worker stated of the unmarried fathers: "Many of them are only frightened boys who are willing to coöperate if they are sure that they are not to be exposed to unreasonable demands and social opprobrium." Some examples of success in securing coöperation were cited. One unmarried father who had been allowed to see his child offered his services when a transfusion of blood was required, and made daily inquiries at the hospital to know how the child was getting along. Another unmarried father arranged to adopt his illegitimate child. Still others were willing to pay for the care of their offspring in an institution or boarding home. All of the agencies attempting a case work approach to the unmarried father were careful to point out that his eagerness to evade his responsibility was due not only to his desire to escape the burden of the child's support, but also to his fear of the social penalties attached to illegitimate parenthood, and that in cases where it was possible to diminish danger of exposure by observing a suitable discretion, the chances of securing the father's coöperation were greatly increased.

The failure of some social agencies to take into consideration the existence of the unmarried father in the treatment of the illegitimate family may result also in the increase of the problem with which they are dealing. There were found, in one maternity home coöperating in this study, two unmarried mothers who named the same man as the father of their illegitimate infants.[2] In the records of one of the specialized agencies, mention was made of an unmarried father who had been named as the father of their infants by three unmarried mothers who had come under the care of this agency at different times. The unwisdom of failing to consider the unmarried fathers was in these and similar cases markedly evident.

The more progressive social workers dealing with questions

[2]Although all of the statistical analyses which follow assume that there were 1,599 different men to be accounted for, such an assumption is not necessarily true, as the statement above suggests.

growing out of the care of the illegitimate family were quick to insist that the same social and economic conditions that lead to illegitimate parenthood in the case of young women also operate to permit illegitimate parenthood on the part of the young men subject to them, and that the failure to include both parents in any scheme of approach to the situation can lead only to results partial and unsatisfactory. It was pointed out also that much importance was attached by social agencies to their program of reëducating unmarried mothers with a view to preventing a recurrence of their difficulties, but that no such measures were taken in the case of the unmarried fathers, and that because of the scarcity of information regarding them it was not known how many of them had become the father of a second or even a third illegitimate child.

While this report has no specific recommendations to offer with regard to policies and procedures, it appears evident from the records available that the possibility of providing help for the illegitimate child through a case work approach to his father has not been diligently exploited in all cases, and that the success of certain agencies in this regard indicates that a fruitful return from such effort might reasonably be expected in a fair percentage of the cases.

In the following pages the data on unmarried fathers which appear on birth certificates and on agency records have been analyzed.

Marital Status

Data on marital status of the fathers appear in agency records for only one-third of the cases. It is impossible to determine whether or not this is a random sampling of all of the cases. There is, however, no obvious reason for supposing that a selective factor has entered into the composition of this group, since it is unlikely that the mothers would be any better informed about, or more inclined to report, men who were or had been married than men who were single. No data on this point appear on birth certificates and hence there are no figures available at the Health Department.

TABLE 26

Fathers of Illegitimate Children Classified by Marital Status

MARITAL STATUS	TOTAL	PERCENT
Total	544	100.0
Single	383	70.4
Married	140	25.8
Divorced	4	0.7
Separated	13	2.4
Widowed	4	0.7

Table 26 reveals the fact that 25.8 percent of the known cases were married, and that an additional 3.8 percent were either widowed, separated, or divorced from their wives. It will be observed that among the known cases a much higher percentage of unmarried fathers than of unmarried mothers were or had been married: 29.6 percent of the former and a little less than 8 percent of the latter. The proportions of the total having marital status reported in the two groups are widely different, however, and strictly speaking, not comparable, but, since the results of our tabulations of marital status agree with the general observations of social workers on the point, they are presented as of interest in offering some support of their views. In any event the actual number of men—160— known to have been previously married exceeds the number of previously married women and girls, which is 122.

A breakdown of the cases by marital status in each nativity group is made in Table 27.

The similarity of proportions of single men in each of the nativity groups is rather striking.

Since the chances of securing adequate support for an illegit-

TABLE 27

Fathers of Illegitimate Children Classified by Marital Status, Color, and Nativity

| | TOTAL | | WHITE | | | | | | NEGRO | | |
| MARITAL STATUS | | | TOTAL | | NATIVE BORN | | FOREIGN BORN | | TOTAL[a] | NATIVE BORN[a] | FOREIGN BORN[a] |
	No.	Percent	No.	Percent	No.	Percent	No.	Percent	No.	No.	No.
Total	394[b]	100.0	332	100.0	203	100.0	129	100.0	62	59	3
Single	286	72.6	241	72.6	146	71.9	95	73.6	45	43	2
Married	92	23.3	77	23.2	50	24.6	27	20.9	15	14	1
Divorced	3	0.8	3	0.9	2	1.0	1	0.8	...	...	...
Separated	10	2.5	8	2.4	4	2.0	4	3.1	2	2	...
Widowed	3	0.8	3	0.9	1	0.5	2	1.6	...	...	...

[a]Percentage not computed, base less than 100.

[b]From this table 1,205 cases were excluded because one or more of the items needed were not recorded.

imate child from his father are somewhat diminished if the latter is married, it can be seen that the marital status of unmarried fathers is of considerable importance in planning social measures for the care of the illegitimate family. It might well be made a matter of more interest than seems to have been the rule with the 1930 grist of cases.

Age

Table 28 presents the age grouping of 716 unmarried fathers about whom this item of information was given in the social agency records.

TABLE 28

Fathers of Illegitimate Children Classified by Age

AGE GROUPS	NUMBER	PERCENT
Total	716	100.0
15–19	45	6.3
20–24	245	34.2
25–29	232	32.4
30–34	95	13.3
35–39	61	8.5
40 and over	38	5.3

It will be observed that a higher percentage of unmarried fathers than of unmarried mothers was found in the upper age groups. Comparatively few of the fathers were under twenty, though nearly half of the mothers were. Matching the considerable number of unmarried mothers who were in the age group twenty to twenty-four years is the comparatively large number of unmarried fathers who were in that group also. A slightly higher percentage of unmarried fathers than of mothers were in the group over thirty. It should be noted that while 74 percent of the unmarried fathers are under thirty years, 93.8 percent of the unmarried mothers are under that age. Even though it is true, however, that larger numbers of young women than of young men of our group are under twenty-five, there were nevertheless 42 percent of the total number of unmarried fathers whose ages were known to be under twenty-five.

The 1,470 birth certificates on file at the Health Department contain age data on only 447 fathers. In these the percentage age distribution is almost identical with that reported by the agencies. Some similarity might reasonably be expected, since some of the agencies doubtless secured their information from the birth certificates and others collaborated in making the birth certificates. But in the additional cases—at least 269 and possibly more—for which they secured data which were not recorded in the Health Department, the same age distribution must have prevailed.

Wide disparity between the ages of the unmarried mother and of the father appeared in a few instances. One Negro girl among those fourteen or less was involved with a Negro man of fifty. Two white girls, in the age group fifteen to nineteen years old, each reported white men of fifty or over as the fathers of their children. Three white men forty to forty-four years old had illegitimate children whose mothers were less than twenty years old.[3]

In the main, however, the ages of the fathers were not widely different from those of the mothers.

Comparison of the age distribution in the nativity groups can be made in Table 29. It is based on agency records.

Of the eighty-two native Negro fathers on whom there are data, 57.3 percent were under twenty-five years of age; of the native white, 40.5 percent were in these age groups; while only

[3]Three cases of incest of fathers and daughters were known to the agencies; one was a native white father of 49, one a foreign white father of 55 and one a Negro father of unreported age. The girls were 17, 15, and 17 years old respectively.

TABLE 29

Fathers of Illegitimate Children Classified by Age, Color, and Nativity

Age Groups	TOTAL		WHITE TOTAL		WHITE NATIVE BORN		WHITE FOREIGN BORN		NEGRO TOTAL	NEGRO NATIVE BORN[a]	NEGRO FOREIGN BORN[a]
	No.	Percent	No.	Percent	No.	Percent	No.	Percent	No.	No.	No.
Total	491[b]	100.0	397	100.0	247	100.0	150	100.0	94	82	12
15–19	27	5.5	15	3.8	11	4.5	4	2.7	12	11	1
20–24	160	32.6	121	30.5	89	36.0	32	21.3	39	36	3
25–29	163	33.2	139	35.0	83	33.6	56	37.3	24	19	5
30–34	70	14.3	61	15.4	35	14.1	26	17.3	9	6	3
35–39	43	8.7	40	10.0	18	7.3	22	14.7	3	3	...
40 and over	28	5.7	21	5.3	11	4.5	10	6.7	7	7	...

[a]Percentage not computed, base less than 100.

[b]From this table 1,108 cases of the 1,599 studied were excluded because one or more items needed were not recorded or not available.

24 percent of the foreign born fathers were under twenty-five. These proportions are undoubtedly affected by the age distribution among the men of the several nativity groups. Among native white males in the general population a little less than one-fifth were in the ages of fifteen to twenty-four; among Negroes this proportion is a little less than a sixth, but among foreign born white men the proportion is only about one-eleventh.

Further discussion of the race and nativity groups appears in the following section.

Color and Nativity

As in the case of the mothers, the data at the Health Department on the fathers are more complete for color or race than for any other type of information.

The 1,470 birth certificates provided data in more instances than did the agency records on the color of fathers. Of the 962 reported, 764 fathers were reported to be white, 196 Negro, 2 Chinese; 508 certificates had no data on this point. The agency records have data on color in 807 instances. The proportions of white and Negro in the total known cases are almost the same as the proportions found among the agencies' cases which are shown in Table 30.

TABLE 30

Fathers of Illegitimate Children Classified by Color
(Social Agency Data)

COLOR	NUMBER	PERCENT
Total	807	100.0
White	646	80.0
Negro	161	20.0

An even 80 percent of the total number whose color was known were white, and 20 percent were colored. As will be observed when this table is compared with that for the unmarried mothers, the proportions differ slightly; but this can be regarded as of no significance, because of the large number of unmarried fathers whose color is not stated in the record.

Among the 962 cases in which the Health Department had data for the race or color of the father as well as of the mother, there were only 18 instances of race crossing reported. Fifteen of these were instances of Negro women who had white fathers of their children, while three were white women who had Negro fathers of their babies. Among the agency cases there were ten instances noted of white women who had Negro fathers for their children, and only four instances of Negro girls who had babies by white fathers. There was one instance of a white girl and an Oriental man. The wide discrepancy between these two groups in type of race crossing suggests that among the cases of fathers of unknown race in each set of data —the birth certificates and the agency records—there were race crosses. How much race crossing there was in the cases of fathers whose race was unreported in both series cannot, of course, be even conjectured.[4]

Some of the child care agencies report much difficulty and perplexity in arranging the foster care of these children of mixed races, of whom they report an appreciable number.

In addition to color, the nativity of 462 white unmarried fathers was stated in the agency records. Of these, about two-thirds were native born, and about one-third were of foreign birth. There were nativity data on only 115 of the 161 fathers known to be colored. Thus there were both race and nativity data for only 577 fathers of the 1,599.

The birth certificates recorded the nativity of only 426

[4]Julius Drachsler. *Democracy and Assimilation*, The Macmillan Company, New York, 1920, p. 129: "In New York City for a period of five years (1908-1912) the ratio of intermarriage between colored and white was 1.08 per cent. For colored men it was 1.78 per cent, for colored women .44 per cent. In other words, the men intermarried about four times as frequently as the women."

TABLE 31

Fathers of Illegitimate Children Classified by Nativity and Color

NATIVITY	TOTAL		WHITE		NEGRO	
	No.	Percent	No.	Percent	No.	Percent
Total	577	100.0	462	100.0	115	100.0
Native	383	66.4	282	61.0	101	87.8
Foreign	194	33.6	180	39.0	14	12.2

fathers. These were all among the 962 fathers for whom color was also reported. Of these 426, the native white numbered 221, foreign born white 127, native Negro 59, foreign born Negro 17, and foreign born Chinese 2.

It will be noted that the proportion of native born and foreign born unmarried fathers in known cases corresponds roughly with these same classifications of unmarried mothers, and also with the proportion which these nativity groups form of the city's population.

As has been stated in the section dealing with unmarried mothers, some few of the unmarried fathers had never been in this country, and the adjustment of these cases was rendered difficult by the practical impossibility of any approach to them.

Country of Birth of Foreign Born Fathers

The two hundred foreign born fathers for which information on country of birth was recorded on the agency records were distributed as shown in Table 32.

In general, this alignment of foreign born fathers shows the same proportions as were found among the foreign born mothers of the several countries of birth. The only marked discrepancy appears in the case of Italians. The Italian mothers were only 5.3 percent of the foreign born mothers, while the Italian fathers constituted 17.5 percent of the known foreign born fathers.

TABLE 32

Foreign Born Fathers of Illegitimate Children Classified by Country of Birth and Color

COUNTRY OF BIRTH	TOTAL	PERCENT	WHITE	NEGRO	COLOR NOT RE-PORTED
Total	200	100.0	180	14	6
The British Empire	86	43.0	69	14	3
England	8	4.0	7	1	0
Scotland	4	2.0	4	0	0
Ireland	48	24.0	48	0	0
Canada	10	5.0	10	0	0
British West Indies	15	7.5	0	12	3
British Guiana	1	0.5	0	1	0
Sweden	6	3.0	6	0	0
Germany	24	12.0	24	0	0
Austria and Hungary	4	2.0	4	0	0
Czechoslovakia, Yugoslavia, and Greece	6	3.0	6	0	0
Russia, Poland, and Finland . .	22	11.0	22	0	0
Italy	35	17.5	35	0	0
France	4	2.0	4	0	0
Spain and Portugal	7	3.5	5	0	2
Central and South American Countries	5	2.5	4	0	1
Syria	1	0.5	1	0	0

In the case of the fathers as in that of the mothers the most enlightening data of this type would be those which indicate the cultural group to which native born men and boys belonged. This can be known only if there is recording of the birthplace of the parents of the person being described.

Since the United States census analyzes the general population in such terms, comparisons of the various groups according to foreign stock are possible, provided the facts on these cases could be recorded.

Crossing of Nationality Groups

There were 214 instances in which one or both parents were foreign born and in which the birthplaces of both parents were known. These are classified in Table 33.

This tabulation accounts for only 137 of the 323 women and girls known to have been foreign born. Twenty-nine were associated with native born men, 82 with foreign born men of approximately[5] their own nationality, and 26 with foreign born men of a different nationality. The 186 others of the 323 contracted relations with men whose birthplace was not reported.

Of the two hundred men known to have been foreign born, 77 were known to have been associated with native women, 82 with foreign born women of approximately their own nationality, and 26 with foreign born women of a different nationality. In 17 instances out of these two hundred, the birthplace of the mother was not reported. Julius Drachsler reported that of 6,714 marriages of first generation immigrant men contracted in New York City (1908–12), 5,170, or 77 percent, were with first generation immigrant women; of 6,249 first generation immigrant women married in New York City (1908–12), 5,170, or nearly 83 percent, married first generation immigrant men.[6] In the figures above, of the 137 instances of foreign born girls associated with men whose nationality was known, 108 or nearly 79 percent were associated with foreign born men; of the 183 foreign born men associated with women whose nationality was known, 59 percent were with first generation immigrant women. These figures would seem to indicate that in cases where the association of these foreign born people is of

[5]The nationalities are said to be "approximately" the same because in a few instances nations closely related in blood and culture have been combined.

[6]Julius Drachsler, *Democracy and Assimilation*, The Macmillan Company, New York, 1920, p. 104.

TABLE 33

Fathers of Illegitimate Children Classified by Birthplace, and by Birthplace of Mother of Child in 214 Cases with Data for Both

BIRTHPLACE OF FATHER

BIRTHPLACE OF MOTHER	Total	United States	England	Scotland	Ireland	Canada	British West Indies	Norway, Sweden, and Holland	Germany
Total	214	29	8	4	50	10	1	6	24
United States . . .	77	..	5	1	6	3	..	1	5
British Empire									
England . . .	4	2	..	..	1	..	..	..	1
Scotland . . .	6	2	..	1	1	..	..	..	..
Ireland . . .	59	12	2	1	39	2	..	1	2
Canada . . .	9	2	..	..	2	5	..	..	..
British West Indies . . .	3	..	..	..	1	..	1	..	..
Norway, Sweden and Holland .	5	1	..	..	..	..	..	4	..
Germany	21	3	..	..	..	..	..	..	16
Austria, Hungary, and Switzerland	3	1	..	..	..	..	..	..	..
Czechoslovakia, Yugoslavia, and Greece	2	..	..	1	..	..	..	..	..
Russia, Poland, and Finland . .	14	3	1	..	..	..	..	..	..
Italy	8	3	..	..	..	..	..	..	..
France	2	..	..	..	..	..	..	..	..
Central and South American countries	1	..	..	..	..	..	..	..	..

TABLE 33 (*continued*)

BIRTHPLACE OF FATHER

BIRTHPLACE OF MOTHER	Total	Austria, Hungary, and Switzerland	Czecho-Slovakia, Yugoslavia, and Greece	Russia, Poland, and Finland	Italy	France	Spain and Portugal	Central and South American Countries	Syria
Total	214	4	7	23	32	4	7	4	1
United States	77	3	4	13	26	1	5	3	1
British Empire									
England	4	..	..	..	..	..	..	..	..
Scotland	6	..	..	1	..	1	..	..	..
Ireland	59	..	..	..	..	..	..	..	..
Canada	9	..	..	..	..	..	..	..	..
British West Indies	3	..	..	..	..	..	1	..	..
Norway, Sweden and Holland	5	..	..	..	..	..	..	..	..
Germany	21	..	..	..	..	..	1	1	..
Austria, Hungary, and Switzerland	3	..	1	1	..	..	..	..	..
Czechoslovakia, Yugoslavia, and Greece	2	..	1	..	..	..	..	..	..
Russia, Poland, and Finland	14	1	1	8	..	..	..	..	..
Italy	8	..	..	..	5	2	.	..	..
France	2	..	..	..	..	..	..	..	..
Central and South American countries	1	..	..	..	1	..	..	..	..

a type that enables the mother to know something of the background of the man, it is not very different as regards mixture of nationalities from the associations which lead to marriage.

It seems probable that the unions of foreign born with native born were often in the same cultural groups, but this cannot be more than surmised. More detailed and explicit data than are now recorded would be required to establish an adequate answer as to the extent of nationality and cultural group crossing in these cases.

That wide differences in race and nationality are barriers to marriage in some of these cases is highly probable. The extent to which this factor has operated is a matter which might well be further studied if data were properly collected by the agencies.

Occupation and Education

In records furnished by the Health Department, only 29 percent of the total number of birth certificates contained any information as to the occupation of the putative father. Of those about whom such information was given, the largest segment, 32.1 percent was in the occupational group "miscellaneous," showing that statements as to their occupations had been vague and difficult to classify. The next largest percentage, 22.9, was listed as engaged in "trades." Obviously, however, information regarding the occupation of the putative father obtained by the attending physician from the unmarried mother for entry on the birth certificate would not have been the subject of social investigation or any other form of verification, and could not be viewed as possessing any high degree of accuracy.[7]

[7]In the proceedings to establish paternity and secure support, the man's occupation and income becomes a matter of primary interest, and considerable effort is expended to secure these facts about him.

Records of social agencies showed that information as to the occupation of the putative father had been entered in about 45 percent of the cases. Again the information obtained had been vague and difficult to classify, so that the largest group, 17.9 percent of the total, was classed as "miscellaneous." Of the remaining, 16.2 percent were engaged in domestic or personal service; 15.2 percent were in the building trades; 14.9 percent were in "trades"; while 11.5 percent were classed as chauffeurs or truck drivers. Other occupational groups of the classification used contained smaller percentages of the unmarried fathers. It may be interesting to note that, of the total number of unmarried fathers whose occupations are stated, 5.9 percent were classed as professional workers, and 4.7 percent were clerical workers. The proportions of unmarried mothers in these two occupational groupings were respectively 5.1 percent and 17.4 percent. It was found that seventeen of the unmarried fathers, or 2.4 percent, were schoolboys. As might be expected from the distribution of the general population in occupational groups, more Negro unmarried fathers than whites were found in domestic and personal service, while a larger percentage of whites than Negroes was found in clerical and professional groups.

Only seventy-five records contained information as to the education of the unmarried father. The distribution of unmarried fathers in the different educational groups of our classification can, therefore, have no significance for the total group under consideration, but it may be of some interest to note the distribution of the seventy-five cases about which such information was given (Table 34).

It will be observed that the percentage of unmarried fathers of this small group of seventy-five who have had some college or professional training is larger than that for the population at large! This is probably due to the quite natural tendency of

TABLE 34

Fathers of Illegitimate Children Classified by Educational Attainment

EDUCATION	NUMBER	PERCENT
Total	75	100.0
Elementary school		
First to fourth grades	5	6.7
Fifth to eighth grades	25	33.3
High school	26	34.7
Trade school	1	1.3
College	13	17.3
Professional school	5	6.7

those unmarried mothers who had been associated with men of some educational attainment to impart this information more readily than did the mothers associated with men about whose education there was nothing of distinction. There were sixty-seven women known to have had some education beyond high school. For eighteen women and girls to have reported men with at least some college or professional training is not inconsistent with what might be expected.

When the seventy-five cases are further analyzed according to the nativity and race of the fathers, the probability of these being a representative sample as regards the proportions of those with higher education becomes still more remote (Table 35).

It will be seen that while only about one-fifth of the native white men were reported as having some higher education, a third of the foreign born, and a quarter of the Negroes are so reported! No Negroes with less than a fifth grade education were reported.

It would seem to have been the tendency of the unmarried mothers to tell little about the education of the fathers of their children unless they could speak well of it.

TABLE 35

Fathers of Illegitimate Children Classified by Educational Attainment, Color, and Nativity

| | | WHITE | | | NEGRO | | |
| | TOTAL | TOTAL | NATIVE BORN | FOREIGN BORN | TOTAL | NATIVE BORN | FOREIGN BORN |
EDUCATION	No.	No.	No.	No.	No.	No.	No.
Total	65	57	45	12	8	7	1
Elementary school							
First to fourth grades	5	5	2	3	..	..	..
Fifth to eighth grades	19	16	13	3	3	3	..
High school . . .	25	22	20	2	3	2	1
Trade school . . .	1	1	1	..	..	..	..
College	11	9	6	3	2	2	..
Professional school	4	4	3	1	..	..	..

Religious Affiliation

Although the number of cases with data on the religious affiliations of unmarried fathers considerably exceeds the number on which health and education are recorded, it yet remains that in only 501 cases was the religion of the unmarried father stated in the record. This is in accord with the general lack of information regarding him on the part of the person furnishing the information for the social record, and is due largely to the fact that the person making inquiries had not considered the unmarried father's religion of any importance in preparing the outline of the record. Illegitimate families, as was mentioned before, usually come to the attention of social agencies through the appeal of the unmarried mother for help, and it was her religion which determined which of the sectarian groups should assume the responsibility for her care and protection. It sometimes happened, however, that religious differences between the parents of an illegitimate child were known to have been the cause for their failure to marry, and thus had come to the attention of the agencies. In these few cases, the fact of the different religious affiliations, of the parents had been carefully noted in the record. Furthermore, in certain of the case work agencies which make it a part of their program to include an approach to the unmarried father as a part of their plans for constructive work, the fact of his religious affiliations had been noted.

TABLE 36

Fathers of Illegitimate Children Classified by Religion

RELIGION	NUMBER	PERCENT
Total	501	100.0
Protestant	180	35.9
Catholic	222	44.3
Jewish	99	19.8

As in the case of the unmarried mothers, it should be noted that these proportions are somewhat at variance with the estimates as to the proportions of these religious groupings in the city's population. However, since information on this point with regard to two-thirds of our cases is missing, no general conclusions can be drawn from these figures.

Health

It seems significant that, out of a total of 1,599 illegitimate families, the records in only 103 cases contained any statement as to the health of the unmarried father. The group of agencies manifesting the greatest amount of interest in this item of information were those child placing agencies which regard an investigation into the child's heredity as of some importance in their work, especially in the protection of foster families from transmissible diseases and from disappointment and unusual hardship and expense in caring for the foster child. Statements as to the health of the unmarried father which had been made by the unmarried mother at the time when she offered her child for surrender had accordingly been supplemented, when this was possible, by information obtained in an interview with the father or with someone who knew him. Of the 103 fathers about whom any entry as to the health had been made, 91 were reported to be in good health. Of the 12 unmarried fathers who were not in good health, 7 were reported as in "poor" health, without any specification as to the nature of their ailments; 3 were reported as suffering from venereal disease; and 2 were said to be suffering from some form of mental ailment.

It will be inferred from the above statements that entries regarding the father's health were seldom based upon the results of a physical examination. One social worker had, however, urged upon unmarried fathers the necessity of a physical examination in order that information as to the child's heredity might be rendered more accurate. While consent to physical examination is obviously more difficult to obtain from the unmarried father than from the unmarried mother, some of the agencies insisting upon a physical examination of the latter were of the belief that in cases where paternity had been legally established a physical examination of the unmarried father should be required as well as a record of his social history. At the present time all such information is conspicuously lacking in the records of illegitimate families.

Insofar as a knowledge of the health and physical endowment of parents is of value in the care of children generally, it would seem to be important to secure such information in these cases.

What They Do for Their Children

The willingness of unmarried fathers to efface themselves from the scene when the question of caring for the illegitimate child is under discussion has already been commented upon.

The fact that there are exceptions to this general behavior pattern has also been indicated, and some examples of the voluntary coöperation of these young men cited. Some social workers believe, however, that the only effective way to hold the unmarried father to his responsibilities is by a swift and immediate resort to legal action, before he becomes aware that an agency is interested in the case. They believe that the efforts of social workers to establish paternity by voluntary acknowledgment on the part of the father are rarely crowned with success, and that the young man merely takes advantage of the opportunity thus allowed to put himself beyond the reach of the law. They report it as their observation that even in cases where a voluntary agreement for the support of the child has been entered into, the father is more than likely to tire of his burden after a short time and make efforts to evade his obligations. Particularly is this said to be true of the younger men, who form new attachments and wish to be relieved of all burdens growing out of former relationships. The instance was cited of a young man of twenty-two who signed a voluntary agreement to give ample support to his illegitimate son, and did so for a period of a little less than two years. At the end of that time he complained bitterly of the burden which such an obligation had placed upon him. When no adjustment satisfactory to him had been reached, he disappeared from view, and his whereabouts could not be learned.

It is to meet the situation encountered in cases of this nature that some social workers have insisted upon an increased use of a lump sum payment by the father, after which he is freed of all further financial responsibility toward his illegitimate child. The assessment of such a lump sum depends, obviously, upon the economic status of the man, or, in the case of a boy, of his parents. This sum, they insist, should be sufficiently large in amount to cover a substantial part of the illegitimate child's support during childhood. The practice of certain foreign countries, notably Germany, is cited in support of the feasibility of the plan. It is pointed out that if the young man is under age the sum can be assessed against his parents, who are presumably liable at law for the obligations which he incurs; or the young man himself, when he is still a minor, may be held responsible for its payment when he does actually become of age. In further support of the plan, its advocates were inclined to urge that the payment of a lump sum is more reasonably adapted to the psychological situation growing out of illegitimate paternity. It is pointed out that under present social conditions it rarely happens that there is any direct association between the unmarried father and his child, and consequently little or no opportunity for the development of paternal affection. Under such circumstances it is not surprising that the young unmarried father becomes weary of the burden of the support of his illegitimate child which continues over many years, and that he accordingly makes strenuous efforts to escape. These workers point out that the history of the exaction of legally imposed payments from the father is one of arrears in payment and arrests, usually ending with the definitive disappearance of the unmarried father. For this reason, they urge that a lump sum payment might be more easily enforced and less stubbornly resisted by unmarried fathers who would see in it a way to be definitely freed of the responsibilities which they had incurred. It does not come within the scope of this report to test the validity of these beliefs by analysis of cases over a period of years, but, since many social workers expressed an opinion with regard to this question, it was thought well to make some mention of it here.

Any procedure to secure financial aid from the father would seem to require a fairly careful case work procedure which would ascertain, first, his property and income, and, second, his other obligations. This is especially needed when the man has other children for whose support he is responsible.

An effort was made to ascertain what action had been taken by the social agencies coöperating in the study to establish paternity. As has been indicated earlier, some agency records made no mention at all of the subject, and some that did refer to it, had entries which were difficult to interpret. Table 37 was prepared from such information as could be obtained through the agencies.

It should be pointed out that these figures by no means represent all the work which had been done to establish the paternity of the illegitimate infants born in New York City in 1930, but only that part of the work which we found in the social records of those agencies coöperating in the study. As was stated in a previous section, proceedings to establish paternity may be initiated by the mother of the child at any time within two years after its birth, so that it is quite conceivable that some of the unmarried mothers who had not instituted paternity proceedings at the time that the study was undertaken would do so later, and would do so without the knowledge of the agencies.

TABLE 37

Method of Establishment of Paternity

METHOD	NUMBER OF CASES
Total	216
Legally	71
Through case work	42
Voluntarily by father	88
Established, but method not recorded	15

It is also possible that in some cases in which paternity had been established through case work or voluntarily by the father, such an admission would be used as a basis for legal proceedings later, in case the father should not live up to his agreement.

Social workers who favor the establishment of paternity by extra-legal means pointed out that under the present system the sums which they can obtain are frequently larger than those awarded by the courts. They insisted, too, that even in cases where paternity has been legally established obligations are difficult to enforce, and that unmarried fathers are not infrequently found to be in arrears with their payments. On the other hand, those who favor the establishment of paternity by legal means were of the opinion that justice to the illegitimate child demands that his paternity be legally established, and that improvement in the legal machinery for establishment of paternity and for enforcing the rights of the illegitimate child can come only through the loyal use of the existing facilities and the study of the experience thus gained.

The amount of support which was given by unmarried fathers was not usually indicated in the records. In some cases, where the amount agreed upon by the father, or ordered by the court, was stated, there was no follow-up record to show how much had actually been paid.

Table 38 shows the volume of the filiation proceedings initiated on new cases through the Department of Public Welfare of New York City in 1929, 1930, and 1931, and the total amount of money collected and disbursed in behalf of these cases each year.

Without more data, it is, of course, impossible to form an idea as to the efficiency and value of the filiation proceedings. It must be clear that with new cases coming into the Department at the rate of eight hundred to a thousand in a year (not all, of course, result in the establishment of paternity), and with fathers theoretically responsible for the support of their children, at least to the age of sixteen, that there would be an accumulation of several thousand children who would be on the rolls of the department to receive support from men who had agreed to give support or who had been adjudged their

TABLE 38

Filiation Proceedings in the Department of Public Welfare

FILIATION PROCEEDINGS	1929	1930	1931
New applications in paternity proceedings	801	842	1,016
Settled in the office	...	349	576
Presented to court	...	493	440
Money received and disbursed for the support of children of unmarried mothers			
Received	$223,405	$234,960	$200,875
Disbursed	222,235	230,633	208,656

fathers. If such open cases numbered as many as four thousand, the collection of $200,000 in a year would represent an average of $50.00 per child actually paid.

It would be enlightening if the Department would report the number of "open cases" classified by the amounts ordered or agreed to be paid and the amounts actually paid for each class of cases.

It seems fairly clear from the figures on the new complaints received and the total amounts paid through the Department that, as the depression progressed, more applications were made to the Department of Public Welfare for its help in securing financial support from unmarried fathers; but it is also clear that the additional effort on the part of the mothers, agencies, and the Department did not yield any noticeable financial results. The amount collected in 1931 was considerably less than the amounts collected in 1929 and 1930.

The Department also reported in 1931 that in addition to the increased number of new cases it received 7,738 complaints on "recurrent" cases. Out of these 375 were presented to court. The rest were adjusted in the office. These complaints related to arrearages, to the reopening of cases by the presentation of new information regarding the whereabouts of defendants, to the annoyance of one party to the case by the other, and to other miscellaneous matters.

It was impossible, within the limitations of this study, to follow through each of the agency cases to see if it had come to the attention of the Department of Public Welfare. Since the names on a considerable proportion of cases were withheld, it was impossible to investigate them further. We cannot, therefore, report how many of the 1,817 cases of which some knowledge was secured, or how many of the 1,599 cases which were studied, were represented in the 1,858 new complaints filed with the Department of Welfare in 1930 and 1931. It does seem likely that perhaps as many as half of the illegitimacy cases known to agencies appear also in the Department of Public Welfare, and that perhaps as many as a quarter finally get to the Court of Special Sessions, where these cases are tried.

The conditions of procedure in the Department and in the court which deter some social workers from advising or urging unmarried mothers to have recourse to the law could not be carefully studied. It was pointed out, however, that a complainant who is sensitive to public exposure of the details of her case would unquestionably suffer some humiliation through the process of making her complaint and seeing it through the court. At the Department of Welfare the unmarried mothers must wait their turn for an interview in a place which is set apart for their exclusive but not private use. The nature of their business with the Department is therefore known to all of the observers who pass by. They must tell their stories in explicit detail several times, and, if the case goes to court, they must submit to public questioning, sometimes of the most prying and humiliating kind.

One of the investigators on this study made three visits to the Court of Special Sessions during July, 1931, when cases of this type were heard. It was warm and the windows had to be opened. The noise of traffic outside made it necessary for the complainants, defendants, and witnesses to speak very loudly in order that they might be heard. Besides the court attendants and an audience of court hangers-on,[8] all of the persons connected with the various cases to be heard were present as cases proceeded. Thus most of the complainants went through an ordeal, not only in the actual conduct of their cases but also as they heard the cases which preceded their own. By the time the later cases were scheduled to be heard, some of the complainants were in a highly overwrought condition, and one observed by the investigator was so terrified that she was almost in a state of collapse. The investigator was at a loss to understand why there need be anyone present at these cases other than the parties at interest, their attorneys, witnesses, and the court personnel necessary to hear and record the case.

With regard to the actual conduct of these cases in the Department and the court, this investigator, a woman of wide experience in social case work with unmarried mothers, reported that the "court procedure was marked by a routinization that was very noticeable." She thought that

Inquiry into facts known to social agencies should be an essential part of the preliminary investigation made for the court. The agencies all know the court procedure and rebel against it. One executive stated that she takes to court only those cases where she is certain that a judgment can be obtained. She never takes cases where there is any question of the girl's promiscuity.

Yet these are the cases in which recourse to court might seem to be most needed for a final determination of the case.

Of the Department of Public Welfare, she reported:

When you realize that the staff at the Department is so limited, that practice is concerned almost wholly with office interviews, and that these interviews are conducted under the most trying circum-

[8]This investigator reported: "Although under the law the court may exclude the public, on the three visits I made the public was not excluded but was present in large numbers."

stances, you again get the impression of the same routinization that characterizes the court. The records are so meager as to be practically worthless. Fragmentary information about the father and mother would seem to be barely in keeping with modern trends in thinking in regard to the complexity of the problem. The nature of the questions asked in the preliminary interviews at the Department of Public Welfare would not even conduce to honesty in reply.

On one of her visits to the Department this investigator observed

a young girl who came into the Department just after closing time. She was a shy, timid little person, refined in appearance, and I could well imagine what had preceded that "bankrupt moment," when, her own resources failing, she made the decision to ask for such outside help as could be obtained from the Department of Public Welfare. She was coldly received, and, when she briefly stated the object of her call, was told that it was past the time for reporting cases and she would have to come back. On my way out I saw the girl standing bewildered before the building. I learned she had come from a distant part of Queens. She was doing housework. This being her only day out, she would probably never come back. On another occasion, I was present at one of the cross examinations that take place prior to the filing of the affidavit. I believe that certain types of women might well feel they had been stripped of every vestige of their "spiritual clothing" after such an ordeal.

The Department began late in 1930 to clear these cases through the Social Service Exchange, so that it now has a means of knowing what other agencies are concerned with the case and know the families involved. Such registration is, of course, of no value unless there is careful study of the data found in the agency records. Without an adequate and carefully chosen staff effective social work with this type of cases is almost impossible.

This whole situation with regard to filiation proceedings

presents another angle of the highly disjointed procedure of the adjustment of relationships between the unmarried mother, the father of her child, and the public and private agencies working supposedly in their behalf. On one sector of the field there is such meticulous regard for secrecy in these cases that even the general problem cannot be studied efficiently and impersonally, and the help which is available from the many agencies and institutions, and sometimes even from the girl's own family, cannot be properly mobilized for her. On the other hand, there is a legal procedure which requires, to get the engines of justice in motion, that these unmarried mothers must expose themselves and their children to the crudest forms of public examination. It is entirely thinkable that the same cases that are "protected" by the medical agencies from careful social study and an intelligent guidance of their affairs are at the same time "aided" by a legal procedure which, when they seek simple justice, exposes them to the gaze of idle curiosity seekers and to newspaper accounts of their misfortune.

Another of the curious contradictions presented by the conduct of these cases, taken as a whole, relates to the completion of the child's birth certificate after paternity has been admitted or adjudged. This would seem to be a matter which could and should be reduced to a routine clerical procedure between the courts and the Department of Health. But such seems not to be the case. It was reported by social workers to be a difficult and laborious process to get the father's name entered on the certificate.

Although these cases often in themselves present serious complications and difficulties, it would seem that the community's efforts, taken as a whole, are not calculated systematically to resolve these difficulties in a direct and kindly way. Some of the procedures unquestionably complicate the problems of the mother and of the father of the child and open the way to confusion, to working at cross purposes, and to actual hardship for these already burdened and often perplexed people. It would seem not to be a superhuman task to devise a procedure, both social and legal—if such a distinction is permissible—which would move toward its objectives with directness and simplicity, and which would consistently follow good practices of health, of mental hygiene, and of justice for the members of these families, and of professional coöperation among the public and private agencies working with them.

XV

THE ILLEGITIMATE CHILDREN
BORN IN 1930

THE individual case schedule was framed to mobilize certain facts regarding the illegitimate infants born in New York City in 1930. Since the field work for the study was begun in the summer of 1931, it is evident that many of the children under consideration were still in their early infancy, that none was yet two years old, and that inquiries regarding their history had therefore to be limited to a very few simple facts regarding them. Many of the agency records available to the study staff, furthermore, were not complete to the date at which access was had to them. In many cases the last entry as to the whereabouts of the illegitimate child had been made several months or even a year previous to the time at which the records were studied. Whether other arrangements for the care of the illegitimate child had been made subsequent to the time indicated by the last record regarding him we had no means of knowing. In the case of the hospital social service records the last entry regarding the illegitimate child was made, in a large proportion of cases, at the time of the dismissal of the mother from the hospital, some ten days subsequent to the birth of the child. Any deductions which are made regarding the care of the illegitimate child from the study data are based only upon the compilation of facts from the last entries regarding him in the hospital and social agency records available for study. The questions of the schedule were accordingly framed to secure only such elementary facts as the date and place of birth of the child, his sex and color, his physical condition, and the type of care which he was receiving at the time when the agency had last made an entry in its records regarding him.

The failure of many of the agencies to make any entry whatsoever regarding the fate of the illegitimate child will be apparent from the statistical tables which follow. The fact that so large a number of our records came from the social service departments of hospitals is in part an explanation of this deficiency of data, for some of these departments, because of the great burden of work which they have been called upon to carry, had not been able even to record what plans had been made for the care of the mother and child after their departure from the hospital, or whether, indeed, any plan for their care had been made at all. An occasional entry in the records indicated that in some cases the unmarried mother and her child had been dismissed from the hospital by a member of the medical staff without the social service department having been informed of their departure. Other reasons for the inadequacy of data regarding these children, so likely to be in need of special measures of protection to insure their survival and proper growth, will be set forth in the analyses of available data which follow.

Place of Birth

There has already been considerable comment to indicate the high proportion of these mothers and children who have hospital contacts. The actual place of birth is indicated in Table 39.

TABLE 39

Illegitimate Children Classified by Place of Birth

PLACE OF BIRTH	NUMBER	PERCENT
Total	1,523[a]	100.0
Own home	44	2.9
Hospital	1,465	96.2
Maternity home	9	0.6
Proprietary hospital	1	0.1
Other	4	0.3

[a]Information on place of birth was not available on 76 of the 1,599 cases studied.

Thus, according to the social agency reports, 96.2 percent of the total number of illegitimate children for which such information was available had been born in hospitals either public or private. This proportion of hospital births was much higher for illegitimate births than for the total number of births for 1930, only about 66 percent of which occurred in hospitals.[1] The reasons for this difference have already been discussed. In another section the difficulties of maternity care in the girl's home were shown to be virtually insurmountable in the case of unmarried mothers, because of the large proportion of those, resident as well as non-resident, who were living separated from their relatives in furnished rooms at the time when they found themselves in difficulties. Even of those who were living with their families, the majority had wished to arrange for their hospitalization, because of the greater facilities thus afforded for avoiding neighborhood comment and criticism.

The large proportion of unmarried mothers who receive maternity care in hospitals would seem to guarantee for the illegitimate infant proper care at birth and a favorable start in life. This apparent advantage was shown from the records to have been offset by the fact that so many of the unmarried mothers had not sought medical aid until the ninth month of pregnancy, and that they had in many cases undergone considerable physical hardship and anxiety.

In virtually all the cases for which such information was given, however, the mother had been attended by a physician at the birth of her child. In only four cases had a midwife attended the birth of the illegitimate child. In nine cases, however, the mother had not been attended by any one at the birth of her child, because she had through fear or ignorance failed to summon any assistance. The peril to the life of both child and mother in such instances is obvious.

Statistics furnished by the Health Department as to the type

[1] The Bureau of Records reports that of a total of 122,811 births recorded in New York City for 1930, 81,587, or nearly 66 per cent, occurred in hospitals.

THE ILLEGITIMATE CHILDREN 195

of place of birth reveal that in 1,325 cases this place was an institution and in 145 cases a tenement or private house. When compared with the agency figures, this implies that there may have been a hundred cases of illegitimate children born in tenements or private dwellings which never came to the attention of any agency. Since, however, there is the possibility of error in the two sets of records and of divergent methods of classification, this discrepancy may not be significant. It again suggests, however, the value which would come from the pooling of data on a year's grist of cases.

While no figures exist to show what proportion of married mothers receive prenatal care and advice,[2] the medical and health workers consulted on the subject were inclined to the view that this proportion was perhaps not as high as in the case of the unmarried mothers. All were insistent, however, that special measures of care and protection were necessary in the case of the latter because of their difficult positions in the social scheme. It was the general belief that there is often extreme social pressure on young women to seek an end to their anxieties by an illegal operation, and that many were not disinclined to do so. Instances were found in social agency records of such measures having been taken by young women contrary to all advice which had been given them by those responsible for their care. It was evident, however, that the majority of the unmarried mothers, subjects of this study, had not been aware, because of their youth and inexperience, of the possibility of such a measure of escape. Some, moreover, had been aware of the possibility, but had refrained from the step because of moral or religious scruples. Still others had wished to seek this way out of their difficulties, but had not been able to raise the sum of money ordinarily required in cash payments for such an operation. A few instances were recorded of applications having been made to social agencies in the vain hope of secur-

[2]See Michael M. Davis and Mary C. Jarrett, *A Health Inventory of New York City*. New York, 1930, Chapter III, "Maternity Hygiene."

ing a loan in order to arrange for an illegal operation. Some young women had registered in prenatal clinics in the hope that they would be able to have an abortion. A few young women under the supervision of case work agencies had notified the latter that their services were no longer required because their anxieties had been ended by resorting to an illegal operation. Thirty-six unsuccessful attempts at abortion by the young women included in the study were reported in addition to those who had successfully evaded the issue in this manner. Of these thirty-six cases, thirty-four were white and two were Negro. Because of the difficulties which we have illustrated above, social workers were of the opinion that the life of the illegitimate child and his mother should be safeguarded by special attention to the mother's health throughout the entire prenatal period, if it could be so arranged that these mothers would come to the institutions and agencies for such care.

In twenty-five cases, the records of social agencies had stated that the illegitimate child was stillborn, but since no entry at all with respect to this item had been made in many cases, it is evident that no deduction as to the proportion of stillbirths can be made from this figure. In 12 cases it was stated that the child had died shortly after birth. There is also no way of knowing how many of the stillbirths and very early deaths of live babies were affected by the measures which the mother might have taken to induce an abortion. Just as the proportion of stillbirths among the total number of illegitimate births could not be estimated because of the incompleteness of the records available, similarly information as to the number of deaths occurring among infants of illegitimate birth during the first year of life was not available, although such data must be regarded as of foremost importance in estimating the social measures necessary to meet the problem of illegitimacy.[3]

[3]Such a determination can be made only by following up individual cases closely and by checking birth and death records, case by case.

From the proportion of illegitimate births which occur in hospitals, it is evident that much can be done by medical and health agencies not only to care for the illegitimate child during the period when he is under their direct supervision, but also to see to it that the proper agencies are informed as to the necessity of his protection after his departure from the hospital.

Detailed information as to the sex and the month of birth of illegitimate infants who were born in the boroughs of New York City in 1930 was available and is given in Appendix 4. These data are for the 1,470 cases recorded on birth certificates.

Health

Despite the emphasis put upon the importance of preserving the life and health of the illegitimate child by all the agencies having to do with the illegitimate family, the entries with reference to this item were disappointingly few. It was obvious from a consideration of the program of work and the general aims of these agencies, many of which were medical and health agencies, that far more had been done to preserve the child's health than the records had indicated.

Nevertheless, entries had been made in some cases, and, when these were sufficiently specific in nature, an attempt was made to classify them. It is evident that such entries as "Jane's baby not doing well," or "Little Edward had not taken on weight" are not susceptible of classification, but they tend to indicate that attention to the child's health had been regarded as of some importance; and, in the case of some agencies, statements followed to show that such observations had been followed up by action designed to remedy the conditions noted: for example, "Took Mary's poor baby to Doctor Smith," or "Saw that Jane registered at clinic." Some entries had been made, too, as to the efforts which had been made by the social worker to encourage breast feeding of the child. In 117 cases it was indicated that the child was so fed. This, however, is certainly an understatement of the total number of infants fed by the mother, for the maternity homes are known to give careful attention to the matter of infant feeding.

In fifty-four cases it was indicated that the child had been born diseased or deformed. Fifteen cases of venereally diseased infants were listed and thirty-nine cases of deformity such as club foot, or absence of the hand, were entered in the records. Since entries with regard to health and physical development were the exception and not the rule, it is evident that no conclusions regarding these matters can be drawn, even for the 1,599 illegitimate infants subjects of this study. The need of full and accurate information on this point is evident, however, if any general measures regarding the protection of the lives and health of these infants are to be framed, or if the agencies are to be able to measure or evaluate the work which they are at present doing in this respect.

It would seem that since baby health work is now regarded as one of the primary functions in the public health field, these children, so severely handicapped, would be regarded as a group requiring special care and adaptations of routine techniques. They are such a relatively small group that, with properly coördinated procedures, it would not be difficult to keep them under observation for the first two years of life, or until they were in the custody of persons and agencies who could be relied upon to safeguard life and health.

What Became of Them

An attempt was made to learn from the records of social agencies what had become of the illegitimate infants born in New York City in 1930. It was thought that some general picture of the way in which these infants born in 1930 were living at the time when the social agencies had last recorded information regarding them might be of worth in portraying the types of problems which their care presents.

It should be emphasized, however, that the information regarding the form of care which these children were receiving, as it is here presented, represents no more than the last entries made by the social agencies regarding them. In the case of the hospital social service records, entries were sometimes made of illegitimate infants who had, so far as the records showed, not received care from any specialized or sectarian agency. Nevertheless the classification of infants according to the religious preferences of the mother has been made and is presented for what interest it may have.

That as many as 381 cases out of a total of 1,599 (Table 38) could not be accounted for is one of the most significant features of this situation.

In nearly 1,200 cases the child was known to be still living and there was some information as to the immediate plans which had been arranged for his care. Of these cases the whereabouts of the child as judged from the last entry regarding him in the social record, was indicated as shown in Table 40.

TABLE 40

Illegitimate Children Classified by Whereabouts,
as Recorded by Social Agencies

WHEREABOUTS	NUMBER	PERCENT
Total	1,181[a]	100.0
Given for adoption	74	6.3
Own home	280	23.7
Relatives' home	275	23.3
Boarding home	128	10.8
Institution	357	30.2
Other	67	5.7

[a]There is definite knowledge that in 37 instances of the 1,599 studied the child was either still born or died soon after its birth. The base figure for total babies for which some disposition had to be made is therefore 1,562 and the cases classified as unknown are 381.

"Own home" in this classification indicates that the child was with his mother in the home of her parents, or with her in any home which she had been able to provide for herself through marriage or otherwise, but always with the understanding that the child's home was the same as that of his mother and that he was under her supervision.[4] In "relatives' home" it is implied that the child was not with his mother but was being cared for by relatives. In the case of the "boarding home" and "institution," it was not assumed that the mother had relinquished the custody of her child but that she had been unable to have him in her own home or in the home of her relatives. In the case of some children in institutions and boarding homes, the mothers had taken preliminary steps to surrender their custody, but if the arrangements had not been definitely completed the child was indicated in these classifications as being still in the custody of his mother but in the care of these agencies. In some cases, too, the child "in the institution" was actually being cared for by his own mother, who had been received into the institution with him and who was able to give him her personal care. It must be assumed, therefore, that some of these children who were in institutions with their mothers would not be left there for any considerable period of time, but would be taken later either into the mother's own home or into the home of her relatives, or else placed with foster parents. In some cases the child who was separated from his mother and in the institution was being cared for temporarily, while arrangements for his placement in a foster home were already under way.

It must also be remembered that in New York City a large part of the boarding-out work is conducted by institutions. All boarding children who are public charges must have been committed officially to institutions. Hence while the child is technically in an institution, he may actually be in a boarding home supervised by that institution.[5]

[4]It does not include the cases of children in institutions with their mothers.
[5]This affords another illustration of the need for a complete follow-up of all cases, if there is ever to be an accurate accounting for these children and a true description of the care that they received.

It will be observed that by the summer of 1931 there were seventy-four of the children, subjects of this study, who were known definitely to have been surrendered for adoption. This does not mean, however, that the adoption had actually been consummated. A much larger number had been offered for such surrender, but, as was indicated above, they were not counted in the classification because arrangements for surrender had not yet been completed at the time that the study was made. Of the remainder, 30.2 percent were in institutions and 10.8 percent were in boarding homes for infants. Forty-seven percent of all the children whose histories were known, however, were with the mother or with her relatives.

Although the numbers were small in each classification, an attempt was made to ascertain whether or not the marital status of the unmarried mother had seemed to influence the immediate plan which she had made for the care of the child. No such relationship, however, could be discovered. Some of the women who were or had been married had wished to keep their illegitimate infants with them and others had not. The same was true in the case of the single woman. Apparently the consideration of what should be done with the infant had been determined by other circumstances than that of the marital status of the mother, since no significant difference appeared when an attempt was made to relate marital status of the mother to the plans actually made for the care of the child, as indicated in the preceding table.

Similarly, no connection was found between the age of the unmarried mother and the plans made for the care of her child. Some social workers were of the opinion that unmarried mothers under twenty years of age should not be encouraged to keep the child. All, however, had not shared this view, and we could not discern in the statistics that were available to us any trend in disposition of the child which was associated with the age of the unmarried mother. The unmarried mothers who were older seemed neither more nor less inclined to keep their infants than those who were younger. Similarly, there was no evident relationship between the educational qualifications of the unmarried mother and her plans for the care of her child.

However, the connection between the color and nativity of the unmarried mother and the plans made for the immediate care of her child appeared evident in the cases where such information was given.

From Table 41 it will be seen that while only 34 percent of the white illegitimate infants of which we had record were with the mother in her own home or in the home of her relatives, of the Negro illegitimate infants 73.7 were so situated. In other words, Negro families appeared to be more than twice as likely as white ones to receive an illegitimate child with his mother immediately into the home or into the home of relatives. Similarly, only two cases were reported of Negro unmarried mothers who had surrendered their children for adoption.

This difference in the type of care which the Negro illegitimate child and the white illegitimate child receive is attributed by social workers to two sets of circumstances. In the first place, it is indicated that the facilities existing for the care of the dependent Negro child are far less adequate than the same facilities for the dependent white child, and that, even if the Negro unmarried mother should wish to surrender her child, she would have more difficulty in doing so. In the second place, it was pointed out by social workers engaged in work for the illegitimate family that the Negro unmarried mother is less likely than is the white unmarried mother to wish to surrender her child. It was said that in the case of the Negro unmarried mother her natural affection for the child is less hampered by strong social pressures, that she is consequently less likely to be willing to give him up. For the same reason, her relatives are likely to be willing to aid her in her difficulties, and willing if necessary to receive the child into their home. It was reported,

TABLE 41

Illegitimate Children Classified by Type of Immediate Care Received and Nativity and Color of Mother

TYPE OF CARE RECEIVED	TOTAL		WHITE						NEGRO				FOREIGN BORN[a]
			TOTAL		NATIVE BORN		FOREIGN BORN		TOTAL		NATIVE BORN		
	No.	Percent	No.	Percent	No.	Percent	No.	Percent	No.	Percent	No.	Percent	No.
Total	1,137[b]	100.0	779	100.0	566	100.0	213	100.0	358	100.0	333	100.0	25
Adoption	73	6.4	71	9.1	57	10.1	14	6.6	2	0.6	2	0.6	...
Own home	261	22.9	166	21.3	127	22.4	39	18.3	95	26.5	84	25.2	11
Relatives' home	268	23.6	99	12.7	81	14.3	18	8.5	169	47.2	162	48.6	7
Boarding home	128	11.3	117	15.1	75	13.3	42	19.7	11	3.1	10	3.0	1
Institution	343	30.2	289	37.1	205	36.2	84	39.4	54	15.1	51	15.4	3
Other	64	5.6	37	4.7	21	3.7	16	7.5	27	7.5	24	7.2	3

[a] Percentage not computed, base less than 100.

[b] From this table 425 cases were excluded because one or more of the items needed were not recorded.

also, that cases of voluntary aid by the unmarried Negro father were not so infrequent as among the whites, although it was impossible to determine from the case records whether this was so or not.

Workers in close touch with the Negro illegitimate family were unanimous in their belief that the facilities at present existing for the care of the Negro unmarried mother are inadequate, and that they should be expanded and given more ample support. It was also suggested that the natural tie between mother and child, so deep and so widespread among the Negro people, should be respected and fostered; and that any aid contemplated for the illegitimate family in the future should be planned in such a way as to accomplish this end. Apropos of this topic, it was pointed out by one social worker that in the case of one of the Negro children surrendered for adoption this step had been taken at the suggestion and even at the insistence of the social worker herself, although the baby's mother and his maternal grandmother had at first been unwilling to consider such a measure.

Differences in the dispositions made of illegitimate children born to native and to foreign born women are of interest. The larger proportion of infants of native born girls in relatives' homes is to be expected, since the foreign born unmarried mother is less likely to have relatives in this country who can come to her aid. For the same reason, perhaps, the proportion of children of foreign born mothers who were in boarding homes or institutions was greater. This also is attributed to the fact that the foreign born mother is more likely than the native born mother to be living away from her relatives.

Table 42 aims to show the relationship between the occupation of the mother and the immediate disposition that she makes of her child.

It should be borne constantly in mind that the numbers in this distribution are small and not to be taken as of general

TABLE 42

Illegitimate Children Classified by Type of Immediate Care Received and Occupation of Mother[a]

TYPE OF CARE RECEIVED	CLERICAL		DOMESTIC		FACTORY		SCHOOL		MISCELLANEOUS	
	No.	Percent	No.	Percent	No.	Percent	No.	Percent	No.	Percent
Total	165	100.0	509	100.0	152	100.0	67	100.0	79	100.0
Given in adoption	22	13.3	21	4.1	11	7.2	4	6.0	6	7.6
Own home	31	18.8	115	22.6	29	19.1	20	29.9	26	32.9
Relatives' home	23	13.9	133	26.1	38	25.0	13	19.4	9	11.4
Boarding home	26	15.8	57	11.2	18	11.8	2	3.0	15	19.0
Institution	55	33.3	139	27.3	53	34.9	26	38.8	18	22.8
Other	8	4.8	44	8.6	3	2.0	2	3.0	5	6.3

[a]From this table 580 cases were excluded because one or more items needed were not recorded.

significance. However, it is interesting to note that they are in harmony with the assumption that the occupation of the unmarried mother may be one of the factors of importance in determining the disposition which is made of her child. It would appear that the clerical workers had surrendered their children for adoption in a somewhat higher proportion of cases than had any other group. This failure of the girl in clerical employment to provide for her illegitimate child in her own home or in the home of her relatives in any large proportion of cases is probably associated with the fear of severe social disapproval from the group of which she is a part and of consequent loss of employment. On the other hand, the domestic servant can, because of the nature of her employment, more easily provide for her child in her own home or with relatives, and accordingly seems to do so. The group of school girls, the younger group, contains many of the Negro unmarried mothers, and explains perhaps why a large proportion of the infants are cared for in the mother's own home or in the home of relatives. Other relationships between the form of care provided for the child and the occupation of the mother are evident from the table, and appear plausible when conditions associated with such employment are considered.

Inquiry was made also to determine whether the forms of care given the illegitimate child differed when considered from the point of view of the religious preferences of the unmarried mother. The results of this inquiry are shown in Table 43. It should be emphasized that these distributions are not significant for the entire group of infants under consideration, but only for the 1,168 for whom such information was given. Of the remaining 431 we only know that 37 had died; the whereabouts of others were not reported. Furthermore, this classification of illegitimate children according to the religious preferences of the mother does not imply that all of the infants were receiving care from agencies of these sectarian groups. As

TABLE 43

*Illegitimate Children Classified by Type of Immediate Care
Received and Religion of Mother*[a]

TYPE OF CARE	PROTESTANT		CATHOLIC		JEWISH	
	No.	Percent	No.	Percent	No.	Percent
Total	584	100.0	443	100.0	141	100.0
Given in adoption .	36	6.2	10	2.3	28	19.9
Own home	151	25.9	110	24.8	15	16.6
Relatives' home . .	204	34.9	65	14.7	5	3.5
Boarding home . .	52	8.9	53	12.0	20	14.2
Institution	104	17.8	179	40.4	69	48.9
Other	37	6.3	26	5.9	4	2.8

[a]From this table 394 cases were excluded because one or more items needed
were not recorded.

has been indicated previously, some of these infants had, so far
as the records showed at the time the study was made, no contact with a social agency other than the social service department of the hospital where they were born. Some had received
care from non-sectarian agencies.

Of the children born to the 745 Protestant mothers, the 584
reported above constitute 78 percent; of the 631 children born
to Catholic mothers, the 443 reported here are 70 percent;
while the 141 children of Jewish mothers here accounted for
constitute 75 percent of the 189 such children.

It will be observed that a large proportion of the infants
whose mothers were Protestant were being temporarily cared
for in the home of the mother or in the home of relatives of the
mother. Of the infants, subjects of this study, whose mothers
were Jewish, 48.9 percent were temporarily in institutions,
and 19.9 percent had been given in adoption. In connection
with this group, it should be recalled that a large proportion of
these young women were engaged in clerical pursuits, and
that, in general, fewer young women of this occupational
group had been able or willing to keep their infants in their

own homes or in the homes of relatives. It is possible, too, that the dread of censure and blame common to clerical workers in general, in addition to the strict ideals of family life known to prevail in this racial and religious group, may have been of influence in determining the form of care which these infants received. The known availability of excellent Jewish adoption homes may also have influenced their course of action.

A large proportion of illegitimate infants whose mothers were Catholic were recorded as receiving temporary care in institutions. As has been pointed out in connection with the other groups, not all of these children were separated from their mothers even temporarily. In some cases, the mother and child together were receiving institutional care. In other cases, arrangements for foster home care were already under way, although the child was receiving temporary care in the institution. Not all of the illegitimate infants whose mothers were Catholic had, at the time the study was made, come into contact with a Catholic social agency. Some in this group, as in others, had had contact only with hospital and health agencies. A few were receiving care from non-sectarian agencies. This situation was accompanied by a relatively small number placed for adoption, and a relatively large number being cared for in the home of the mother and in the home of relatives of the mother. It should be recalled also that a comparatively large proportion of the young women of this group were engaged in some form of domestic service, and that the keeping of the child by mothers of this occupational group has been shown in a preceding section to be characteristic of that occupational group. In general it may be said that the forms of care which the illegitimate infants of all of these sectarian groups are receiving is as readily associated with the occupational pursuits of the mothers of these infants and the social and economic levels at which they are living, as with the beliefs and traditions of the group itself.

It may be of interest to observe further the relation between the temporary disposition of the child and the color of the unmarried mother in the three sectarian groups. Table 44 indicates the disposition of the child of the white unmarried mothers of these groups, and of the Negro mothers.

It will be readily seen that when the Negro unmarried mothers are omitted from the statistics, the proportion of illegitimate infants in the Protestant group kept in the home of the mother or her relatives is noticeably diminished. On the other hand, the proportion given in adoption or placed by the mother in boarding homes or institutions is higher than when the Negro group is included. In general, it might be observed that among the white unmarried mothers for whom we have information the Protestant had a smaller, and the Catholic and Jewish unmarried mothers had a higher, proportion of their infants temporarily in institutions at the time that the data used in the study were recorded. The white Catholic and white Protestant unmarried mothers had about the same proportion of infants in the mother's own home, while the Jewish had the largest percentage of infants surrendered for adoption. Whether or not a later check-up would reveal a change in the types of care provided for these illegitimate children, we have no means of knowing.

The high proportion of Negro illegitimate infants kept by their mothers or relatives and the reasons for this have already been discussed. The small number of Negro unmarried mothers who were Catholic make comparisons between the Protestant and the Catholic Negro unmarried mothers of little value, but the figures are given for what they may be worth.

It must be clear that the alternatives presented in the care of an illegitimate child depend to some degree on the responsibility which his father assumes or can be induced to assume toward him. Until there has been a thoroughgoing attempt to secure for each illegitimate child the assistance in his support

TABLE 44

Illegitimate Children Classified by the Type of Immediate Care Received
and by the Race and Religion of Their Mothers

| | WHITE | | | | | | NEGRO | | | |
| | PROTESTANT | | CATHOLIC | | JEWISH | | PROTESTANT | | CATHOLIC | |
DISPOSITION	No.	Percent	No.	Percent	No.	Percent	No.	Percent	No.	Percent
Total	239	100.0	385	100.0	137	100.0	316	100.0	32	100.0
Given in adoption . .	33	13.8	10	2.6	28	20.4	2	0.6	...	...
Own home . . .	55	23.0	93	24.2	14	10.2	83	26.3	10	31.3
Relatives' home . .	41	17.2	52	13.5	4	2.9	154	48.7	9	28.1
Boarding home . .	42	17.6	51	13.2	20	14.6	9	2.8	2	6.3
Institution	58	24.3	156	40.5	67	48.9	43	13.6	9	28.1
Other	10	4.2	23	6.0	4	2.9	25	7.9	2	6.3

ᵃFrom these tables 453 cases were excluded because one or more items of information needed were not recorded.

that is due and can be collected from his father, when paternity can be established, there can be no final judgment as to the proportion which might properly be enabled to stay with their own families and there will be no real determination of the extent to which these children are genuinely and properly a responsibility of the community.

In this connection it should be remembered that, although child-caring agencies and institutions of New York City are almost wholly under private auspices, a large majority of them receive financial assistance from public sources, and a large proportion of the children accepted for care in institutions and boarding homes are at least partially supported from public funds. The children kept with their mothers and with relatives may, of course, also be dependents upon public or private charity if they are members of families on relief. It is unlikely, however, that in ordinary times these children are, directly or indirectly, supported by charity to the same extent as are children in boarding homes and in institutions. It is, however, only by means of more intensive and prolonged observation of these cases that the question of the financial support of these children can be accurately answered.

It is of less consequence to the community to assure itself with regard to the financial support of these children than it is to make sure that the care which they are receiving is such that it will foster their health, physical and mental, and will develop in them the character to offset the handicaps of their birth and to make of them good members of the community. A clearly defined, systematic community program that insures that the parents of these children will not shift their responsibilities to other shoulders, and that safeguards the health and fosters the growth of these children, is not a part of New York City's social scheme. Undoubtedly, many are now being well reared by one method or another, but this is by virtue of the interest and devotion of voluntary groups, acting with some financial and legal assistance from the city, but proceeding each as it sees fit. What is happening to the rest of these children nobody now knows or can find out. It is only as a thorough program of action and study that undertakes to account for all of these children can be put into operation that there can be assurance that they are being properly cared for, and that their parents are meeting the obligations that parents ordinarily assume.

APPENDICES

APPENDIX 1

INDIVIDUAL CASE SCHEDULE FOR EACH UNMARRIED MOTHER WHOSE CHILD WAS BORN BETWEEN JAN. 1, 1930 AND JAN. 1, 1931

THE MOTHER

1. Name_____
   (Alias) _____
2. Address _____
3. Agency_____
4. Case No._____ active ( )
                                              closed ( )
5. Source of application: in person ( ) relatives ( ) doctor ( )
   ( ) clergyman ( ) police ( ) social agency ( ) others_____
   _____
6. Date of birth_____
7. Marital status at birth of child: single ( ) married ( )
   divorced ( ) separated ( ) widowed ( )
8. Occupation previous to birth of child_____
   weekly earnings _____
   Occupation after birth of child_____
   weekly earnings _____
   Occupation at present time _____
   weekly earnings _____
9. Religion: Protestant ( ) Catholic ( ) Jewish ( )
10. Country of birth_____
11. Citizenship: Yes ( ) No ( ) Not reported ( )
12. Color_____ 13. Resident in N. Y. C. ( )
                              Non-resident ( )
14. Education _____
    (last school grade attended)

15. Health as reported_____
    "   not reported _____
16. Previous pregnancies? No ( ) Yes ( ) Number_____
17. Child living? Yes ( ) No ( )
18. If any other child or children, present whereabouts?_____
    _____

19. Any form of abortion attempted? Yes ( ) No ( ) Not reported ( )
20. Check month in pregnancy when application was made: 1 2 3 4 5 6 7 8 9 or what month after birth of child was application made? 1 2 3 4 5 6 7_____
21. Nature of aid asked_____
22. Was complete social history obtained?_____

THE FATHER

23. Name_____ 24. Age_____

	single ( )
	married ( )
25. Marital status:	divorced ( )
	separated ( )
	widower ( )

26. Occupation_____ Weekly earnings_____
27. Religion: Protestant ( ) Catholic ( ) Jewish ( )
28. Country of birth_____
29. Citizenship? Yes ( ) No ( ) Not reported ( )
30. Color_____ 31. Education_____
                                  (last school grade attended)
32. Health (as reported)_____
    "   not reported _____

THE CHILD

33. Date of birth_____ 34. Color _____
35. Sex _____ 36. Certificate No. _____

37. Place of birth: in what city_____

38. Birth registered? Yes ( ) No ( ) Legitimate? ( ) Illegitimate? ( ) Not reported_____

39. Place of delivery: own home ( ) hospital ( ) maternity home ( ) proprietary hospital ( ) Other_____

40. Attendance at birth: physician ( ) midwife ( ) other_____

41. Breast fed? Yes ( ) No ( ) How long?_____

42. Any physical defects? Yes ( ) No ( ) Describe_____
_____

43. How long kept with mother?_____

44. If given in adoption, reasons assigned_____

45. If mother has kept child, present whereabouts? Own home ( ) Relatives' home ( ) Boarding home ( ) Institution ( ) Elsewhere _____

46. If child not given in adoption, and not kept by mother, to whom committed? _____

SERVICES RENDERED TO MOTHER

47. Physical examination secured? Yes ( ) No ( )

48. Recommendations followed? Yes ( ) No ( )

49. Psychometric test given? Yes ( ) No ( )
M.A._____ I.Q._____

50. Vocational training? Yes ( ) No ( ) If yes, describe_____
_____

51. Vocational placement? Yes ( ) No ( ) If yes, describe_____
_____

52. Special educational opportunity secured? Yes ( ) No ( ) If yes, describe _____

53. Special cultural opportunities? Yes ( ) No ( ) If yes, describe_____

54. Special recreational opportunities? Yes ( ) No ( ) If yes, describe _____

55. Special opportunity for religious training? Yes ( ) No ( )
If yes, describe_____

56. Supervision after placement? Yes ( ) No ( ) How long?_____
_____

57. Material relief: money_____ clothing_____ food_____

58. Other relief (such as confinement care, other medical or dental service, payment of board)

59. Any other services?

60. Paternity established? Yes ( ) No ( )
Legally? ( ) Through case work? ( )
Voluntarily on part of father? ( )

61. Amount of court settlement, if any_____
    "   " voluntary "   "   " _____

62. Was money paid direct to mother? Yes ( ) No ( )

63. If not, who is responsible for disbursement?_____

64. Are payments regular? Irregular? ( ) In arrears? ( ) How long in arrears? _____

65. Any services rendered father? Yes ( ) No ( ) If yes, describe
_____

66. Does agency consider this case successful? If so, why?_____
_____

If not, why? _____
_____

67. Did unmarried mother pay for any service rendered? Yes ( )
No (˙) How much?_____

Name of person filling in schedule_____
Date_____

AGENCY SCHEDULE

Name of reporter_____
Date of report_____

1. Name of agency_____

2. When founded_____ 3. When incorporated_____

4. Name of person furnishing information_____

5. Position _____

FUNCTION

6. What is the present function of agency? (See explanation of function, last page.)

7. Has the function changed since agency was founded? Yes ( ) No ( )

8. In what way?

9. What function discontinued?   10. Why?

11. What new function assumed?   12. Why?

POLICY (See explanation of policy, last page.)

13. What is the present policy with regard to:

    a) area served   f) second offenders
    b) age limit of patients   g) patients with venereal disease
    c) race   h) patients from commercial homes
    d) color   i) patients of low mentality
    e) creed   j) patients who refuse to coöperate

14. Any other limitations of intake?

15. What is the present policy with regard to discharge?

    a) Average length of stay of unmarried mother
    b) Basis of decision with regard to discharge
    c) Responsibility for decision: superintendent ( ) board ( ) committee ( ) other

16. Has there been any change in the policies pursued by the agency? Yes ( ) No ( )

17. Describe and give reasons.

18. Who is responsible for policy making?

19. Is governing board active? (Determine by regular meetings, participation in planning and policy making, interest in other community projects.)

20. How often does it meet?   Minutes kept? Yes ( ) No ( )
Has a policy book or other statement been formulated?

21. Who makes social investigations?

22. Is Social Service Exchange consulted in every case?

23. Yearly intake: *a)* new cases: 1930____ 1929____ 1928____
           1927____ 1926____
       b) old or reopened cases: 1930____ 1929____
           1928____ 1927____ 1926____

24. Total active unmarried mother cases, January 1, 1931.

25. What is the capacity of the institution?
(If hospital, greatest number of unmarried mother cases carried at one time.)
Any seasonal fluctuations? Yes ( ) No ( ) When?_____

26. Has the proportion of cases increased or decreased over a ten-year period?
Percentage increase_____ Percentage decrease_____

27. Reasons ascribed for increase or decrease.

28. Sources of applications for year 1930: in person ( ) relatives
( ) friends ( ) clergy ( ) doctors ( ) police ( ) hospital
( ) others (list) _____

SERVICES RENDERED BY THE AGENCY

29. Case work, including: social investigation ( ) treatment ( )
reëducation ( ) supervision before confinement ( ) arranging for confinement ( ) case work supervision after confinement ( ) placement of mother ( ) placement of child ( )

30. Prenatal care: clinic ( ) institutional ( ) other_____

31. Confinement care: hospital ( ) maternity home ( ) own
home ( ) other _____

32. Postnatal care: clinic ( ) maternity home ( ) shelter ( )
other _____

33. Vocational training—skilled trades: dressmaking ( ) millinery ( ) list others_____
    —unskilled trades: domestic service ( ) laundry ( ) mother's helper ( ) list others _____
    —semi-professional: typing and stenography ( ) bookkeeping ( ) infant's nurse ( ) list others _____

34. Vocational placement: is agency in touch with employers who can offer opportunities for which training is provided? Yes ( ) No ( ) List and describe these opportunities_____

35. Other special features of agency's program:
    a) formal classes ( ) subjects taught _____
    b) clubs ( ) c) cultural opportunities ( ) d) religious training ( ) e) library facilities: own ( ) traveling ( ) f) recreation ( )

36. List special equipment for above:
    a) material equipment _____
    b) trained leadership _____

37. Adoption work:
    a) Does the agency place children in adoption? Yes ( ) No ( )
    b) What is basis of decision in regard to adoption?_____
    c) Through what means are adoptive homes found?_____
    d) Who investigates them? (Attach forms.) If children placed in another state, is case referred for investigation to a local or state-wide social agency?_____
    Give names of agencies recently used_____

    e) Is there any follow-up after adoption? Yes ( ) No ( )
    f) How long?_____ g) By whom?_____

38. Placement of child (other than adoption):
    a) boarding home ( ) b) free home ( ) c) institution ( )

d) mother's own home (   ) *e*) relatives' home (   )

f) describe amount and kind of supervision given in each case

39. Material relief for child: *a*) payment of board: full (   ) partial (   ) *b*) clothing provided: full (   ) partial (   ) *c*) other services _____

40. Material relief for mother: *a*) payment of board: full (   ) partial (   ) *b*) clothing provided: full (   ) partial (   ) *c*) other forms of relief (medical, dental service, etc.)_____

41. Paternity proceedings: *a*) initiated by agency? Yes (   ) No (   )

　　　　　　　　　　　　 b) carried through court? Yes (   )
　　　　　　　　　　　　 No (   )

　　　　　　　　　 · *c*) referred to other agency? Yes (   )
　　　　　　　　　　　　 No (   )

　　　　　　　　　　　　 d) name of agency to which referred
　　　　　　　　　　　　 _____

　　　　　　　　　　　　 e) number of paternity proceedings
　　　　　　　　　　　　 carried through court in 1930_____
　　　　　　　　　　　　 1929_____ 1928_____

42. Personnel:

a) what special training has superintendent had?

b) case workers: give number on staff July 1, 1930.

Full time_____ Part time_____

c) trained nurse	" " _____	" " _____
d) chaplain	" " _____	" " _____
e) physician	" " _____	" " _____
f) psychiatrist	" " _____	" " _____
g) psychologist	" " _____	" " _____
h) teacher	" " _____	" " _____

i) recreation leader: give
number on staff July
1, 1931　　"   " _____　　"   " _____

    j) volunteers   Full time_____ Part time_____

    k) clerical   "   " _____   "   " _____

    l) labor

    m) check special opportunities for staff training extended during the last two years: staff meetings ( ) institutes ( ) special courses ( ) attendance at local, state, national conferences ( ) service on committees ( ) list other_____

---

43. Cost of care:

    a) number of days' care given unmarried mothers in 1930

    b) what is the usual charge for care?_____

    c) "   "   "   " payment for care?_____

    d) how paid? (actual money or service from mother in institution?)

    e) how much actually collected from unmarried mothers in 1930? _____

44. Does the agency have any projects through committees, individuals, or other means for:

    a) improvement of legislation on illegitimacy_____

    b) reform of administration in courts_____

    c) study of causes or any fact-finding with reference to the problem as a basis for future planning_____

    d) development of case work service for unmarried mothers

    e) participation in community projects having similar objectives _____

45. Records:

    a) who is responsible for records?

    b) nature of records kept: good ( ) fair ( ) poor ( )

46. Agency's evaluation of its work:

    a) basis of judgment of success

    b) basis of judgment of failure

DIGEST OF LAWS ON CHILDREN BORN OUT OF WEDLOCK IN THE STATE OF NEW YORK

In this digest[1] reference is made to the various statutes specifically applying to children born out of wedlock; but procedural technical details, not of particular interest, are not digested. In a few cases, it seemed wiser to present the statutory provisions substantially in full rather than in the form of a digest.

With reference to the filiation proceedings, under the second subject, it was thought that a comparative digest of the pertinent laws of the State and of the city of New York would be useful.

I. Designation of Child

The term "bastard" or "illegitimate child" in a statute means a child born out of wedlock. Hereafter in any local law, ordinance, or resolution, or in any public or judicial proceeding, or in any process, notice, order, decree, judgment, record, or other public document or paper, the term "bastard" or "illegitimate child" shall not be used, but the term "child born out of wedlock" shall be used in substitution therefor and with the same force and effect. [Cahill's *Consolidated Laws, 1930,* "General Construction Law," sec. 59. Added by *Laws of 1925,* ch. 515.]

II. Support and Education of Children Born out of Wedlock, and Proceedings to Establish Paternity

STATE LAW

Definitions

"child born out of wedlock;" and child begotten and born: *a*) out of lawful matrimony; *b*) while the husband of its mother was separate from her a whole year previous to its birth; or *c*) during the separation of its

LAW FOR THE CITY OF NEW YORK[2]

* * *

"Natural child" is substituted for "child born out of wedlock"; and "support" is defined to include *a*) the necessary support and education of the child either before or after the order of filiation, *b*) the funeral ex-

[1]This digest is based on the laws in force, January 1, 1933.
[2]Substantially or in effect the same provisions are indicated by asterisks.

STATE LAW

LAW FOR THE CITY OF NEW YORK

mother from her husband pursuant to a judgment of a competent court.[3] * * * [Cahill's *Consolidated Laws,* 1930, "Domestic Relations Law," sec. 119.]

penses in case of the child's death, *c*) the expenses of the mother's confinement and recovery and those incurred during pregnancy.[4] [*Laws of 1930,* ch. 434, sec. 35-a.]

Liability for Support and Education

1. The parents are liable for the necessary support and education of the child, and its father for the expenses of the mother's confinement and recovery, and such expenses in connection with her pregnancy as the court may allow. In case of neglect or inability of the parents, the public local unit to which the child is chargeable must support and educate it.

1. * * * In case of neglect or inability of parents, the city supports the child.

2. If the father dies, the court order in any settlement before his death is enforceable against his estate, but with due regard to the age of the child, the ability of the mother to support, and the rights of the surviving widow and children. [*Ibid.,* sec. 120.]

2. * * * [*Ibid.,* sec. 35-b.]

3. If the mother of a child born out of wedlock has property and fails to support or educate such child, the court [see sections 122(3) and 135 for jurisdiction], on application of the guardian or next friend of the child, or the local welfare official where the child is a charge upon a local unit, may order the mother to pay for support and education. A bond may also be required for payment of the order; and, in default of the security, she may

3. Proceedings may be against both father and mother and the liability apportioned between them. [*Ibid.,* sec. 35-m.]

[3] The law, sections 119-139, was enacted in 1925 (ch. 255), and supersedes former antiquated legislation of this type.

[4] This law was first enacted in 1929 (ch. 434), as Art. III-B of the Inferior Criminal Courts Acts (L. 1910, ch. 659). The law of 1929 is repealed and superseded by the above law of 1930 and the article is redesignated Art. III-C by L. 1931, ch. 407.

STATE LAW

be committed to jail, subject to discharge within one year, or put on probation [see also section 134, following, as to probation]. But these provisions shall not relieve the father's liability for such support and education. [*Ibid.*, sec. 132.]

Agreement or Compromise

An agreement or compromise by the mother, or child, or by some authorized person, with the father, as to the support and education of the child, is binding upon the mother and child only when a court has found that adequate provision is fully secured and has given its approval; such approval is not to be granted until notice and opportunity to be heard has been given to the public welfare official of the local unit where the mother resides or the child is found. Performance of an approved agreement or compromise bars other remedies for support and education. [*Ibid.*, sec. 121.]

Proceedings for Support and to Establish Paternity

A proceeding for support and education may be brought by the mother, or her representative, or, if the child is or may become a public charge, by

LAW FOR THE CITY OF NEW YORK

If the parent of a natural child absconds from the city, leaving it a public charge or to the other parent, the commissioner of public welfare may apply to the local court or to the court where any of the parent's property may be, for authority to take the same. [*Ibid.*, sec. 35-n.]

* * * Notice and opportunity to be heard must be given to the commissioner of public welfare. [*Ibid.*, sec. 35-c.]

Jurisdiction

* * * Proceedings may be brought by the mother, "whether a minor or not" and also by an incorporated society doing charitable work, or, if the

STATE LAW

the public welfare official of the local unit where the mother resides or the child is found. Complaints may be made in the county where she or the child resides or is found, or in the county where the putative father resides or is found, although the child may have been born outside of the State of New York. In case of the mother's death or disability, the child may complain through its guardian or next friend. [*Ibid.*, sec. 122(1).]

Proceedings to establish paternity may be instituted before or after the child's birth, but not after more than two years from such birth, unless paternity has been acknowledged by the father in writing or by furnishing support. But local public welfare officials may sue in behalf of any child under sixteen who is or is liable to become a public charge. [*Ibid.*, sec. 122(2).]

The complaint must be in writing, or oral and reduced to writing by the judge or the clerk, and must be verified by the complainant. The complainant must charge the defendant as being the father and demand that he appear to answer the charge. [*Ibid.*, sec. 122(4 & 5).]

A warrant may be issued for the arrest of the defendant wherever he may be found in the state; or the court may issue a summons, to be personally served. [*Ibid.*, sec. 122(6).]

a) Jurisdiction is given to the children's courts, where established; and the county courts in the counties of Chautauqua, Monroe, and Ontario. [*Ibid.*, sec. 122(3), as amended by Laws

LAW FOR THE CITY OF NEW YORK

child is a public charge, by the city department of public welfare. Proceedings may be brought in any county of the city irrespective of where they were started. The city of New York is, of course, the local unit for purposes of residence, or where the child is found, etc. [*Ibid.*, sec. 35-d(1).]

* * * [*Ibid.*, sec. 35-d(1).]

* * * [*Ibid.*, sec. 35-d(2).]

* * * [*Ibid.*, sec. 35-d(3).]

The court of special sessions of the city of New York has exclusive jurisdiction of all proceedings under this law. [*Ibid.*, sec. 35.]

STATE LAW

of 1931, ch. 219.] *b*) The court is given continuing jurisdiction over proceedings for support and education and to increase or decrease the amount fixed by the order of filiation until the judgment has been completely satisfied. [*Ibid.*, sec. 131.] *c*) Jurisdiction over proceedings to compel support of a child born out of wedlock is also vested in the courts specified in section 122 (3), above. The jurisdiction is not barred where the child or the mother lives in another county or state, if the defendant is a resident of New York. [*Ibid.*, sec. 135.]⁵

LAW FOR THE CITY OF NEW YORK

Continuing jurisdiction * * * and the court may "also entertain new support proceedings should a previous support order [*not?*] have been fulfilled or satisfied." [*Ibid.*, sec. 35-l.]

Proceedings Preliminary to Trial

1. When the defendant is arrested he must be taken before the court issuing the warrant [see sec. 122(3&6)], or, if arrested in another county, before the county judge, the judge of the children's court, or the county magistrate. The court must take from the defendant an undertaking for not less than $500 with security to the effect: *a*) that, if suit is brought by the local public-welfare authority, he will indemnify the local unit against any expense for the support and education of the child and for support of its mother during confinement and recovery and will pay any order of filiation that may be made; or *b*) that he will appear in court and obey its order.

1. When a defendant is arrested within the city of New York he shall be taken before the court or justice thereof. * * * and under the security the defendant also promises that he will "remain subject to its jurisdiction until determination" of the case and failing to do so will allow the security to be applied to payments directed by the court. Indemnification for support by local authorities is found in section 35-k herein. [*Ibid.*, sec. 35-e(1).]

⁵Jurisdiction.—The children's courts are now also given this jurisdiction in the city of Syracuse [Laws of 1930, ch. 396, sec. 37(3)] and in Erie County [Laws of 1931, ch. 219, sec. 3]. In the city of New York, under the new law for such proceedings, the court of special sessions has exclusive jurisdiction [Laws of 1930, ch. 434, sec. 35]. The State children's court act confers upon such courts the "exclusive original jurisdiction in the hearing and determination of the cases of children born out of wedlock" [Laws of 1922, ch. 547, sec. 6(3)].

STATE LAW

2. If summons has been issued the defendant must appear in the court where the complaint was made.

3. When he is arrested in another county and fails to give security, he must be taken before the court which issued the warrant.

4. When an undertaking is given he must be discharged.

5. If he fails to give an undertaking the court may commit him to jail. [*Ibid.*, sec. 123.]

The court may adjourn trial; but must bind him over or held him in jail until the trial if he requests adjournment, and may do so if the complainant requests adjournment. [*Ibid.*, sec. 124.]

In case of death or insanity, or if the mother cannot be found, after complaint, the child may be substituted as complainant. [*Ibid.*, sec. 125.]

The Trial

1. The trial must be by the court without a jury. Both the mother and alleged father are competent witnesses, but he may not be compelled to give evidence. The general public may be excluded from any proceedings.[6]

1. If the defendant fails to appear, his security for appearance is forfeited and must be applied to the payment of the order of affiliation, but the trial must proceed and orders be made as if he were present. [*Ibid.*, sec. 126.]

LAW FOR THE CITY OF NEW YORK

2. No corresponding provision. [Such appearance may be taken for granted.]

* * * [See below.]

* * * [*Ibid.*, sec. 35-e(2).]

* * * If he fails to give security and is arrested in a county outside of New York City, he must be placed in custody of a peace officer or the city for arraignment therein. [*Ibid.*, sec. 35-e (3).]

* * * [*Ibid.*, sec. 35-h.]

* * * [*Ibid.*, sec. 35-f.]

* * * [*Ibid.*, sec. 35-g.]

* * * [*Ibid.*, sec. 35-g.]

[6]Section 4 of the State Judiciary Law also provides that in trials in cases of illegitimacy, the court may exclude all persons not directly interested.

The Judgment

2. If the finding be against the defendant, the court must make an order of filiation, declaring paternity, and must order support and education.

Such order must specify the sum to be paid until the child reaches the age of sixteen. The order must also provide for payment of expenses during confinement and recovery of the mother; for funeral expenses if the child has died; for support of the child prior to the order; and for such other expenses of the mother as are proper. [*Ibid.*, sec. 127.]

The court may require the payment to be made to the mother, or to some trustee designated by it, but if the child is or may become a public charge upon a local unit, the local public welfare official must be the trustee. The payment must be to a trustee if the mother does not live within the court's jurisdiction. The trustee must at least annually report to the court the sums received and paid over. [*Ibid.*, sec. 128.]

Appeals may be taken by the defendant, a guardian *ad litem* for the child, the mother, or a local public welfare official, from any final order or judgment to the appellate division of the supreme court within thirty days. But the appeal shall not stay the execution unless the defendant gives security for the payment of the order of filiation and of the costs of appeal. [*Ibid.*, sec. 136.]

Enforcement of Judgment

Bonds may be required of the father to secure the payment of the order of

* * * [*Ibid.*, sec. 35-i.]

* * * Subsequently to the age of sixteen, for good cause, support may be ordered up to the age of twenty-one or longer. [*Ibid.*, sec. 35-i.]

* * * And the court may cancel arrears of payments and may for good cause shown substitute another trustee. [*Ibid.*, sec. 35-j.]

1. Appeals may be taken by the "complainant or by the defendant" * * * If defendant appeals, he must deposit with the court $100 to pay the costs of his appeal, should the order appealed from be affirmed.

2. If the complainant appeals, the court may grant payment for printing costs by the city. [*Ibid.*, sec. 35-p.]

* * * Should the defendant [after discharge from jail] continue to fail to

STATE LAW

filiation, and, if suit was brought by a public welfare official, also for the indemnification of the local unit against any expenses for the support and education of the child and for the support of the mother during confinement and recovery. In default of the security, the court may commit him to jail, subject to discharge within one year, or put him on probation. [*Ibid.*, sec. 129(1).]

In case of default of a bond, judgment may be given against the sureties on such bond, and the amount recovered may be used for the mother and child. [*Ibid.*, sec. 129(2).]

Upon failure to give security, under sections 129 and 132, the court, instead of imposing sentence or committing the father or mother to jail, or as a condition of his or her release from jail, may place him or her on probation on such terms as to payment of support to or on behalf of the mother or child, and as to personal reports, as the court may direct. If they violate these terms, the court may commit or recommit them to jail. [*Ibid.*, sec. 134.]

If at any time after an order of filiation has been made and an undertaking been given but not complied with, or recovery thereon cannot be had, or if complied with and the sureties are discharged, or if money deposited instead of bail is exhausted, and the child still needs support, the local welfare officials, where the child lives, shall apply to the court for arrest of the father; and the court must then require a new undertaking, or, if he fails

LAW FOR THE CITY OF NEW YORK

provide support, proceedings may be renewed. [*Ibid.*, sec. 35-k(1).]

* * * But where the security deposited consists of money or government obligations, judgment is not required and the court may order sale of such obligations and apply the proceeds to payments for support. [*Ibid.*, sec. 35-k (3).]

* * * [*Ibid.*, sec. 35-k(2).] Under section 35-m, these proceedings would also apply to the mother for nonsupport of her child.

* * * In such cases "the trustee [instead of the public welfare official, as for state] may apply to the court." [*Ibid.*, sec. 135-k(4).]

STATE LAW

to give it, commit him to jail or put him on probation. [*Ibid.*, sec. 129(3).]

No corresponding provision in the state law.

The court also may, on such default, adjudge the father in contempt and commit him to jail, but this shall not stay the execution upon the judgment of the bond. [*Ibid.*, sec. 130.]

Protection of Mother and Child in Records

In all records, certificates, or other papers, other than birth records and certificates or records of judicial proceedings involving questions of birth out of wedlock, touching on the relationship between the mother and child, no reference shall be made to illegitimacy. [*Ibid.*, sec. 138.]

Miscellaneous Provisions

Making false complaints as to the identity of the father, or aiding therein, is punishable as for perjury. [*Ibid.*, sec. 133.]

In case the complainant is a public welfare official, the local county attorney, or the attorney named by the board of supervisors, or the corporation counsel of a city, or their assistants, must prosecute cases on children born out of wedlock. [*Ibid.*, sec. 137.]

LAW FOR THE CITY OF NEW YORK

The pertinent judgment of any court of competent jurisdiction in the state, or of a like court in any other state, is enforceable by the court in New York City with the same remedies as in New York judgments; and any order of filiation of the latter court may be enforced in any county where the defendant or his surety has property. [*Ibid.*, sec. 35-k(5).]

No corresponding provision in this law.

No corresponding provision in this law.

* * * but is misdemeanor, instead of perjury. [*Ibid.*, sec. 35-o.]

The corporation counsel of the city must prosecute all cases in which the complainant is the commissioner of public welfare. [*Ibid.*, sec. 35-q.]

STATE LAW	LAW FOR THE CITY OF NEW YORK
Statutory criminal provisions inconsistent with this law (secs. 119-138) are made inapplicable to cases arising under such law. [*Ibid.*, sec. 139.]	Instead of making such inconsistent provisions merely inapplicable, this law repeals them. [*Ibid.*, sec. 35-r.]

III. Local Public Care and Supervision of Children Born Out of Wedlock

Residence for Purposes of Public Welfare

The settlement of a minor born out of wedlock shall be that of his mother. [Cahill's *Consolidated Laws*, 1930, "Public Welfare Law," sec. 55 (2).][7]

Relief and Care of Children

A county public welfare district is responsible for the expense of providing relief and care for children born out of wedlock having a settlement in a town or city [apparently such cities as form part of a county district][8] in such district. The cost of such relief and care, administered by the county commissioners, may be charged back to such town or city if the regulations established by the board of supervisors so direct. [*Ibid.*, secs. 25-26.]

Commissioners of public welfare and city public welfare officers responsible under the provisions of a special or local law for the children hereinafter named shall have powers and perform duties as follows: . . .

5. As to children born out of wedlock:

a) Provide for such children and their mothers in need of public relief and care.

b) Institute proceedings to establish paternity and secure the support and education of such child or make a compromise with the father of the child, under the law on such children. [See "Domestic Relations Law," secs. 119, et seq.]

[7] The public welfare law was enacted in 1929 (Laws of 1929, ch. 565) and supersedes the former poor-relief legislation.

[8] A "public welfare district" shall mean a division of the State which is a unit for the administration of all public relief, care, and support. [*Ibid.*, sec. 2.] It is to be noted that the city of New York and certain other cities are constituted city public welfare district [*Ibid.*, sections 4 to 13, 17]; and in such districts the city performs the pertinent duties as to children born out of wedlock.

c) Hold the money received from such a compromise or pay it to the mother if she gives security for support of the child.

d) Care for such child with his mother in her own home or in a family free or boarding home or institution, and, when practicable, require the mother to contribute to the support of the child. [*Ibid.*, sec. 106(5).]

6. . . . The following provisions on further duties of public welfare officials, as to certain classes of children, would seem to apply also to children born out of wedlock.

a) Investigate the family circumstances of each child reported to him as destitute, neglected, delinquent, defective, or physically handicapped in order to determine what care, supervision or treatment, if any, such child requires.

b) Provide for expert mental and physical examination of any child whom he has reason to suspect of mental or physical defect or disease, and pay for such examination from public funds, if necessary.

c) Provide necessary medical or surgical care in a suitable hospital, sanitorium, preventorium, or other institution, or in his own home, for any child needing such care, and pay for such care from public funds, if necessary.

d) Ascertain the financial ability of the parents of children who become public charges, and collect toward the expense of such child's care such sum as the parents are able to pay.

e) Collect from parents whose children have been discharged to his care by any children's court such sums as they are ordered to pay for the maintenance of such children, and report any failure to comply with such order to such court.

f) When in his judgment it is advisable for the welfare of the child, accept the surrender of a child by an instrument in writing in accordance with the provisions of the state charities law.

g) Place children in suitable instances in family homes or institutions under the proper safeguards, either directly or through authorized agencies as defined by the state charities law.

h) Supervise children who have been cared for away from their families until such children become twenty-one years of age or until they are discharged to their own parents, relatives within the third degree, or guardians, or adopted by foster parents.

The State board of social welfare or the department of social welfare is required to: "Supervise the work of public-welfare officials and advise them in the performance of their official duties"; and "Collect statistical information in respect to the number of recipients of aid in each public welfare district . . . together with such other facts as the board or department may deem advisable." [*Ibid.,* sec. 138.]

Penalty for failure to support children: the local public welfare officials, whose duty it is to provide for the support of any child born out of wedlock and aid to its mother, who neglect such duty, are guilty of a misdemeanor, punishable by a fine of $250, or by imprisonment for not over one year, or by both. [*Ibid.,* "Penal Law," sec. 1843.]

IV. Legitimacy of Certain Children

Legitimation by marriage

All children born out of wedlock are legitimated by the subsequent intermarriage of their parents and thereby become legitimate for all purposes and entitled to all the rights and privileges of legitimate children, except as to an estate or interest vested or trust created before the marriage. [*Ibid.,* Domestic Relations Law, sec. 24.]

Legitimacy of children in cases of annulment of marriage

The following digest shows the effect upon the legitimacy of children of parents whose marriage is declared void or is annulled for reasons set forth. [Civil Practice Act, Cahill's *Codes,* 1931, sec. 1135.]

GROUND OF ANNULMENT	EFFECT
Where one or both parties were under the age of legal consent.	Their child is the legitimate child of both parents.
Idiocy or lunacy of one person.	The child is deemed the legitimate child of the parent of sound mind, and the court may decide the same as to the unsound parent.

Same—of both persons.	Court may decide the child legitimate child of either or both parents.
Marriage obtained by force, duress, or fraud.	Legitimate child of both parents.
Incestuous marriage.	Legitimate child of both parents.
Because former husband or wife was living.	The child is the legitimate child of the parent competent to contract; and the court may decide the child a legitimate child even though either or both parents were incompetent to enter marriage.
For any other cause.	The court may hold the child legitimate as to either or both parents.[9]

Legitimacy of children in action for divorce by wife

Where the action for divorce [for adultery] is brought by the wife, the legitimacy of any child of the marriage, born or begotten before the commencement of the action, is not affected by the judgment dissolving the marriage. [*Ibid.,* sec. 1154.]

Legitimacy of children in action for divorce by husband

Where the action for divorce [for adultery] is brought by the husband, the legitimacy of a child born or begotten before the commission of the offence charged is not affected by a judgment dissolving the marriage; but the legitimacy of any other child of the wife may be determined as one of the issues in the action. In the absence of proof to the contrary, the legitimacy of all the children begotten before the commencement of the action must be presumed. [*Ibid.,* sec. 1157.]

V. Rights of Inheritance

Descent and distribution of estate of decedent

The real property of a deceased person, male or female, not devised, shall descend, and the surplus of his or her personal property after payments of debts and legacies, and if not bequeathed,

[9] Under this law, the court, in deciding a child legitimate as to either or both parents, may limit the effect of the legitimization to rights other than the succession to real and personal property of a deceased parent.

shall be distributed to the surviving spouse, children, or next of kin or other persons, in manner following: . . .

7. If the deceased was illegitimate and leave a mother, and no child, or descendant, and no surviving spouse, such mother shall take the whole and shall be entitled to letters of administration in exclusion of all other persons. If the deceased shall leave a surviving spouse, the surviving spouse shall take five thousand dollars and one-half of the residue, and the mother shall take the balance. If the mother of such deceased be dead, the relatives of the deceased on the part of the mother shall take in the same manner as if the deceased had been legitimate, and be entitled to letters of administration in the same order.

13. If a woman die, leaving illegitimate children, or the illegitimate descendants of deceased illegitimate children and no lawful issue, such children or descendants inherit her real and personal property as if such children were legitimate. [Cahill's Consolidated Laws, 1930, Decedent Estate Law, sec. 83.]

Children born out of wedlock

If an intestate who shall have been illegitimate die without lawful issue, or illegitimate issue entitled to take, under this section, the inheritance shall descend to his mother; if she be dead, to his relatives on her part, as if he had been legitimate. If a woman die without lawful issue, leaving an illegitimate child, the inheritance shall descend to him as if he were legitimate. In any other case illegitimate children or relatives shall not inherit. [*Ibid.*, sec. 89.]

Distribution of personal property of decedent

(9) If the deceased was illegitimate and leave a mother, and no child, or descendant, or widow, such mother shall take the whole, and shall be entitled to letters of administration in exclusion of all other persons. If the mother of such deceased be dead, the relatives of the deceased on the part of the mother shall take in the same manner as if the deceased had been legitimate, and be entitled to letters of administration in the same order.

15. If a woman die, leaving illegitimate children, and no lawful issue, such children inherit her personal property as if legitimate. [*Ibid.*, sec. 98.]

VI. Adoption of Children

Consent to adoption

Consent of the mother of a child born out of wedlock is required before such a child may be adopted. [*Ibid.*, "Domestic Relations Law," sec. 111.]

Records of adoption

"The fact of illegitimacy shall in no case [in cases of adoption of children born out of wedlock] appear upon the record." [*Ibid.*, sec. 113.]

Effect of adoption

Where a husband or wife adopts a natural child of the other spouse such child shall thereafter for all purposes be regarded and treated as the legitimate offspring of the marriage of its natural parent and its foster parent. [*Ibid.*, sec. 114, as amended by *Laws of 1931*, ch. 562.]

VII. Miscellaneous Provisions

Registration of births

"The name of the putative father shall not be entered without his consent but the other particulars relating to the putative father may be entered if known, otherwise as 'unknown.'" [*Ibid.*, "Public Health Law," sec. 383.]

Inclusion of child under workmen's compensation legislation

The word "child" is defined to include an acknowledged illegitimate child dependent upon the deceased. [*Ibid.*, "Workmen's Compensation Law," sec. 2(11).]

APPENDIX 3

NOTES ON BIRTH REGISTRATION IN NEW YORK CITY

The system for the registration of births in New York City is operated by the Health Department in accordance with the provisions of the Sanitary Code of the Board of Health, Article III, Sections 31, 33, 36, and 357. These sections are as follows:

Sec. 31. *Births and still births; parents, and every person to report; physicians and professional midwives to keep registry and file written copy.* It shall be the duty of the parents of any child born alive or dead in the City of New York (and if there be no parent alive that has made such report, then of the next of kin of said child born), and of every person present at such birth or still birth, to file with the Department of Health, within ten days after such birth and within thirty-six hours after such stillbirth, a report, in writing, stating, as far as known, the date, borough, street, and street number of said place of birth or still birth, the name, sex, and color of such child born, the name, residence, birthplace, and age of the parents, respectively, the occupation of the father and mother, and the maiden name of the mother. It shall also be the duty of physicians and professional midwives to keep a registry of the several births or still births in which they have assisted professionally, which shall contain the date of birth or still birth, the borough, street, and street number of premises wherein such birth or still birth took place, the sex and color of the child, and also, as nearly as can be ascertained, the name of the said child, the number of previous children born of the mother, the number now living, the name, residence, birthplace and age of the parents, respectively, the occupation of the father and mother, and the maiden name of the mother; and it shall be the duty of such physicians and professional midwives, also, to file a written copy of the said registry of birth, or still birth with the Department of Health in the borough office of the borough wherein the birth or still birth occurred, within ten days after such birth and within thirty-six hours after such still birth, upon blank forms furnished by the said Department. Such physicians and professional midwives shall also certify that they assisted professionally at the birth or still birth so reported, and that all the other facts stated in the copy of the said registry are true to the best of their knowledge, information and belief. (S. C. Sec. 159.) (As amended by the Board of Health, December 28, 1917.)

Section 33. *Births, still births, marriages and deaths, a copy of registry to be filed; refusal to file such certificates.* It shall be the duty of every person required to make or keep a registry of births, still births, marriages or deaths, to present to the Bureau of Records of the Department of Health a copy of such registry signed by such person within ten (10) days after the birth or marriage and within thirty-six (36) hours after the death or still birth of any person to whom such registry relates, which copy of such registry shall thereupon be placed on file in the said Bureau; nor shall any person required by this article to fill out a certificate of birth or death and file same with the Bureau of Records of the Department of Health, refuse to perform such duty, nor shall such person charge, demand or exact any fee for the issuance of a birth or death certificate. (S. C. Sec. 161.) (As amended by the Board of Health, December 28, 1917 and further amended April 2, 1929.)

Sec. 36. *False certificates, statements, and reports.* No person shall make, prepare, deliver, or issue any false certificate, statement, or report, of a birth, marriage, or death, or any certificate, statement, or report which is not in accordance with the facts of the birth, marriage, or death. All certificates, statements, and reports, of births, marriages, or deaths, shall be signed by the person purporting to make the same, and no person shall sign or forge the name of another to any such certificate, statement, or report. (S. C. Sec. 162.)

Sec. 357. *Births, marriages, and deaths; duty of officers, surgeons, and others to report.* The master, chief officer, ship's surgeon, or the company, corporation, charterer, or person having the management and control, of any vessel which shall arrive at the port of New York shall report, in writing, to the Department of Health of the City of New York, within three days after the arrival of such vessel, the death or marriage of any resident of said City, or the birth of any child, whose parents are residents or parent is a resident of said City, occurring thereon at sea, and shall file in the Bureau of Records of said Department a transcript of the entry made in the log book of such vessel, in respect to any such death, marriage, or birth. A transcript of any death, marriage, or birth filed as aforesaid may be issued, in the discretion of said Department, to any person entitled to receive the same. (S. C. Sec. 151a.)

It will be noted that among the items of information required for a New York City birth certificate, there is no reference to legitimacy. This differs from the requirements of the rest of the State, other parts of the Birth Registration Area of the United States where the standard birth certificate is used, and most of the countries in Europe.

APPENDIX 4

SUPPLEMENTARY TABLES

TABLE 45

Illegitimacy Rates in American Cities with Population of
100,000 and Over in 1930

CITY	TOTAL NUMBER OF BIRTHS		TOTAL NUMBER OF ILLEGITIMATE BIRTHS		NUMBER OF WHITE AND NEGRO ILLEGITIMATE BIRTHS PER 1,000 TOTAL WHITE AND NEGRO BIRTHS	
	WHITE	NEGRO	WHITE	NEGRO	WHITE	NEGRO
Birmingham, Ala. . .	3,070	2,134	98	356	31.92	166.82
Denver, Col.	5,083	101	279	9	54.88	89.10
Bridgeport, Conn. . .	3,005	97	24	3	7.98	30.92
Hartford, Conn. . .	4,099	200	80	12	19.51	60.00
New Haven, Conn. .	3,282	149	51	15	15.53	100.60
Wilmington, Del. . .	2,063	242	49	42	23.75	173.55
Washington, D.C. . .	6,322	3,054	127	562	20.08	184.02
Jacksonville, Fla. . .	1,689	759	47	131	27.82	172.59
Miami, Fla.	1,446	576	14	66	9.68	114.58
Tampa, Fla.	1,500	330	15	63	10.00	190.90
Atlanta, Ga.	3,493	1,808	87	249	24.90	137.72
Chicago, Ill.	53,344	4,739	1,091	405	20.45	85.46
Peoria, Ill.	1,940	40	72	3	37.11	75.00
Evansville, Ind. . .	1,688	82	32	14	18.95	170.73
Fort Wayne, Ind. . .	2,219	51	40	2	18.02	39.21
Gary, Ind.	1,975	326	20	17	10.12	52.14
Indianapolis, Ind. . .	5,957	849	145	72	24.34	84.80
South Bend, Ind. . .	1,928	85	19	10	9.85	117.64
Des Moines, Iowa. . .	2,649	100	121	12	45.67	120.00
Kansas City, Kan. . .	1,953	409	48	39	24.57	95.35
Wichita, Kan.	2,154	126	129	5	59.88	39.68
Louisville, Ky. . . .	5,003	727	102	88	20.38	121.04
New Orleans, La. . .	6,179	3,158	160	480	25.89	151.99

CITY	TOTAL NUMBER OF BIRTHS		TOTAL NUMBER OF ILLEGITIMATE BIRTHS		NUMBER OF WHITE AND NEGRO ILLEGITIMATE BIRTHS PER 1,000 TOTAL WHITE AND NEGRO BIRTHS	
	WHITE	NEGRO	WHITE	NEGRO	WHITE	NEGRO
Baltimore, Md. . . .	11,725	3,269	189	699	16.11	213.82
Detroit, Mich. . . .	30,253	2,713	740	189	24.46	69.66
Flint, Mich.	4,037	132	78	6	19.32	45.45
Grand Rapids, Mich. .	3,366	55	165	6	49.01	109.09
Duluth, Minn. . . .	1,919	8	69	2	35.95	250.00
Minneapolis, Minn. .	8,049	67	283	5	35.15	74.62
St. Paul, Minn. . . .	5,036	49	227	1	44.83	20.40
Kansas City, Mo. . .	5,880	621	505	110	85.88	177.13
St. Louis, Mo.	12,623	1,873	294	249	23.29	132.94
Omaha, Neb.	4,270	254	187	22	43.79	86.61
Camden, N. J. . . .	2,672	341	22	44	8.23	129.03
Elizabeth, N. J. . . .	2,409	207	27	19	11.20	91.78
Jersey City, N. J. . .	5,518	363	91	35	16.49	96.41
Newark, N. J. . . .	8,721	1,100	105	64	12.03	58.18
Paterson, N. J. . . .	2,955	96	31	6	10.49	62.50
Trenton, N. J. . . .	2,612	242	78	31	29.86	128.09
Albany, N. Y.	2,566	58	64	8	24.94	137.93
Buffalo, N. Y. . . .	11,215	345	321	36	28.62	104.34
New York, N. Y. . .	114,980	7,293	1,140	409	9.91	56.08
Bronx Borough . .	17,982	370	85	25	4.72	67.56
Brooklyn Borough .	47,150	1,912	259	91	5.49	47.59
Manhattan Borough	34,364	4,742	718	285	20.89	60.10
Queens Borough . .	12,798	221	39	7	3.04	31.67
Richmond Borough	2,686	48	39	1	14.51	20.83
Rochester, N. Y. . .	5,607	53	116	5	20.68	94.33
Syracuse, N. Y. . . .	4,210	45	126	1	29.92	22.22
Utica, N. Y.	1,864	6	26	1	13.94	166.66
Yonkers, N. Y. . . .	2,093	62	14	2	6.68	32.25
Akron, Ohio	5,030	240	100	20	19.88	83.33
Canton, Ohio . . .	2,037	75	43	3	21.10	40.00
Cincinnati, Ohio . .	7,671	1,045	134	103	17.46	98.56

CITY	TOTAL NUMBER OF BIRTHS		TOTAL NUMBER OF ILLEGITIMATE BIRTHS		NUMBER OF WHITE AND NEGRO ILLEGITIMATE BIRTHS PER 1,000 TOTAL WHITE AND NEGRO BIRTHS	
	WHITE	NEGRO	WHITE	NEGRO	WHITE	NEGRO
Cleveland, Ohio . .	16,391	1,515	368	124	22.45	81.84
Columbus, Ohio . .	4,762	609	186	53	39.81	87.02
Dayton, Ohio . . .	3,386	279	76	31	22.44	111.11
Toledo, Ohio	5,310	243	96	23	18.07	94.65
Youngstown, Ohio . .	3,480	309	61	18	17.52	58.25
Oklahoma City, Okla.	3,504	231	88	28	25.11	121.21
Tulsa, Okla.	2,202	164	53	15	24.06	91.46
Portland, Ore. . . .	4,158	91	146	3	35.11	32.96
Erie, Penn.	2,500	24	56	2	22.40	83.33
Philadelphia, Penn. .	30,855	4,963	482	691	15.62	139.23
Pittsburgh, Penn. . .	13,679	1,315	508	129	37.13	98.09
Reading, Penn. . . .	1,656	43	57	10	34.42	232.55
Scranton, Penn. . . .	2,802	12	35	1	12.49	83.33
Providence, R. I. . .	5,551	158	100	12	18.01	75.94
Chattanooga, Tenn. .	1,850	485	42	64	22.70	131.95
Knoxville, Tenn. . .	2,138	269	64	36	29.93	133.82
Memphis, Tenn. . .	3,106	1,797	126	321	40.56	178.63
Nashville, Tenn. . .	2,631	829	85	143	32.30	172.49
Salt Lake City, Utah .	3,459	34	36	1	10.40	29.41
Norfolk, Va.	1,504	750	31	144	20.61	192.00
Richmond, Va. . . .	2,376	1,204	99	250	41.66	207.64
Seattle, Wash. . . .	5,011	270	109	8	21.75	29.62
Spokane, Wash. . . .	1,990	22	105	2	52.76	90.90
Tacoma, Wash. . . .	1,843	34	55	2	29.84	58.82
Milwaukee, Wis. . .	11,529	77	269	4	23.33	51.94

TABLE 46

Unmarried Mothers Classified by Occupation, Color, Nativity, and Religion
(Social Agency Data)

OCCUPATION	TOTAL (White and Negro) No.	Percent	NATIVE BORN Protestant No.	Percent	Catholic No.	Percent	Jewish[a] No.	FOREIGN BORN Protestant[a] No.	Catholic No.	Percent	Jewish[a] No.
WHITE											
Total	1,178[b]	100.0	205	100.0	321	100.0	93	50	151	100.0	41
Professional . .	60	5.1	15	7.3	16	5.0	7	3	7	4.6	4
Clerical . . .	206	17.5	60	29.3	77	24.0	46	4	9	6.0	8
Domestic service .	614	52.1	85	41.5	116	36.1	4	38	123	81.4	10
Factory . . .	191	16.2	24	11.7	82	25.5	27	3	11	7.3	16
School . . .	85	7.2	15	7.3	25	7.8	5	2	1	0.7	1
Miscellaneous . .	22	1.9	6	2.9	5	1.6	4	…	…	…	2
NEGRO											
Total	1,178[b]	100.0	277	100.0	23	…	1	10	6	…	…
Professional . .	60	5.1	7	2.5	…	…	…	…	1	…	…
Clerical . . .	206	17.5	1	0.4	1	…	…	…	…	…	…
Domestic service .	614	52.1	210	75.8	16	…	1	7	4	…	…
Factory . . .	191	16.2	20	7.2	4	…	…	3	1	…	…
School . . .	85	7.2	34	12.3	2	…	…	…	…	…	…
Miscellaneous . .	22	1.9	5	1.8	…	…	…	…	…	…	…

[a]Percentage not computed, base less than 100.

[b]From this table 421 cases of the 1,599 studied were excluded because one or more items needed were not recorded.

TABLE 47

Illegitimate Births in the Boroughs of New York City, 1930, Classified by Sex and Month of Birth (Health Department Data)

MONTH OF BIRTH	TOTAL			MANHATTAN		BRONX		BROOKLYN		QUEENS		RICHMOND	
	TOTAL	MALE	FEMALE	MALE	FEMALE	MALE	FEMALE	MALE	FEMALE	MALE	FEMALE	MALE	FEMALE
Total . . .	1,470	763	707	397	359	86	72	193	181	68	70	19	25
January . .	99	53	46	27	23	10	2	11	14	4	4	1	3
February . .	127	68	59	35	33	8	2	14	14	9	5	2	5
March . . .	128	59	69	36	39	5	7	11	16	7	7	..	..
April . . .	147	68	79	33	40	8	7	19	23	5	7	3	2
May	125	63	62	42	29	4	9	14	13	1	10	2	1
June . . .	110	55	55	30	20	10	8	11	20	4	6	..	1
July . . .	130	60	50	33	28	6	8	13	12	6	2	2	..
August . .	115	65	50	28	27	6	1	22	14	8	7	1	1
September . .	107	60	47	27	27	8	6	18	11	7	3	..	..
October . .	107	54	53	23	28	7	7	20	6	2	7	2	5
November . .	138	74	64	40	29	5	6	18	18	7	7	4	4
December . .	157	84	73	43	36	9	9	22	20	8	5	2	3

APPENDIX 5

LIST OF AGENCIES WHOSE SERVICES
ARE DESCRIBED IN PART TWO

City hospitals[1]

Bellevue Hospital
City Hospital
Coney Island Hospital
Cumberland Hospital
Fordham Hospital
Gouverneur Hospital
Greenpoint Hospital
Harlem Hospital
Kings County Hospital
Lincoln Hospital
Metropolitan Hospital
Morrisania Hospital

Private hospitals[2]

Beth David Hospital
Beth Israel Hospital
Bronx Hospital
Brooklyn Hospital
Columbus Hospital
Fifth Avenue Hospital
Flower Hospital
Jewish Maternity Hospital
Knickerbocker Hospital
Lebanon Hospital
Lenox Hill Hospital
Lutheran Hospital of Manhattan
Lying-in Hospital

[1]All furnished schedules on individual cases.
[2]Four furnished schedules on individual cases; others received cases from and referred cases to agencies and shelters that furnished schedules.

Manhattan Maternity and Dispensary
Methodist Episcopal Hospital
Misericordia Hospital
Mount Sinai Hospital
New York Infirmary for Women and Children
New York Nursery and Child's Hospital
New York Polyclinic Hospital
People's Hospital
Presbyterian Hospital, Sloane Division
St. John's Hospital
Staten Island Hospital
Sydenham Hospital
United Israel-Zion Hospital
Woman's Hospital

Other medical and health agencies[3]

Henry Street Nursing Service
Jamaica District Nursing and Social Service Association
John E. Berwind Free Maternity Clinic
Maternity Center Association

Homes for mothers and babies (shelters)[4]

Brooklyn Nursery and Infants' Hospital
Brooklyn Welcome Home for Girls
Council Home for Jewish Girls
Guild of the Infant Saviour
Heartsease Home for Women and Babies
Katy Ferguson House-Sojourner Truth Board
Lakeview Home
New York Foundling Hospital
St. Faith's House
Salvation Army Home and Hospital
The Shelter
Washington Square Home for Friendless Girls

[3]None furnished individual schedules.
[4]Six of these furnished individual schedules; some of the others were parts of a coordinated plan and received their cases through other agencies or hospitals that furnished schedules.

The family welfare and the protective agencies[5]

    Big Sisters of Queens Borough
    Brooklyn Bureau of Charities
    Brooklyn Society for the Prevention of Cruelty to Children
    Charity Organization Society of the City of New York
    Church Mission of Help, Diocese of Long Island
    Church Mission of Help, Diocese of New York
    Crime Prevention Bureau
    Girls' Service League of America
    Jewish Board of Guardians
    Jewish Social Service Association
    New York Association for Improving the Condition of the Poor
    New York Society for the Prevention of Cruelty to Children
    Queens Children's Society
    State Charities Aid Association, Mothers' and Babies' Department
    United Jewish Aid Societies of Brooklyn
    Vocational Adjustment Bureau

Agencies and institutions for delinquents[6]

    Correction Hospital
    Inwood House
    New York State Reformatory for Women, Bedford Hills
    New York State Training School for Girls, Hudson
    Wayside Home School for Girls
    Women's Prison Association and Isaac T. Hopper Home

Child placement societies[7]

    Alice Chapin Adoption Nursery
    Children's Aid Society, Foster Home Department
    Free Synagogue Child Adoption Committee

[5]Twelve furnished schedules for individual cases.
[6]Five furnished schedules for individual cases.
[7]Some of the agencies classified in other groups above also carry on child placement, notably the Foundling Hospital; three agencies furnished individual schedules; some of the others received their cases from agencies that furnished schedules.

Infants' Home of Brooklyn
Israel Orphan Asylum
Sophia Fund
State Charities Aid Association, Child Placing Agency

Day nurseries[8]

Halsey Day Nursery
Lisa Day Nursery
Wayside Day Nursery

[8]Eleven other day nurseries were visited but were not found to be eligible for inclusion in the study; the three nurseries listed above furnished individual schedules.

ANNOTATED BIBLIOGRAPHY ON ILLEGITIMACY

ANNOTATED BIBLIOGRAPHY ON ILLEGITIMACY

1. Abbey, Charlotte, M.D. Illegitimacy and sex perversion. [A] Child welfare symposium, edited by W. H. Slingerland, p. 24-31. New York, Russell Sage foundation, Department of child-helping, 1915.

   The article describes the work of the Woman's directory in Philadelphia in helping the mother to keep her child. The mothers dealt with are of the domestic service or factory groups. The Directory helps the mother find a situation when the infant is over two months old. A case is given of a girl who became a prostitute to pay the board of her two-year-old child. The Directory now guarantees to place the child if the mother can not support it. Many of the girls marry but there are cases of repeated illegitimacy. The women are of average intelligence. The records of the Directory show an increase of Negro illegitimacy.

2. Acerboni, A. F. Recent conferences on illegitimacy. Catholic charities review, v. 4, p. 82-83, March 1920.

   The article discusses the stand taken by the two regional conferences in New York and Chicago (1920). "The resolutions adopted by the two conferences show a striking similarity though they were worked out by two separate groups and without any collaboration." The registration of illegitimate births was desirable in the opinion of the Chicago group; and the New York group went further, asserting that it should be compulsory.

3. Addams, Jane. Disturbing conventions. Survey, v. 37, p. 1-5, October 7, 1916.

   The story of a grandmother of an illegitimate child, showing modification of the former severe attitude toward the unmarried mother.

4. Allan, Robert Marshall, M.D. Report on maternal mortality and morbidity in the state of Victoria, Australia. Medical journal of Australia, v. 1 of 1928, p. 668-83, June 2, 1928.

   The report presents the findings and recommendations from a research investigation for the period November 1925—April 1928, carried on by the author as Director of obstetrical research under the Obstetrical research committee. "The illegitimate birth rate in Victoria averages 4.46% of the total births. . . Besides the unmarried woman there are many others whose children have been born within nine months of marriage. In both groups ante-natal supervision is largely inadequate and complications are more likely to occur."

5. Anderson, M. M. (The) Welfare of the illegitimate child and the Norwegian laws of 1915. Child [London], v. 11, p. 136-38, January 1921.

An interpretation of the "Children's laws" passed in Norway in 1915.

6. Anthony, Katharine. Feminism in Germany and Scandinavia. 260 p. New York, Henry Holt, 1915.

Pages 83-116, 133-41, 142-68 deal with illegitimacy in Germany, Sweden, and Norway; maternity insurance for unmarried mothers; protection of children born out of wedlock in Norway; general discussion of illegitimacy.

7. ——— Norway's treatment of the illegitimate child. New republic, v. 4, p. 70-71, August 21, 1915.

The article is an elaboration on the Castberg laws of Norway.

8. ——— Outlawed children. New republic, v. 10, p. 41-42, February 10, 1917.

Injustice to the illegitimate child is shown by legislation in Illinois, which requires not more than fifty dollars a year from the father for the support of his illegitimate child, no matter what income he may have. The proposed law for Illinois contains a provision that the birth of the child should be sufficient to establish a common law marriage. This method is manifestly impossible. Forced marriage as the solution is social unwisdom.

9. Ashby, Hugh T., M.D. Infant mortality. 229 p. Cambridge, University press, 1915.

Pages 178-86 (Chapter XII). (The) Children act—Infant life protection—Infant life protection visitors. The "Children Act and the Infant Protection Visitors" are essential to see that all goes as well as possible with the illegitimate infant. The high infant mortality of illegitimate children is stressed.

10. Axmann, Julius. Social work in Austria. International conference of social work, Proceedings, v. 1 of 1928, p. 175-98.

Pages 179-98 (II). Specialized social work.

Pages 179-87 (II. 1). Maternity, infancy, childhood. Provisions for the illegitimate child by law, and details of state guardianship are given. "There is a general wish to avoid placing children in institutions. . ." Day nurseries, both publicly and privately supported, are scattered throughout Austria.

11. Babbitt, Ellen C. (The) Foundling asylum and the unmarried mother. American association for the study and prevention of infant mortality, Transactions, 1913, p. 363-65.

The "foundling" asylum is discussed in relation to breast-feeding and its other responsibilities to the mother, such as payment to the mother that otherwise goes to a foster-mother. The "statistics given by Hungary show that the mortality of the illegitimate babies supported by the Government and kept by their own mothers is lower than that of such babies boarded with foster-mothers."

12. Bang, Dagny, M.D. Illegitimacy in Norway. International conference of women physicians, Proceedings, 1919, v. 6, p. 33-37. New York, Woman's press, 1920.

Legislation passed in Norway relative to illegitimacy is discussed.

13. Barlow, T. W. N., M.D. Illegitimacy in relation to infant mortality. Medical officer [London], v. 15, p. 235, June 17, 1916.

A discussion of the poor law of Great Britain and needed revisions to reduce infant mortality.

14. Barnes, Annie E. (The) Unmarried mother and her child. Contemporary review, v. 112, p. 556-59, November 1917.

A plea to change the old type of "rescue" work to constructive means of keeping the mother and child together for at least the first year.

15. Barrett, Robert South. (The) Care of the unmarried mother. 224 p. Alexandria [Virginia], Author, 1929.

Introduction by George B. Mangold, Ph.D.

This book represents the results of investigations made by Dr. Kate Waller Barrett, mother of the author. Chapter I deals with the unmarried mother in the United States: extent of unmarried motherhood among Negroes, age of mothers, urban and rural areas, occupation and education of mothers. Chapter II considers primary causative factors. Chapter III considers the minor causative factors. Chapter IV has to do with organized agencies to assist the unmarried mother and her child. Chapter V discusses legal protection for the child and particularly a uniform law and the establishment of paternity. Chapter VI is entitled "Keeping mother and child together." The rest of the book deals with the maternity home, and an appendix gives a list of "philanthropic maternity homes" in the United States.

16. Bartlett, C. A. H. Illegitimates and legitimation. American law review, v. 54, p. 563-86, July 1920.

Refers to England and the question of legitimation of the child by the subsequent marriage of the parents. "Legitimation in England would seem to depend upon the status of the putative father." England's law relating to illegitimacy is "obsolete," for England is the only civilized country to refuse to permit legitimation by subsequent marriage of the parents. "Their neglect to modernize legislation in regard to illegitimate children has been responsible for the death of thousands and the lowering of the physical standard of life of tens of thousands of children who otherwise might have grown up vigorous and healthy citizens. . ."

17. Battis, R. J. Laws regulating placement of illegitimate babies in homes for adoption. Illinois medical journal, v. 52, p. 299-301, October 1927.

"An expose of conditions surrounding the placement of illegitimate babies in homes for adoption;—laws regulating the procedure;—and suggested improvements wherein the medical profession may assist welfare agencies in protecting the future of Illinois."

18. Baylor, E. M. H. Necessary changes to be effected in the methods of social service agencies working with unmarried mothers. Hospital social service, v. 6, p. 144-56, September 1922.

Case work with the unmarried mother is presented from many different angles: the proper social agency, type of investigation, personality of the worker, prenatal care [preferably at home], maternity homes, medical-social service, breast-feeding, convalescent care, follow-up of child, mental hygiene, recreation, vocational training, marriage and adoption.

19. Bench, P. J. (The) Child of the unmarried mother. Public health journal [Toronto], v. 11, p. 282-85, June 1920.

A discussion from the "viewpoint of his legal status in this Province [Toronto]," and of "reforms by way of legislation" which the author believes "would work in the best interests of the child. . ."

20. Bingham, Anne T., M.D. Determinants of sex delinquency in adolescent girls; based on intensive study of 500 cases. Journal of American institute of criminal law and criminology, v. 13, p. 494-586, February 1923.

Pages 535-38. Pregnancy. Median age of the 500 when they were referred is 17. It is therefore "striking to find that over one-third of all our cases (177, or 35.4 per cent) had been pregnant at some time" to the extent of 249 pregnancies, only 7 percent of which were legitimate. "Regarding abortions, 53 (10.6 per cent) reported having had one or more, but this is regarded as a conservative statement."

"Our study of sex delinquents leads us to believe that illegitimacy should be considered rather as an incident in irregular living than as a distinctly isolated condition. . . Forty-four per cent of all who had been pregnant were mentally abnormal. Amentia obscured all other conditions by its frequency occurring in 40 per cent of these pregnant cases."

The "answer to the question why girls were sex delinquents lay primarily not in any hereditary, environmental, physical or mental factors . . . but . . . in the girls' own individual make-ups which reacted to condition and circumstances in ways peculiar to themselves."

21. Boston, Conference on illegitimacy. Manual of laws relating to illegitimacy in Massachusetts. 86 p. Boston, The Conference, 1917.

Pages 25-60. Part II deals with the marriage law of Massachusetts. According to this law, children are illegitimate if the marriage of the parents is annulled on the ground of duress or fraud. Act of 1913, Chapter 563, is an act relative to illegitimate children and their maintenance. The aim of this act was to compel the father to contribute reasonably to the support of the child. Registration of illegitimate births is required by law in Massachusetts.

22. —— Studies on illegitimacy. 48 p. Boston, The Conference, 1914.

Reports on Massachusetts "bastardy" laws, syphilis and gonorrhoea, feeblemindedness, public opinion, "normal" girls, present conditions in Boston. Questionnaires sent out, replies tabulated, and tables showing the number of illegitimate births in Boston in 1913 are included.

23. Boston, Research bureau on social case work. Report on a study of applications for illegitimacy cases, by Ada E. Sheffield. 16 p. Boston, The Bureau, 1920.

A study of applications received between September 1, 1919 and March 1, 1920, including pregnant unmarried women, illegitimate children under three years of age, and unmarried mothers with or without children under three years of age. Twenty-seven agencies responded. A total of 792 applications, of which number 160 were duplicates, 74 cases beyond the time limit, and 8 anonymous, were received.

24. Boston, Society for helping destitute mothers and infants. Final report . . . including a study of the records of the Society of five hundred cases. 46 p. Boston, The Society, 1919.

Based on the "records of five hundred unmarried mothers who applied consecutively to the Society in the period between January, 1914, and October, 1918 [exclusive of married women, or those whose marriages were belated or forced]."

Characteristics of the mother and of the father and the care of the child are outlined. "When it comes to pass that every child has a complete physical and mental examination before it leaves school, many of the potential mothers of illegitimate offspring will have been discovered and cared for before they become a menace to the community."

25. ———— (The) Story of an invisible institution; forty years' work for mothers and infants, by Lilian F. Clarke. Part I, 12 p. Part II, 17 p. Part III, 19 p. Boston, Press of Geo. H. Ellis, 1912?-1914.

The aim of this organization is to assist the mother to keep her child. No date is given for Part I. Part II (1913) includes cases of care given to unmarried mothers. Part III is dated 1914.

26. Bowen, Louise de Koven. Safeguards for city youth at work and at play. 241 p. New York, Macmillan, 1914.

Preface by Jane Addams.

Pages 131-54. A study of "bastardy" court cases by the Juvenile protective association of Chicago.

27. ———— Some legislative needs in Illinois. 28 p. Chicago, Chicago juvenile protective association, 1914.

Pages 4-9. Need for a uniform state birth registration law is pointed out. The present "bastardy" law is inadequate, providing only that if an unmarried woman can prove the paternity of her child, the man is obliged to pay a sum not exceeding $100 for the first year of the child's life, and not more than $50 for each succeeding nine years.

Brooke, Elisabeth W. joint author see entry 114.

28. Buffalo foundation, Foundation forum. (The) Child born out of wedlock (unsigned). Buffalo foundation, Foundation forum, no. 41, p. 19-25, 1925.

A brief analysis of Buffalo birth certificates (1922-24) of children registered as illegitimate, covering the age of the mother, occupation, and residence by ward in Buffalo.

29. ——— For the child born out of wedlock (unsigned). Buffalo foundation, Foundation forum, no. 38, p. 16-19, 1924.

Discussion of the proposed change in the New York State illegitimacy laws proposed by the New York State commission to examine laws relating to child welfare.

30. ——— How Buffalo cares for the unmarried mother and her child, by Maud Bozarth. Buffalo foundation, Foundation forum, no. 65, p. 14-21, 1928.

A summary of the organized care, medical and social, given in Buffalo in an attempt to meet the situation.

31. ——— (The) Number of children born out of wedlock in Buffalo (unsigned). Buffalo foundation, Foundation forum, no. 65, p. 22-46, 1928.

A study of illegitimacy based on material gathered in connection with the "Five year infant mortality study" made by the Foundation (1922-26), to which information for 1927 was added. The basis was locally filed birth and death certificates, and comprised 1,883 live births registered as illegitimate, a rate of 3 out of each 100 live births. The mother's color, age, number of present births, occupation, residence, place of birth, and institutional delivery are tabulated.

32. ——— What the community may owe the unmarried mother and her child, by Mildred P. Carpenter. Buffalo foundation, Foundation forum, no. 65, p. 5-13, 1928.

The function of the maternity home, the type of social investigation needed, and the economic burden on the community of the girl not belonging there, are discussed.

33. Bury, Mary. (The) Unmarried mother and her child in Scotland; the present law. Woman's leader and common cause [London], v. 22, p. 176, July 11, 1930.

Legislation relating to illegitimacy in England does not affect Scottish law. In Scotland, responsibility for the maintenance of the child is regarded as equal between father and mother. The sum of 4s.6d. is allowed by the court until the child is fourteen, although if the child is either mentally or physically incapable of earning his own living at that time, the obligation continues for life. The mother cannot bring action against the putative father until after the birth of the child. The provisions of the new bill, called (The) Illegitimate children bill [Scotland] are given.

Cabot, Hugh, M.D. joint author see entry 297.

34. Cahn, Leni. (The) Child of nobody. Welfare magazine [Illinois], v. 19, p. 795-98, June 1928.

Of all European countries, it is Germany which has taken the leading rôle in the care and protection of the unmarried mother and her child. American legislation has been decidedly influenced by different European laws. For instance, the law of Minnesota closely follows the Castberg laws of Norway. Switzerland aids both the unmarried mother and her child. By the Swiss civil code of 1917, registration of illegitimate births is compulsory and is very strictly observed.

35. Canadian council on child welfare. (The) Legal status of the unmarried mother and her child in the province of Quebec, by John Kerry. (Publication no. 22.) 10 p. Ottawa [Canada], The Council, 1926.

The methods of recourse of the mother against the father of her child include criminal proceedings, in certain cases, to punish the father, and civil proceedings to recover damages from him. For the child there are civil proceedings to have the father judicially declared to be the father and criminal proceedings if the father fails to support his child.

36. ———— Legislation (as of date, January 1, 1929); Canada and her provinces; affecting the status and protection of the child of unmarried parents. (Publication no. 46.) 30 p. Ottawa [Canada], The Council, 1929.

An analysis of the laws of the nine provinces and a cumulative summary of principles and provisions. "Related legislation within the various provinces" is operative along the following "general lines": legislation "dealing specifically with children born out of wedlock"; legislation "dealing with children who are neglected or dependent . . . who may be found in need of maintenance and protection"; legislation "dealing specifically with the custody of the person and the individual legal guardianship of . . . minors, generally under 21 years of age"; inheritance and succession rights. Accompanying Publication no. 46 is a chart, Comparative summary (Publication no. 46A).

37. Carr, James D. Treatment of unmarried mothers and fathers. New York City conference of charities and correction, Proceedings, 1920, p. 123-32, + 140-41.

The problem of forcing upon the man the duty of providing for the support of his natural child is discussed. Under the old common law, there was no liability resting upon the father. The procedure in New York State requires that the mother must be a bona fide resident if she appeals to the courts to have her child's paternity declared. The proceedings, under a section of the Code of civil procedure, may now be conducted in private, and the child of an annulled marriage declared legitimate.

38. Case, Janet. (The) Rights of children in Norway. Contemporary review, v. 112, p. 683-89, December 1917.

The Castberg law of Norway makes the father equally responsible with the mother. The article quotes Mr. Castberg and explains the law. The Children's rights law went into effect in January 1916, and the new law of inheritance applies to children born after January 1917.

39. Castro, Diego de. Observations on prenuptial conceptions. (Qualche osservazione sui conceptimenti antenuziali.) Bollettino del instituto stat.-econ. di Trieste, v. 6, p. 135-50, July-September 1930.

"De Castro has gathered unpublished data regarding prenuptial conceptions in two zones of the Istrian region, from which it is noted that in the agricultural zone of Salvare, inhabited by peasants of low intellectual and moral level, prenuptial conceptions are very numerous (66% of first-born are conceived before marriage)."—[S.s.a.]
Quoted from Social science abstracts, v. 3, no. 7, p. 1047, July 1931.

40. Catholic encyclopedia, v. 7. New York, Robert Appleton company, 1910.

Pages 650-53. Illegitimacy, by John A. Ryan. The percentage of illegitimate births in the "principal countries of Europe at different periods during the last thirty years . . . all authorities agree that the rate has decreased during the last twenty years. . . The decline does not necessarily indicate an improvement in sexual morality. The number of illegitimate births implies at least an equal number of sins between the sexes. . . Illegitimacy is subject to many social influences . . . some of which increase it in the statistical records without increasing it in the eyes of God. . . It is not difficult to enumerate all the important factors that tend to increase or diminish illegitimacy, but it is practically impossible to measure accurately the relative weight of each. . . In this article nothing more will be attempted than a general description of the significant factors and their influence," if any: poverty, ignorance, climate, city vs. rural residence, heredity ("undoubtedly a factor, but to what extent cannot be determined even approximately"), legislation, late marriage, prostitution, religion, preventives of conception, and devices for procuring abortion. "In all probability it is to the knowledge and practice of these perverse devices, rather than to improved moral conditions, that we must attribute the slight decline in illegitimacy that has taken place in some countries during the last twenty years. . . We believe that the influence of our religion for morality in general, and the special stress that our teaching lays upon the importance of chastity, renders the proportion of sexual immorality considerably less among our people than it is among those without the Catholic fold."

41. Charity organization society of the City of New York. Handbook of information on non-support, desertion and illegitimacy, compiled by Nathaniel J. Palzer. 31 p. New York, The Society, 1916.

Describes the organization and procedure prevailing in those courts in New York City which have jurisdiction over cases of non-support, desertion, and illegitimacy. These include the court of domestic relations, the court of general sessions, the court of special sessions, other courts and bureaus.

42. Chesser, Elizabeth Sloan. Woman, marriage and motherhood. 287 p. New York, Funk and Wagnalls, 1913.

In part, a discussion of the relation of illegitimacy to other social problems, such as crime and prostitution; and of such aspects of illegitimacy as the handicap of the child, infanticide, support of the child by the father, and legislation.

Pages 279-82 (Appendix II) give the laws of various countries regarding the unmarried mother and her child.

43. Chicago, Juvenile protective association. Baby farms in Chicago, by Arthur Alden Guild. 27 p. Chicago, The Association, 1917.

An investigation made for the [Chicago] Juvenile protective association showing the conditions found, particularly the lack of medical supervision. The investigation showed a total of 337 children, of which number 108 were either admitted by the mothers to be illegitimate, or were established as illegitimate through hospital or court records of cases in which the mother had prosecuted the father. The interest of the mothers of these children is also indicated.

44. —— Care of illegitimate children in Chicago, by Howard Moore. 37 p. Chicago, The Association, 1912. (Out of print.)

What becomes of the illegitimate child? This question is answered here insofar as it concerns those children who cannot be kept with their mothers. Many are simply given away; others are adopted. The incomplete records show the necessity for enforced birth registration. Tables are given showing the facts secured by interviews with hospitals and the rate of illegitimate infant mortality in Chicago.

45. Child welfare league of American. (An) Evaluation of work with unmarried mothers, by George B. Mangold, Ph.D. Child welfare league of America, Bulletin, v. 7, p. 817, October 15, 1928.

Two studies to be made—one dealing with the outcome for the child, the other with the identity of the father. The first study to deal with the whereabouts and social conditions of children who were handled not less than five years ago.

46. ——— (An) Inquiry into the case work policy and practice of thirteen hospitals in the treatment of the unmarried mother. Child welfare league of America, Bulletin [monthly], v. 8, p. 8, June 1929, and v. 8, p. 8, September 1929.

A study undertaken by the Pittsburgh section of the American association of hospital social workers, at the request of the [Pittsburgh] Conference on parenthood. Of the 1,211 prenatal and postnatal patients treated through the obstetrical dispensaries of these hospitals, "132 or almost 11% were unmarried. Approximately one-third of all the patients treated were colored. Most of the departments reported that they found it easier to readjust the colored mother and baby in her own home. One hundred and fifty-eight unmarried maternity cases were handled" by these hospital social service departments. "For 79 of these, or exactly one-half, complete responsibility for case work treatment was focused in the department, and for the remaining 79, responsibility was shared with some other agency . . . only 19% of cases referred to Hospital Social Service were referred by outside agencies, the remaining number being referred either through direct contact of the social worker in the ward or dispensary, or by the patient himself or some near friend or relative approaching Hospital Social Service for advice and plan. One function of Hospital Social Service then, it is clear, is this first contact. . . The stress of the case work method of the majority of Hospital Social Service Departments seems to be upon speedy adjustment."

"The following general tentative outline for future procedure is presented:

"1. The unmarried mother in ward or dispensary presents a medical social problem which it is the responsibility of the Hospital Social Service Department to treat on a case work basis.

"2. The successful handling of unmarried mother cases involves so many facets of case work adjustment, legal procedure and special technique that when the number of such cases in any department is large, a specialized worker or workers should be engaged to handle these. (Two Departments are so equipped.)

"3. When transfer to another social agency is determined upon it should take place at the earliest possible time in the handling of the case.

"4. When social case work is determined upon, it should continue as long as the exigencies of the case demand.

"5. When the community is equipped through children's agencies to give adequate care to an additional number of illegitimacy cases according to the highest case work standards, Hospital Social Service should endeavor to focus the responsibility for the social adjustment of the majority of these cases in children's agencies."

47. ——— Inter-city conference on illegitimacy. Child welfare league of America, Bulletin [monthly], v. 3, no. 1, 1924— v. 10, no. 6, 1931.

Recommendation of resolutions pertaining to birth registration, paternal responsibility, inheritance from and use of name of father, legitimation, care of child by mother, state supervision.

48. ——— (The) Problem of the unmarried mother and her child, by Ruth I. Workum. 13 p. (Child welfare league of America, Bulletin, no. 11, May 1924.) New York, Child welfare league of America.

A constructive program including supervision, legislation, a uniform law, a comprehensive mental and physical examination of the unmarried mother, is needed if we are to plan for the future of mother and child and to reduce illegitimacy. A table shows the mentality of the unmarried mothers studied.

49. ——— Protecting illegitimate children through new California adoption law, by Lavonne Stanton. Child welfare league of America, Bulletin [monthly], v. 7, p. 8 + p. 7, November 1928.

"In July, 1927, a new adoption law became effective in California whereby greater protection was given to children," whether "relinquished to an organization licensed by the State Department of Social Welfare" or directly to foster or adopting parents—such surrender or consent to be made on a form prescribed by the State department of social welfare. "It is the duty of the Department to verify the allegations of the petition and to ascertain whether the child is a proper subject for adoption, and to determine whether the foster home is a suitable home for the child. . .

It was discovered that prior to the new law, child placing organizations handled about one-fourth of the adoptions for the State of California— of the remaining three-fourths, no accurate statistics were obtainable. An estimate based on the records of the child placing organizations, indicates that three-fourths of the children adopted are illegitimate. . . From August 29, 1927, to Sept. 21, 1928, the State Department investigated 907 petitions for adoption and 226 were investigated by licensed agencies. That is, approximately 77 per cent were handled by the State Department and 23 per cent by the agencies . . . under the old law little was known of the hundreds of children placed in family homes by independent agencies or persons. . . The State is constantly urging that an ever increasing number of adoptions go through a licensed agency. . . During the last year the work of the child placing organizations has increased at least fifty per cent. . . An increasing number of children are being returned to the parent or parents or adjusted with relatives. . . Children are assured of better and more suitable homes. . . Foster parents are safeguarded also. . . It is true that many imperfections are apparent in the law, but it is decidedly forward-looking. . ."

50. ——— Report of a round table held at the Child welfare league regional conference in New York City, January 6, 1928, by Edith M. H. Baylor. Child welfare league of America, Bulletin [monthly], New series, v. 7, p. 8, February 15, 1928.

The subject under discussion was the unmarried father. There was some difference of opinion expressed in regard to his responsibility for the support of his child. That this would depend upon his age and his ability to support the child was expressed by some who felt the father should not be held responsible under certain circumstances.

51. ——— Study of New York foundling hospital, by Bryan J. McEntegart. Child welfare league of America, Bulletin [monthly], v. 8, p. 8, December 1929, and v. 9, p. 8, January 1930.

A brief review of the study made in 1927 under the direction of Rose McHugh. The hospital was established in 1869. "Romantic is the picture of two women starting out with a pitiable endowment of five dollars to combat the work of the notorious abortionist . . . then reigning arrogantly in her Fifth Avenue mansion. . . Each generation has presented its own problems and has necessitated an adjustment of the work of the Foundling Hospital. . . The proportion of illegitimate children admitted and the number of unmarried mothers under care also greatly decreased. These changes showed the need for a revision of the program to meet changing conditions. To set forth an intelligent plan, it was necessary to make case studies of the unmarried mothers under care. This resulted in an analysis of their home environment, education, attitude toward pregnancy, character and habits, religious training, predominating factors in plans for their future, and their attitude toward their child. As far as was possible, putative fathers were interviewed. On the basis of these findings, recommendations were made calling for a case work service covering the admission, the treatment and after-care of mothers, and their classification and vocational training while in the institution."

"The 117 mothers studied were those under care in the hospital who had been confined. . To the information already in the records of the hospital was added what was found in the records of the social agencies. . . This was supplemented by a social history taken in interviews with the unmarried mother herself and with the staff of the hospital. . . It must be borne in mind that these mothers do not represent a cross-section of the women who become mothers of illegitimate children. . . Their ages . . . fell into somewhat the same groupings as in other studies. . . The homes of 99 had been broken or seriously disorganized by death or other conditions. . . Only 13 came from homes where moral and economic standards were good and there was sufficient protection for the children [of 87 that could be graded]. . . As in other studies it was found that the number coming from domestic service was large. . . Certainly these facts point to the need of careful scrutiny of all homes in which unmarried mothers are placed by social agencies as domestics after the birth of their children. Of the 93 girls who were given psychological tests, only 8 rated normal. Twenty-six of the girls professed having had no previous sex information or instruction, while 75 stated that they had such. . . In 28 cases the mother's family was able to assist with the care of the child and willing to do so, in 86, they were not able."

52. —— What of the father, by Joseph H. Crowley. Child welfare league of America, Bulletin, v. 5, p. 8, December 15, 1926.

There is little material about the father. A study of the files of the Cleveland humane society indicates that the average age of the father is 19, but ranges from "under 21 to 70."

53. Clarke, Walter. (The) Norwegian illegitimacy act. Journal of social hygiene, v. 9, p. 146-49, March 1923.

The provisions of the Castberg law of 1915 are given in full. The author states that the results have been satisfactory and that illegitimacy is decreasing: "In evaluating for other countries the experience of Norway under the Castberg law, several facts must be borne in mind. First, the population of the country is small and almost entirely village or rural. . .

The population is racially homogeneous. . . The people are frugal, indus-
trious, sober and intelligent. There is very little illiteracy."

54. Cleveland conference on illegitimacy. (The) Unwed mother
and her child; reports and recommendations. 19 p. Cleveland,
Cleveland federation for charity and philanthropy, July 1916.

A report of the findings concerning Cleveland's birth records showing
place of birth. Of 175 births, there were 121 in hospitals or special institutions; 41 of these 121 were institutional births in "rescue" homes. Only
18 of the 175 births were under the care of midwives.

55. Cleveland health council. (An) Analysis of the illegitimate
births in the city of Cleveland for the year 1926, by Howard
Whipple Green. 35 + [4] p. Cleveland, The Council, 1928.
(Mimeographed.)

Foreword. "Vital Statistics . . . has presented one of the few sources of
compiled information available. Four years ago the Study Group on Inter-
City Relations [of the Cleveland Conference on Illegitimacy] . . . requested
Mr. Howard W. Green to make an analysis of the registration of illegitimate births in Cleveland in 1923." Thinking that an analysis of 1926
statistics in comparison with the analysis of 1923 would be helpful, the
Group last year requested this second study.

Preface. "The illegitimate births taking place in the City of Cleveland
and registered during 1926 have been analyzed. The births to mothers
resident in the City proper have been considered as resident births, all
other as non-resident. The analysis of the illegitimate births occurring
outside of the City of Cleveland and within Cuyahoga County is given in
the appendix."

Pages 1-5. An analysis of Cleveland, 1926, with some of the data contained
in the 1923 analysis, for comparison. The object has been to serve as the
"fact basis of further studies of the problem of illegitimacy."

Pages 6-7. An analysis of the data for Cuyahoga county outside of the city
of Cleveland.

Pages 8-32. Data on illegitimate births, Cleveland, 1923 and 1926. There
are 21 tables with classifications according to color of mother, residence
of mother, stillbirths, illegitimacy rate (births per 1,000 total births),
hospital delivery, home delivery, occupations of mother and of father,
ages of mother and of father, countries of birth of mother and of father.

Pages 33-34 + [35-38] (Appendix). Analysis of illegitimate births, Cuyahoga county. Four tables and four maps.

56. Cleveland, Welfare federation of Cleveland, Cleveland conference on illegitimacy. Report on a survey of community

care for children of illegitimate birth. 12 p. Cleveland, The Conference, May 1921. (Mimeographed.)

A report from the Cleveland conference to the Inter-city conference on illegitimacy.

Contents: I. Laws affecting children of illegitimate birth; II. Local facilities, administration of laws and general conditions governing care of children of illegitimate birth; III. Case study [Brief of case of illegitimacy covering period of four years].

57. ———— (The) Unmarried mother whose confinement takes place outside of institutions; report of Study group. 5 p. Cleveland, The Conference, [1926]. (Mimeographed.)

A study undertaken to inquire into the unmarried mother who does not come to the maternity home or hospital, based on "records of closed cases of the Unmarried Mother Department of the Cleveland Humane Society; the records of the out-patient department of Maternity Hospital, and the statistics of the Bureau of Vital Statistics for the year 1925. Forty case records, representing 1.4% of the number of unmarried mother cases closed in 1925 by the Society were analyzed," only 9 of which came to the attention of the Society during the pregnancy. About "40% of all confinements took place in hospitals during 1925 [of all mothers, married and unmarried, in Cleveland]."

"It has not been possible to arrive at a fair estimate of the ratio of first confinements in hospitals and at home of married women, as compared to the ratio of illegitimate confinements in institutions and outside." Thirty of the 40 cases were delivered in the woman's home, several reasons for which are suggested. Assistance given is analyzed, as is also the disposition of the child. "The Committee is of the opinion that they [mothers at home] do not as a rule receive care equal to that of unmarried mothers in institutions or in many cases equal to that of married women confined outside of hospitals."

The Committee "urges that the subject be suggested as the theme of a thesis for graduate work . . . under the direction of this Conference," and that "publicity material on the facilities both medical and legal of the social agencies" be prepared, and "distributed by some such agency as the Visiting Nurse Association to all unwed mothers registered by the Bureau of Vital Statistics."

58. Cleveland, Welfare federation of Cleveland, Cleveland conference on illegitimacy, Study group on adoptions. Study of adoptions in Cuyahoga county, July 1, 1922 to June 30, 1923. 13 p. Cleveland, The Federation, 1925. (Mimeographed.)

During the year 311 adoptions, involving 339 children, were consummated; 127 schedules were filled out from the court records and 66 of these cases were intensively studied.

"The unmarried mother in a hospital maternity ward is in no fit condition to decide the future of herself or her child and all too often gives up her child, to her future distress. Often well-meaning, but misguided doctors, nurses or other individuals, urge her to give the child up, with the hope of hiding her shame, only to find that her sacrifice has been useless and instead she has lost what might have been a real incentive to right living. Out of 66 cases intensively studied at least 23, that is over one-third are definitely known to be adoptions of illegitimate children. . . . Do we not take too legal a point of view of the parent giving up the child? Is it not more than a mere legal contract between two parties? Does not the State have the right to intervene . . . ? "

Pages 12-13. Statistical summary of 66 cases studied intensively, and of 311 total cases for the year, under the captions: sex, age, consent given by, parents' status, illegitimacy, special report form filed, length of time in home, relative adoptions, agencies knowing consenting families, total families identified, total agencies knowing these families, agencies knowing adoptive parents.

59. Colbourne, Frances. For unmarried mothers abroad. Survey, v. 51, p. 96, October 15, 1923.

"England and France have shown greater interest in infant mortality than has been indicated in this country." There are institutions in those countries for the care of the unmarried mother, but no organized attempt at constructive work is made when the mother leaves the institution although the child may remain for three years before being placed. At the Margaret club in England, mothers may live with their children.

60. Colby, M. Ruth. (The) Unmarried mother and her baby. Welfare magazine, [Illinois], v. 17, p. 5-8, June 1926.

An account of the practical working of the Minnesota law.

61. Colcord, Joanna C. Need of adequate case work with the unmarried mother. Family, v. 4, p. 167-72, November 1923.

"Minnesota is the only state which has made effective case work with the unmarried mother practicable." The Children's code provides that the illegitimate child shall be the ward of the state during his minority. In New York State, there is no central agency to get in touch with the unmarried mother. The article also refers to the study of "forced marriages," made by the [Chicago] Juvenile protective association; Spann's study of illegitimacy in Germany; and the study of the [Boston] Research bureau on social case work, dealing with the adjustment in life being made by the unmarried mother.

62. Cole, L. C. Need of the case work method in dealing with illegitimacy. Hospital social service, v. 13, p. 430-42, May 1926.

"There is if anything more need for investigation of the unmarried mother than in the normal family problem." Requisite are the "most intensive kind of community education . . . an unprejudiced, open-minded sympathetic understanding and the recognition of the power of natural laws of constructive forces." This is discussed in detail, from the angles of disposition of the child, non-residence, rights of the illegitimate family and of the community.

63. Cordemans, L. Social work in Chili. International conference of social work, Proceedings, v. 1 of 1928, p. 248-67.

Pages 253-67 (II). Specialized social work.
Pages 253-62 (II. 1). Maternity and infancy. The provision made by agencies for the social and health care of the unmarried mother are very briefly described.

64. Curry, H. Ida. (The) Girl with a second or third illegitimate child. National conference of charities and correction, Proceedings, 1915, p. 115-17.

Case of an unmarried mother with three illegitimate children.

65. Darwin, Leonard. Divorce and illegitimacy. Eugenics review, v. 9, p. 296-306, January 1918.

This article refers to divorce law reform in England. "Greater frequency of divorce might be accompanied by a diminution in the number of illegitimate unions," states Major Darwin, who is opposed to divorce law reform and prefers to give the unmarried mother fairer treatment. He discusses the question whether the legitimate child is more likely to be eugenically superior to the illegitimate child. In his opinion, this is true.

66. Davis, Otto W. Children of unmarried and of illegitimate parents; recent legislation in Minnesota and elsewhere. National conference of social work, Proceedings, 1918, p. 94-101.

Recent progressive legislation. Minnesota and North Dakota passed laws in 1917 but the law failed to pass in Missouri. A detailed explanation of the Minnesota plan is given.

Déak, Francis. joint author see entry 276.

67. Deardorff, Neva R., Ph.D. "(The) Welfare of the said child . . ." Survey, v. 53, p. 457-60, January 15, 1925.

"During the last several months the Children's Commission of Pennsylvania has been making an intensive study of the adoption laws and practices of the state. Through its own staff it has accumulated information on 1022 adoptions consummated in Philadelphia County during the period from January 1, 1919, to June 30, 1924." Through the coöperation of the [State] Department of welfare and the [Federal] Children's bureau, adoptions in a number of other counties in the state were studied. "In all, over 2,200 recent adoptions have been subjected to study as the basis for the Children's Commission's suggestions to the Legislature, meeting in 1925." The Philadelphia county findings are here summarized. The "Children's Commission has not found that adoption is practiced extensively in Philadelphia County as a method of adjusting the problems of illegitimate or otherwise dependent children. A conservative estimate of the illegitimate children born in the county during the five and a half year period covered by the study of the Children's Commission would place the number in excess of 6,000. The adoption records show, however, that only 365 illegitimate children, of whom only 281 were under six years, found their way into adoption homes good, bad and indifferent." Illegitimacy is tabulated in relation to: minors adopted by relatives; minors adopted by non-relatives with natural families unknown to social agencies; minors adopted by non-relatives with natural families known to social agencies; minors placed for adoption by social agencies. Suggested amendments to the adoption statutes are outlined.

de Castro, Diego. see Castro, Diego de.

68. de Ford, Miriam Allen. Brood of folly. Outlook, v. 159, p. 46-47, September 9, 1931.

"There are no illegitimate children—only illegitimate parents." Illegitimacy is being regarded more leniently but we lack laws for the support of such children. The highest rate of illegitimacy is in South Carolina, which is the only state absolutely without provision for divorce. The fitness of the mother to care for her child is the important thing.

69. de Lukaco, Charlotte. Social work in Hungary. International conference of social work, Proceedings. v. 1 of 1928, p. 407-37.

Page 410. The welfare of unmarried mothers is here briefly discussed, from the legislative angle. State guardianship is provided for.
Page 448. Relief for "foundlings."

70. Deming, Julia. Problems presented by children of parents

forced to marry. American journal of orthopsychiatry, v. 2, p. 70-82, January 1932.

"Forced marriage was one of the factors considered in an attempt to evaluate and compare emotional and social situations and their bearing on the behavior of 200 children from the New England Home for Litttle Wanderers . . . "—[S.s.a.]
Quoted from Social science abstracts, v. 4, no. 5, p. 807, May 1932.

71. De Vilbiss, Lydia Allen. Who is the father? Survey, v. 41, p. 923-24, March 29, 1919.

History of legislation regarding illegitimacy. The Castberg law of Norway was the first law to protect the rights of the child born out of wedlock. The proposed law for the state of Kansas would make it mandatory that proceedings be instituted to determine paternity.
The New York law is virtually the law of 1828. There has been little change in other state laws.

72. Dick, J. T., M.B. Some observations on the illegitimate child. Journal of the Royal sanitary institute [London], v. 40, p. 146-54, November 1919.

A discussion of certain illegitimacy statistics throughout Great Britain. Certain "preponderating influences and diseases which stand out pre-eminently as slayers of illegitimate infant life" in figures for England and Wales, 1917, are "indicated chiefly in the relative death-rates for prematurity, injury at birth, overlying, syphilis, diarrhoea, wasting diseases and tuberculosis, all of which cause" from "two and a half times to three times, and in the case of syphilis ten times as many" deaths of illegitimate as of legitimate children. A chart shows the "excess of illegitimate deaths at each age-period, England and Wales, 1910-15."

73. Donahue, A. Madorah. Case of an unmarried mother who has cared for her child, and succeeded. National conference of social work, Proceedings, 1917, p. 282-84.

Case study of an unmarried mother with a second illegitimate child showing depth of her maternal feeling. "Many of our institutions will not receive a woman who had had a second illegitimate child."

74. ——— Case of illegitimacy, where mother and baby have been dealt with separately. National conference of charities and correction, Proceedings, 1915, p. 121-26.

Case of an illegitimate child who was adopted by an unusual family. Later the child's mother married the father of her child although she had given up the child.

75. —— Children born out of wedlock. Annals of American academy of political and social science, v. 151, p. 162-72, September 1930.

"Illegitimacy is a problem of youth. The great majority of mothers of children born out of wedlock are under 25 and almost one-half of them are under 21. The age groups for fathers of such children fall somewhat higher but the fathers are, in the main, young men." The article further states that illegitimacy rates are higher in urban than in rural areas, higher among colored women than among white women, and higher among native white women than among those of foreign birth.

76. —— (A) Diocesan program for the care of unmarried mothers and their infants; [II] from the case work viewpoint.[1] National conference of Catholic charities, Proceedings, 1931, p. 114-19.

"Two states, South Dakota and Texas, are not yet in the birth registration area. Two other states, California and Massachusetts, do not differentiate in their registration of vital statistics, between legitimate and illegitimate births. . . Paternal responsibility" is seldom assumed or fixed in more than one-third of the cases in any group. A disproportionate number of children born out of wedlock are cared for by social agencies. In Boston in one year the illegitimate children "constituted 11 per cent. of all children handled by the public child-caring agency of Boston, 17 per cent. of those dealt with by the private child-caring agencies; 9 per cent. of those handled by the protective agency—with an average of nearly 13 per cent for all of these. . . There is available material in the records of child-caring organizations which points to illegitimacy as a contributing factor, at least, in child neglect and in behavior problems of children. . . Anxiety, worry about family relationships, the unsatisfied demand for answers to the child's questions in regard to his parentage—all contribute to strain and stress which sometimes are manifest in delinquency trends and acts of delinquency."

"Children of void and voidable marriages and children of common law marriages present special problems which can not be discussed here. In some states statutory provision has been made for including these children in the benefits provided for other children; even for giving them a legitimate status. . . Too great emphasis cannot be laid on the function of the Catholic agency in setting the standard on the spiritual and moral values in case treatment."

(A) Discussion by Sister Mary de Paul, p. 120-25.

[1] See M. F. McEvoy's (A) Diocesan program for the care of unmarried mothers and their infants; [I] from the administrative viewpoint.

77. Dreyer, Erik. (The) Social legislation of Denmark. International conference of social work, Proceedings, v. 1 of 1928, p. 305-34.

Pages 319-20. Children's aid; illegitimate children. The support of the illegitimate child is here outlined.

78. Drury, Louise. Mile-stones in the approach to illegitimacy. Family, v. 6, p. 40-42, 79-81, 95-99, April-June 1925.

A series of three articles gives the history of illegitimacy in the last seventy-five years, traces the processes of case work, and considers illegitimacy as a public health problem.

79. Edlin, Sara Boudin. Jewish unmarried mothers; a reply to L. W. Wise. Survey, v. 44, p. 408-9, June 19, 1920.

"Adoption may be the best solution when the mother is extremely young, helpless, and otherwise unfit to care for her baby. But whether adoption should be advocated in general, on the ground that it offers greater opportunity to the child than the average unmarried mother can give, is debatable. Eighty per cent keep their babies in spite of all odds. It is true that most unmarried mothers cannot earn enough to provide a home for the baby; but this is no argument for adoption. It is rather for the state to step in and make it possible for every mother, married or unmarried, to carry out her natural function in the caring for her child."

80. Ehrenfest, Hugo, M.D. Illegitimacy as a child welfare problem; a review. Modern medicine, v. 2, p. 522-24, 1920.

"A digest and analysis of the report by Emma O. Lundberg and Katharine F. Lenroot, United States Department of Labor, Children's Bureau Report, Publication no. 66, Washington, D. C."

81. Emerson, Francis V. (The) Place of the maternity home. Survey, v. 42, p. 772-74, August 30, 1919.

Medical, social, and moral care is given the unmarried mother in the maternity home. We should raise the standards in these homes but not abolish them.

82. Encyclopaedia Britannica, v. 12. London and New York, Encyclopaedia Britannica company, 1929.

Pages 84-85. Illegitimacy, by S. de Jastrzebski. Extent of illegitimacy. Influence of the World war shows an increase in England, Germany, and France, but a decrease in Italy and Austria. Illegitimacy rates are given for the United States and certain Central and South American countries.

83. Encyclopaedia of the social sciences, v. 3. New York, Macmillan, 1930.

Pages 397-98 Child marriage; United States, by Fred S. Hall, Ph.D. "Where the legal minimum age is highest exceptions are usually allowed, the most frequent reason for such discrimination being expectancy of motherhood. . . Some parents . . . consent to child marriage because sex relations have taken place; in such cases some insist upon marriage under threat of criminal action against the boy or man concerned."

Pages 403-6. Neglected children, by C. C. Carstens. A general discussion of such children, with brief reference to illegitimacy. "Illegitimate children are a group particularly likely to be neglected, and special if not altogether adequate legislation, such as regulation of baby farms, has been enacted through the efforts of protective agencies."

Pages 424-27. Child welfare legislation, by Elsie Glück. Among other phases treated are legislation with refence to "children born out of wedlock" and to adoption, the latter being "closely related to the welfare of children of unmarried parents, since such children are those most likely to be considered for adoption."

84. Encyclopaedia of the social sciences, v. 7. New York, Macmillan, 1932.

Pages 579-86. Illegitimacy.

Pages 579-82. Social aspects, by Frank H. Hankins, is largely historical, and gives the extent of illegitimacy, statistics, and causation of infant mortality. "Illegitimacy is an important cause of infanticide, abortion, premature births and stillbirths." Social work inquiries have revealed illegitimacy closely associated with poverty, with drunken, quarrelsome, unsympathetic, or immoral parents, with broken homes, unsupervised recreation, and early employment. The author discusses the effect of certain occupations upon illegitimacy, rural problems, and governmental care and protection.

Pages 582-86. Legal aspects, by A. C. Jacobs, gives a historical summary with a discussion of the present law in France and the German civil code. "In all but a few countries legitimation by subsequent marriage of the parents is now recognized." The article refers to the Legitimacy act of 1926 in England and in regard to the laws of the United States says: "In the United States there may be found illegitimacy laws of practically all known types from the most backward to the most advanced."

Bibliography, p. 586.

85. Engel, Sigmund. (The) Elements of child protection. (Translated from the German by Dr. Eden Paul). 276 p. New York, Macmillan, 1912.

Pages 90-105 (Special part, Chapter III). (The) Protection of illegitimate

children. Outlines the legal protection of such children, causes of the
great infant mortality of illegitimate children. "Baby-farming is in actual
practice nothing but a cruel method of infanticide." The author points
out the relation between illegitimacy and criminality.

Essex, Lou R. joint author see entry 201.

86. Farmer, Gertrude L. Case work with the unmarried mother.
Hospital social service, v. 4, p. 285-88, November 1921.

The function of a department of hospital social work in dealing with
unmarried mothers is to assist in the after-care of such patients and to
restore them to health and social and economic efficiency. There is a lack
of adequate community resources for convalescent care for maternity
cases.

87. Field, Alice Withrow. Protection of women and children in
Soviet Russia. 241 p. New York, Dutton, 1932.

Conditions in Russia, where there is no illegitimacy. "The Revolution
banished the illegitimate child." Abortion was first legalized in 1920.

88. Finkelpearl, (Mrs.) Henry. (The) Problem of the illegitimate
child. [A] Child welfare symposium, edited by W. H. Slingerland, p. 19-23. New York, Russell Sage foundation, Department of child-helping, 1915.

A study of one hundred illegitimate infants under one year of age admitted to the Pittsburgh home for babies. The records of their antecedents, as well as their careers for some time after they left the home, were
studied. Eighteen children were returned to their mothers or relatives.
The mothers of 6 of these one hundred babies married reputable men;
28 of the children were placed in families and legally adopted. The remaining 48 died. The primary cause of their death was the treatment
of the mother before birth.

89. Fish, Ruth G. Some uses of the intelligence quotient in the
adjustment of the delinquent girl. Hospital social service,
v. 17, p. 441-44, May 1928.

A few cases are cited from the University hospital, Ann Arbor, Michigan,
where a psychometric examination is made of all "delinquent girls who
come to . . . attention as unmarried mothers, in the Obstetrical Department. . . . The.intelligence quotient is, of course, not alone the deciding
factor in making our plans. It is an index in every case but it is from the
psychological and psychiatric analysis that we usually take our leads."

90. Fisher, H. A. L. (The) Problem of the illegitimate child. Journal of state medicine [London], v. 34, p. 596-602, October 1926.

Approached as a problem of infant welfare, requiring social and legal measures. The "reformer has two aims in view; try to diminish the number of illegitimate births . . . and secondly to do everything that is possible to save the unhappy babes from suffering, ill-health and disease. . ." Death rates among illegitimates are higher than the official figures suggest, because the rate might well exclude deaths of illegitimates born to "people who live together, who have more or less stable homes, more or less stable families. . ."

91. Fisher, H. M. Legal aspects of illegitimacy. National conference of social work, Proceedings, 1917, p. 294-99.

The author, Judge of the Municipal court, Chicago, who also presided over the Chicago court of domestic relations, states that the "law is rotten" on the subject of illegitimacy. In regard to the law and procedure in Illinois, he says: "The law is inadequate, unfair and entirely out of harmony with every modern idea of justice."

92. Fisher, Lettice. Illegitimacy. Englishwoman, v. 46, no. 137, p. 81-90, May 1920.

There is a crying need for hostels or other accommodations for unmarried mothers and their children in England. The illegitimacy rate is increasing and there is a high death rate among illegitimate children. Postwar conditions have increased the problem. The author discusses the provisions of a bill drafted by the National [English] council.

93. ——— Unmarried mother. Fortnightly review, v. 116, p. 623-26, October 1921.

Pertains to England. Discusses the difficulty the mother has in supporting her child. The amount she can obtain for the child from the father is negligible. The death rate among illegitimate children is roughly twice that among legitimate children.

94. Fordyce, A. D., M.D. (The) Care of the illegitimate baby. British medical journal, v. 2 of 1915, p. 178-79, July 31, 1915.

An "investigation into the welfare of poor illegitimate babies throughout the early years of life" born in the Royal maternity hospital, Edinburgh, "January 1st to June 30th, 1911, and their history for three years. . ." It was possible to trace 82 out of the 127 cases. "It seems reasonable to conclude that an illegitimate baby in 1 out of 4 cases does not receive the ordinary attention given to his legitimate brother."

95. Fowler, H. Handling illegitimacy cases in general hospitals. Journal of social hygiene, v. 8, p. 387-91, October 1922.

The hospital social worker's responsibility for unmarried mothers is outlined on the basis of agency referring, and place delivered (home, hospital, boarding home, maternity home). Advantages of the latter are stressed.

96. Frazier, E. Franklin. (An) Analysis of statistics on Negro illegitimacy in the United States. Social forces, v. 11, p. 249-57, December 1932.

"On the whole the trend of the illegitimacy rate has been slightly upward, in spite of the decrease for the three years from 1923 to 1925." A study was made of 612 families in Macon county, Alabama, which showed that 122 women in 114 of these families had had 191 illegitimate children. This "reflects the simple and naïve behavior of peasant folk. It is not licentious and could scarcely be called immoral. Of course, in some cases it does represent degeneration. . ." Statistics show a marked difference between the rates of northern and southern states. Comparison is made with the illegitimacy rate among Negroes in Chicago.

97. Freeman, Frank N. (The) Effect of environment on intelligence. School and society, v. 31, p. 623-32, May 10, 1930.

Pages 628-29. "The entire group of foster children was also divided into the legitimate and the illegitimate groups in order to avoid any complications that might arise due to the difference between these two groups. The average intellignce quotient of the legitimate children in the good homes was 101 and in the poor homes 89. For the illegitimate group the average in the good homes was 109 and in the poor homes 96."

98. Freund, Ernst. Uniform illegitimacy law. Survey, v. 49, p. 104, October 15, 1922.

Recommendation of a uniform law by the National conference of commissioners on uniform state laws. The proposed law is not a revolutionary reform. It falls short of what some American states have attempted, but would improve existing laws in most states, and permit coöperation between states in securing relief for mother and child.

99. Gallichan. Notes on illegitimacy. American journal of urology and sexology, v. 14, p. 417-21, September 1918.

Abstracts from the literature on illegitimacy, from various countries at different periods of time.

Gallichan, (Mrs.) W. M. see Hartley, Catherine Gasquoine.

100. Gane, E. Marguerite. (The) Children's case working agencies of Pittsburgh. (Pittsburgh child welfare study, Report no. 2, summary.) 63 p. Pittsburgh, Pittsburgh federation of social agencies, 1930.

Pages 39-61. Illegitimacy in Pittsburgh. The extent of the problem in Pittsburgh. Tables show age and residence of parents, and number of parents of illegitimate children known to one or more social agencies during three months of 1927. A list of agencies working with the unmarried mother is given, and tables indicate the number of cases brought before the courts and the disposition made of the illegitimate child.

101. Gesell, Arnold, M.D., Ph.D. (The) Guidance of mental growth in infant and child. 322 p. New York, Macmillan, 1930.

Pages 192-217 (Chapter XIII). Clinical guidance in infant adoption; reducing psychological risks in adoption. Illegitimacy is not directly discussed, but "foundlings" receive brief notice in the findings of the [New York] State charities aid association's How foster children turn out.

102. ——— (The) Pre-school child from the standpoint of public hygiene and education. 264 p. Cambridge [Massachusetts], Houghton Mifflin, 1923.

Pages 143-50. A discussion of illegitimacy in relation to children deprived of parental care, and adoption as it sometimes ensues.

103. ——— Reducing the risks of child adoption. Child welfare league of America, Bulletin [monthly], New series, v. 6, p. 1, column 1, + p. 2, May 15, 1927.

"This article will deal briefly with what might be called the psychological risks of adoption."

104. Gillin, John Lewis. Poverty and dependency; their relief and prevention. Revised edition. 836 p. New York, Century, 1926.

Pages 422-44 (Chapter XXIII). Dependent children; children born out of wedlock. A general discussion of illegitimacy with summary of the literature.
Pages 428-35. Development of the treatment of the illegitimate child.
Pages 435-41. Principles of the care of illegitimate children.
Pages 441-44. Prevention of illegitimacy.

105. —— Social pathology. 612 p. New York, Century, 1933.

Pages 267-85. Illegitimate parenthood. The factors to be considered are economic, social, and personal. The author discusses low wages, home conditions, lack of sex education, desire for luxury, feeblemindedness, emotional instability, precocious physical and sexual development as factors in illegitimate parenthood. The results of illegitimate parenthood are twofold: a menace to the future welfare of the child, and a threat to the stability of the family. Tables are given showing the number and percent of illegitimate births in leading countries of Europe, Australia, and New Zealand, and in 16 states, and 20 cities of over 100,000 population, in the United States.

Pages 359-74. (The) Unmarried.

Pages 369-69. One paragraph discusses prostitution and delinquency of the unmarried.

Goldberg, Bronett. joint author see entry 192.

106. Goodsell, Willystine. Problems of the family. 474 p. New York, Century, 1928.

Pages 234-63 (Chapter XIV). Illegitimacy as a problem in child welfare. This chapter is a general discussion of illegitimacy, stating the laws in England and the United States, and devoting a few paragraphs to the mentality of the unmarried mother. The author refers to studies and statistics estimating a possible 35 percent of feeblemindedness among unmarried mothers.

107. Gray, (Mrs.) Edwin. Illegitimacy in Norway; the Castberg laws. Maternity and child welfare [London], p. 115-17, April 1923.

A discussion of the Norwegian laws relating to illegitimacy and their working. Illegitimacy does not appear to have decreased. Fathers are not paying satisfactorily and there is a small number of legal proceedings instituted to establish paternity. Many mothers go to Denmark or Sweden to escape the law.

108. Great Britain, Medical research council. (The) Effect of maternal social conditions and nutrition upon birth-weight and birth-length, by M. B. Murray. (Special report series, no. 81. Child life investigations.) 34 p. London, His Majesty's stationery office, 1924.

An inquiry into the possible "effects varying social and financial conditions have on birth-weight," from records of 1914, 1915, and 1918 on

primiparous "Maternity patients available at St. Thomas's Hospital and the General Lying-In Hospital, York Road," both the social and the medical records being used.
Pages 18-20 (Section 6). "Circumstances" of unmarried mothers.
Bibliography, p. 31-32.

109. —— Maternal syphilis as a cause of death of the foetus and of the new-born child, by John Norman Cruickshank. (Special report series, no. 82. Child life investigations.) 67 p. London, His Majesty's stationery office, 1924.

Page 8. "The incidence rate of syphilis, as shown by the Wassermann reaction, was 8.91 per cent. in married mothers and 11.16 per cent. in unmarried mothers. These figures agree with the findings of a number of other workers on similar lines."
Page 40 (Table XIII). Infant deaths (by age, marital status of mother, and positive or negative Wassermann reaction of the mother).
Bibliography, p. 66-67.

110. Great Britain, Ministry of health. High maternal mortality in certain areas; reports by Dame Janet Campbell, D.B.E., M.D., M.S., Isabella D. Cameron, M.D., and Dilys M. Jones, M.B. (Reports on public health and medical subjects, no. 68.) 96 p. London, His Majesty's stationery office, 1932.

Pages 3-23 (I). Introduction, by Dame Janet Campbell. "The difficulty remains of getting in touch with all pregnant women, especially primiparae, sufficiently early to make it really useful. . . Yet the value of supervision, especially when difficult and complicated labor may be anticipated has been overwhelmingly proved, and its desirability is reinforced by an examination of the large number of maternal deaths in which no advice has been sought or accepted. . . The experiment of voluntary notification of pregnancy which has been tried in Huddersfield offers one possible solution, at any rate in urban areas."
Pages 62-85 (IV). Maternal mortality in Wales, by Dilys M. Jones. "With the exception of Montgomery, which has a high proportion of illegitimate to total births but a relatively low maternal mortality rate for 1923-29, there is a coincidence between a high percentage of illegitimate births and a high maternal mortality rate. It may be assumed that the circumstances associated with illegitimacy have some effect in increasing the mortality from child-bearing."

111. Great Britain, Registrar-general. Statistical review of England and Wales for the year 1931. (New annual series, no. 11

[in 3 volumes].) London, His Majesty's stationery office, 1932.

Includes standard tables on illegitimacy and text. Superseded the annual report of the registrar-general, beginning 1921.

Part I. Tables. Medical. 410 p. Deaths of infants under 1 year per 1,000 live births by legitimacy, 1838-1931, p. 3; deaths at various periods of the first year of life, 1931, by legitimacy and sex, p. 52; deaths under 1 year and various subdivisions of the first year per 1,000 live births, 1931, by sex, cause, and legitimacy, p. 53-63; deaths under 1 year of all infants and illegitimate infants, numbers and death-rates per 1,000 live births, 1931, p. 66-69; births (number and rate), by legitimacy and sex for the various geographical areas, 1931, p. 70-120; stillbirths allocated to the usual residence of mother by legitimacy and ratio per 1,000 total births, 1931, p. 121-23.

Part II. Tables. Civil. 120 p. Live births, by illegitimacy, per 1,000 population, per 1,000 single and widowed women, 15-45, per 1,000 total births, p. 6; births, by legitimacy and sex, for the various geographical areas, 1931, p. 8-58.

Part III. Text [not yet published].

Part III. Text [*1930*. Abstracted here, as indication of standard tables]. Deaths during various parts of first year of life by sex and legitimacy, 1930, p. 12-13. Deaths within 30 minutes of birth, by legitimacy, sex, and causes of death, showing "the same startling differential incidence upon the illegitimate as in 1928 and 1929, especially so far as those causes of death are concerned which imply, or are likely to mask the operation of violence or neglect. For violence and lack of care as a whole a rate of 6,266 per million for illegitimate infants compares with one of 78 for the legitimate. . . Of the 186 deaths of illegitimate infants assigned to these headings [violence and lack of care] 116 or 62 per cent. relate to abandoned infants of unknown parentage," p. 14-15. Mortality of male infants "greater for the legitimate than the illegitimate," and excess "for the illegitimate . . . as usual, very much greater for syphilis than for any other cause," p. 17. "Percentage of live births occurring in institutions" in several geographic regions, by legitimacy, shows London occupying the most "favorable position" due to "more adequate provision of lying-in accommodation," p. 76. Maternal mortality by civil condition, age and cause of death, p. 78-80. Increase in proportion of illegitimate to total births, 1930 over 1929, p. 123.

112. Groves, Ernest R. Social problems and education. 458 p. New York, Longmans, Green, 1925.

Pages 179-204 (Chapter VII). (The) Unmarried mother. A general discussion of illegitimacy including social causes.

113. Guibord, Alberta S. B., M.D. and Ida R. Parker. What becomes of the unmarried mother; a study of 82 cases. 76 p. Boston, Research bureau on social case work, 1922.

This study comprises babies born between November 1914 and July 1918, and shows the work done in agency placement of the unmarried mother with relatives or in employment and the attempt made to secure marriage for the mother.

114. Hall, Fred S., Ph.D. and Elisabeth W. Brooke. American marriage laws in their social aspects; a digest. 132 p. New York, Russell Sage foundation, 1919. (Out of print.)

Pages 14-17. Common law marriages in relation to proposed legal reforms are discussed.
Pages 31-32. Common law marriages of the various states are summarized.
Pages 51-131 (Part III). The marriage laws by states.

Hall, Fred S., Ph.D. joint author see entries 274 and 275.

115. Hall, G. E. Moral conditions in rural New England. Journal of social hygiene, v. 9, p. 267-70, May 1923.

Suggestions for lessening illegitimacy and assisting unmarried mothers through instruction in sex hygiene, based on a study of one hundred rural illegitimate births in Maine, are given.

Hall, Justin Clarke. joint author see entry 117.

116. Hall, W. Clarke. (The) State and the child. 195 p. New York, F. A. Stokes, 1917. (Printed in England.)

Pages 132-44 (Chapter V). Considers the illegitimate child. Most of the material is prior to 1912. The author discusses the mortality of illegitimate children and legislation in England, especially the Affiliation orders act (1914) dealing with the contribution of the father toward the support of his child.

117. Hall, W. Clarke, and Justin Clarke Hall. Law of adoption and guardianship of infants, with special reference to courts of summary jurisdiction; together with the Legitimacy act, 1926. 171 p. London, Butterworth, 1928.

History of English legislation pertaining to illegitimacy, with the text of the Legitimacy act of 1926.

118. Hanauer, Dr. Illegitimate births among the Jews. (Uneheliche geburten bei den Juden.) Jahrbuch für nationalökon und statistik, v. 132, p. 902-11, June 1930.

" . . . The present study on illegitimacy among the Jews is based on material concerning Prussia, Bavaria, Saxony, Württemberg, Baden and Hesse and five large towns. The figures show that everywhere illegitimacy is much less frequent among the Jews than among the general population, a fact which finds an easy explanation in the social and economic structure of the Jewish community. . ."—[S.s.a.]
Quoted from Social science abstracts, v. 3, no. 1, p. 153, January 1931.

119. Harris, Henry, M.D. Abortion in Soviet Russia. Has the time come to legalize it elsewhere? Eugenics review, v. 25, p. 19-22, April 1933.

An analysis of Soviet Russia's thirteen-year-old experiment in legalizing abortions. "Any woman in Russia, who is not more than three months pregnant, can demand an abortion as her indisputable right. . . If more than three months pregnant, it may be granted her for medical reasons or even eugenic, social, and economic reasons. . . Where she is unattached to a man . . . she is considered to have an adequate reason."

120. Harrison, Austin, For the unborn. English review, v. 20, p. 231-36, May 1915.

What is to be the future of children born out of wedlock during the war? England owes legitimacy to these children.

121. Hart, Hastings H. (The) Illegitimate child; a life-saving problem. 7 p. New York, Russell Sage foundation, 1912. Also American association for the study and prevention of infant mortality, Transactions, 1912, p. 34-38.

A program to give to the illegitimate child the benefits of general infant mortality prevention; in which program are included registration of pregnancy, complete birth registration, care by the mother for at least one year and breast-feeding for at least six months, probation of the mother for the first year, effort to trace parents of "foundlings," and wet-nursing of "foundlings."

122. ——— Registration of illegitimate births; a preventive of infant mortality. 19 p. New York, Russell Sage foundation, 1916.

"The most important part of this paper is entitled A Life Saving Plan for Babies, found on page 15 and following."

123. Hartley, Catherine Gasquoine (Mrs. W. M. Gallichan). (The) Child of the unmarried mother. Nineteenth century and after, v. 90, p. 511-20, September 1921.

This article pertains to England. It outlines the high mortality rate among illegitimate children, the establishment of the paternity bill, and legislation in England, which is still far behind Norway in reform of its laws. "Child welfare should be a national and not a private work."

124. ——— (The) Unmarried mother. English review, v. 18, p. 78-90, August 1914.

The results of illegitimacy to the welfare of the race and reform legislation in various countries discussed.

125. Hartley, Frida. (The) Problem of illegitimacy in South Africa. Child welfare, National council for child welfare [S. Africa], v. 9, p. 1-7, February 1930.

The standard of "idealism and responsibility" is "falling." Of illegitimate births of unmarried mothers, 87 percent are to women under 30 years, namely 1,000 births among 148,800 women. Birth control, maternity homes and hospitals, and sex education are discussed.

126. Healy, William, M.D. and others. Reconstructing behavior in youth; a study of problem children in foster families. (Judge Baker foundation publication no. 5.) 325 + ix p. New York and London, Knopf, 1929.

A study of "accomplishment or failure in the modification of behavior tendencies during a period of years," the modification being "arrived at in a changed situation during placement of the young individual in a foster family." Legitimate problem children are not discussed to any extent as distinct from illegitimate problem children.

Chapter XXIV. Results. "Is illegitimacy a bar to success in placing? This can be readily answered: Of all the problem children taken by the private agencies (Table 24) 27 were illegitimate, and 81 per cent of these were successes in placing. This is favorable in comparison with the legitimate group."

127. Hecke, Wilhelm. Illegitimacy in Austria. ([Die] Unehelichen in Österreich.) Jahrbuch für nationalökon und statistik, v. 132, p. 572-91, April 1930.

"In 1927, 25.2% of Austrian births were illegitimate, the highest ratio among the European states. The rate has been rising since 1921. The

Austrian districts having the highest rates are those characterized by few cities, little industry, and larger agricultural holdings, which in the main give employment only to family members and domestics. Economic conditions and customs make for a postponement of marriage; there is practically no social stigma attached to illegitimacy, the offspring being regarded as legitimized by a subsequent marriage. . . In the district with the highest rate, Kärnten, the majority of the illegitimate children lived with the mother, only 5% being cared for by others. . . "—[S.s.a.]
Quoted from Social science abstracts, v. 3, no. 9, p. 1336, September 1931.

128. Heisterman, Carl A. State supervision of children born out of wedlock. Social service review, v. 7, p. 254-62, June 1933.

History of American legislation on the subject of illegitimacy is summarized. Early laws in Wisconsin and Minnesota are described. Legislation has been passed in several states providing for state supervision by authorizing the state public welfare authorities, under certain conditions, to prosecute the father for the purpose of establishing his paternity and compelling him to support his child. In Wisconsin the maternity hospital is required to report the fact of illegitimacy to the state board of control within 24 hours after the discovery of such fact. Reference is made to legislation relating to state supervision in the following additional states: North Dakota, Rhode Island, Colorado, Alabama, Virginia.

Hemenway, H. B. joint author see entry 133.

129. Henderson, L. M. and others. (The) Legal status of illegitimates in the Commonwealth of Australia. Journal of comparative legislation and international law, third series, v. 3, p. 13-20, 1921.

Legislation has alleviated the harshness with which illegitimate children were treated by the common law. Such legislation includes: legitimation; right to inherit; maintenance, including the establishment of paternity; government bodies and institutions; compensation. Of particular importance was the Maternity allowance act [1912].

130. Hewins, Katharine P. Hazards in illegitimacy; adoptions and mortality. Survey, v. 46, p. 206-7, May 14, 1921.

The second of a series of three articles by the author interpreting the [United States] Children's bureau's Publication no. 75. "Illegitimate children become public charges and a fianancial burden. Birth registration is not yet required in all states and is incomplete in some of the states. There is no satisfactory system in any state."

131. —— Illegitimacy in a rural community. Survey, v. 46, p. 305-6, June 4, 1921.

The third of a series of three articles by the author interpreting the [United States] Children's bureau's Publication no. 75. A study of Cape Cod, Massachusetts, as a rural community. Hospitals and maternity homes are practically non-existent in this section. Here illegitimate children are born in the home; or, in any event, with relatives.

132. —— Study of illegitimacy. Survey, v. 46, p. 115-16, April 23, 1921.

The first of three articles by the author interpreting the [United States] Children's bureau's Publication no. 75. "Illegitimacy is a complex problem with roots that go down and down into the heredity and the environment of both boys and girls. Nobody really knows whether the evil is increasing or decreasing . . . the chance of survival for these children [is] so much less than that for legitimate children, and the appalling cost of their care to the community so great . . . certain very definite and far-reaching, constructive measures" are proposed in the report made by Massachusetts in 1914. The report stresses the connection between mental defect and illegitimacy. From one-third to one-fourth of the mothers had more than one child. The report indicates that the mentality is, on the whole, poorer for this group of second offenders.

133. Howard, Sheldon L., and Henry B. Hemenway. Birth records of illegitimates and of adopted children. American journal of public health and the Nation's health, v. 21, p. 641-47, June 1931.

Part I, by Sheldon L. Howard. The "dual rôle" of registrars of vital statistics is discussed: namely, insisting on "accuracy of the basic data," and furnishing "only such copies of birth records as will best promote the welfare of the persons concerned." The "existing conditions surrounding illegitimacy in this country," and the "more or less progressive legal steps taken by various states" are summarized.

Part II, by Henry B. Hemenway. The author's plan for the correction of birth records of children legitimatized, and of adopted children, and also for the registration of "foundlings," is outlined, together with the resolution, embodying his plan, adopted by the Vital statistics section of the American public health association at its annual meeting, 1930.

134. Howland, Goldwin W., M.B. Illegitimate mothers. Hospital social service, v. 16, p. 6-10, July 1927.

"It is my intention to show that illegitimate mothers usually lapse, not so much from excessive sexual instinct, but from a lack of control over other instincts, which predominate in them." The author decries the "lack of study of the mental makeup of the women themselves" by social workers, full as are their reports in other respects.

135. Hutchcroft, L. W. Wisconsin's illegitimate birth problem. Wisconsin state board of health, Bulletin, v. 5, p. 3-4, + 18-20, December 1932.

A brief discussion of illegitimate births in 1930 reported in Wisconsin's vital statistics.

136. Hutzel, E. L. (The) Social treatment of the unmarried mother with her child. Hospital social service, v. 6, p. 157-64, September 1922.

Discussion chiefly of the "normal" unmarried mother who is kept with her child. Work for legislation to gain support from the father, for gaining the respect of the community, for good medical care, for increase of the mother's earning capacity, and for her reëstablishment in her home, is urged.

137. Indianapolis, Council of social agencies. Supervising unmarried mothers in family boarding houses—a review of twenty-nine situations under the care of the Family welfare society; submitted by the Conference on illegitimacy. 12 p. Indianapolis, The Council, 1925. (Mimeographed.)

Ninety-eight white unmarried mothers were cared for. Of this number, twenty-nine were placed in homes of private families. Facts given about these unmarried mothers include age, education, occupation, marital status, number of other children, mental condition, physical condition, economic provision after birth of child, and length of time under supervision.

138. Irish Free State, Department of local government and public health. Annual report of the registrar-general, 1931. 177 p. Dublin, Stationery office.

A few standard tables on illegitimacy are included:
Page xiii. Illegitimate birth rates by provinces, based on total births, for each year, 1925-1931.
Page 6. Births by sex and legitimacy, 1864-1931.
Page 7. Birth-rates per thousand population and per hundred total births, by legitimacy, 1864-1931.
Page 22. Mortality by certain causes and by age-periods, among illegiti-

mate infants under one year, 1931. Mortality and mortality rates per thousand of corresponding births, by legitimacy and age-periods, 1923-1931.

Page 23. Number of deaths of illegitimate infants under one year in each county and borough, 1931, by age-periods, distinguishing deaths in institutions (corrected for transfers).

Page 24. Illegitimacy birth rate based on total births, by provinces, counties, and county boroughs, 1931.

Pages 32-39. Births by legitimacy, registered in 1931, in each province, county, and county borough, with the results arising from correction for births in institutions.

139. Jewish encyclopedia, v. 2. London and New York, Funk and Wagnalls company, 1902.

Page 587. Bastard, by Lewis H. Dembitz.
The Jewish law in relation to illegitimacy is summarized. "In the English use of the word, a child neither born nor begotten in lawful wedlock. . . There is no Hebrew word of like meaning. The mamzer, rendered 'bastard' in the A. V., is . . . the offspring of a father and mother between whom there could be in law no binding betrothal. . . "

140. Jewish encyclopedia, v. 5. London and New York, Funk and Wagnalls company, 1903.

Pages 440-41. Foundling, by Julius H. Greenstone.
"The question as to the status of such a child in the Jewish community was chiefly decided by the condition in which it was found. If there was evidence that its parents had abandoned it willfully, its legitimacy was under suspicion and it was therefore treated as doubtfully legitimate. If, however, there were indications that its abandonment was caused by the inability of the parents to support it, the child was regarded as legitimate. . . Those foundlings which were suspected of having been born through illegitimate connections were placed outside of the fold, and they might not intermarry with Israelites, nor with other foundlings or illegitimates. The only persons whom they were permitted to marry were proselytes and liberated slaves; and the offspring of such marriages were in the same status as the foundlings themselves. . . There is no trace of institutions for foundlings in Talmudic literature."

141. Jewish encyclopedia, v. 6. London and New York, Funk and Wagnalls company, 1904.

Pages 559-60. Illegitimacy, by Julius H. Greenstone.
In Jewish law illegitimacy is the "state of being born of any of the marriages prohibited in the Bible and for which the punishment is exci-

sion. . . Three kinds of illegitimates ('mamzer') are recognized in Jewish law"; these are here discussed, as is the Jewish law in general in relation to illegitimacy.

142. Johnson, Kate Burr. Problems of delinquency among girls. Journal of social hygiene, v. 12, p. 385-97, October 1926.

Case illustrations of illegitimacy from among the "individual girls whom the State Board of Charities and Public Welfare has tried to help" are given, together with suggestions for a constructive program.

143. Johnson, Roswell H. Determination of disputed parentage as a factor in reducing infant mortality. American association for the study and prevention of infant mortality, Transactions, 1918, p. 100-105.

A presentation chiefly of the use of anthropometry, measures being taken on the child, on the suspected parent, and on the known parent, as a means of determining disputed parentage.
Bibliography, p. 104-5.

144. Jones, Cheney C. (A) Tentative outline for a study on illegitimacy. National conference of social work, Proceedings, 1918, p. 91-94.

"Illegitimacy as a social problem is recognized as a social menace. . . " Part of this article points out the relationship of illegitimacy to other social problems such as infant mortality, prostitution, and divorce.

145. Jones, George L. How does our treatment of the unmarried mother with the second or third child differ from our treatment of the unmarried mother with her first child? National conference of social work, Proceedings, 1919, p. 81-85.

The solution for the unmarried mother with one child has been domestic service. This is not true if there are two children but in that case the first child can be removed from the mother so she can care for the second child and continue to work.

146. Kammerer, Percy G. Social consequences of illegitimacy. Journal of social hygiene, v. 6, p. 161-80, April 1920.

An estimate of the effects upon: I. (The) Institution of the monogamous family. The monogamous home "is too deeply rooted in human history and in human psychology to be withdrawn by such a phenomenon as that of illegitimacy." II. (The) Unmarried father. Public disapprobation (though less severe than toward the mother) and the stabilizing influence on the father, are discussed. "There is room for a study of the unmarried father. . . " III. (The) Unmarried mother. "Causative factors" and "consequences" of illegitimacy are discussed. That the "greatest single determinant in the rate of illegitimacy" is "biologically ordained" is the point of view of Prinzing, who ascribes causation of illegitimacy to the "ratio of the number of unmarried males capable of paternity to the number of females capable of maternity. . ." The discussion is chiefly of the attitude of the public toward illegitimacy. IV. (The) Illegitimate child. The higher infant mortality rate among illegitimate children, and the attitude of the public are discussed.

147. ——— Unmarried mother; a study of five hundred cases. 342 p. Boston, Little, Brown, 1918.

Introduction by Dr. William Healy.
A discussion of the extent and "causative factors of illegitimacy." The author includes in his discussion of "causative factors": bad environment; bad companions; recreational disadvantages; educational disadvantages; bad home conditions; early sex experience; heredity; abnormal physical condition; sexual suggestibility; sexual suggestibility by one individual; abnormal sexualism; mental conflict; assault, rape, and incest. These factors are illustrated by case studies. The author also considers conditions in various countries regarding the occupation of the unmarried mother and legislation.
Bibliography, p. 335-37.

148. Keegan, Robert F. Policies of public and private agencies in dealing with illegitimacy.[2] National conference of Catholic charities, Proceedings, 1918, p. 159-68.

Presented under four headings: "the present laws on the subject, proposed legislation, Catholic teaching, and whether or not the Catholic moral law as we know it harmonizes well with the modern tendencies of legislation in this direction." There is an analysis of the Castberg law of Norway, which gives to the child its "natural right to two parents. . . Since January 1, 1918, the word 'bastard' has been banished from Minnesota law. A comprehensive scheme of vital statistics has been placed in operation. It compels complete returns from physicians and midwives. The records relating to illegitimacy cannot be consulted without a court order." The bill presented to the legislature of Illinois is summarized. "A note of solemn warning must be sounded to direct attention to the great truth that this whole problem is one essentially bound up with morality rather than economics. The one distressing feature of all the attempts at proposed reform in our legislation is the seeming conviction

[2]Discussion, p. 168-74.

on the part of our social workers that this thing has to be. . . With proper education, with God and the truth of eternity put into our education, with sound principles of morality increasingly inculcated into the minds of our youth, such provisions as are at present deemed a necessary feature of every proposed reform in this direction might properly be passed over. . . Let no legislation be enacted which while preventing the birth of illegitimate children will cause those who gratify their animal senses to resort to contraceptive methods."

149. ───── (The) Practicable ideal of protection and care for children born out of wedlock. Catholic charities review, v. 4, p. 99-102, April 1920.

This article discusses the rights of the children of illegitimate birth, the mother, and the father.

150. Kellogg, Foster S., M.D. (The) Unmarried mother before and after confinement. Mother and child, v. 2, p. 74-80, February 1921.

A "central clearing house composed of a representative of each agency" is urged, the cost to be met by the agencies interested, including the Commonwealth. "Illegitimacy should be handled as an entity—directed legally, sociologically and medically—loosely at first until knowledge is accumulated—under one office. . . "

151. Kenworthy, Marion E., M.D. Mental hygiene aspects of illegitimacy. Mental hygiene, v. 5, p. 499-508, July 1921.

"It is my purpose merely to urge the importance of seeking to discover the motive behind every act and to recognize the elements at work in the personality of every individual who comes to attention because of failure in dealing with the problems of life. In such studies . . . we may often find the key to the real situation in the problem of the unmarried mother." In some women there may be a definite correlation between "illicit sex practice and mental pathology." In some others "illicit or promiscuous sex expression exists as a definite behavior tendency." The author analyzes other groups of unmarried mothers. In handling such mothers, success is achieved only when their urges are "directed into socially acceptable channels." The essential qualities of the worker in this field are a "satisfactory adjustment" of her own "sex life, even after many difficulties, and an objective point of view." The most satisfactory solution is brought about usually by the worker with "mental-hygiene training." A center in "every large community," for the treatment of unmarried girls under the care of agencies, and for research, is urged.

152. ——— Mental hygiene aspects of illegitimacy, read before the Inter-city conference of illegitimacy, Milwaukee, June 29, 1921. [8] p. New York (?), The Author (?), 1921 (?).

The article points out the relation between mental hygiene and illegitimacy, showing the need for mental hygiene study. The basic reason given for illicit sex relations is social maladjustment. The author also discusses other factors: urge for sex expression, lack of ordinary inhibitory faculties, younger sister "grudge" attitude, "so-called electra complex," feeble-mindedness, and points out the relation between mental pathology and prostitution.

153. King, H. D. (The) Importation of foundlings; a sociological problem; a protest. New Orleans medical and surgical journal, v. 65, p. 851-55, 1912-13.

A protest before the Orleans parish medical society, March 10, 1913, against the importation of "foundlings" from New York City, which had been going on for five or six years. The author suggests as an alternative the "adoption of children from local institutions, whose family and personal histories are at least better known than those of the imported foundlings from New York City."

154. Klumker, Christian J. (The) Draft of a law of illegitimacy and the public bureaus of youth welfare. ([Der] Unehelichenentwurf und die jugendaemter.) Zentralblatt für jugendrecht und jugendwohlfahrt, v. 20, p. 313-15, March 1929.

"The JA (Jugendamt) was created by the RJWG (Reichsgesetz fuer Jugendwohlfahrt) to take care of all dependent children. Its main task is guardianship of illegitimate children. . . "—[S.s.a.]
Quoted from Social science abstracts, v. 2, no. 9, p. 1491-92, September 1930.

155. ——— Parental authority according to the draft of the law on illegitimacy. ([Die] Elterliche gewalt im entwurf eines unehelichengesetzes.) Zentralblatt für jugendrecht und jugendwohlfahrt, v. 21, p. 73-77, June 1929.

Indexed in Social science abstracts, v. 2, no. 10, p. 1642, October 1930.

156. Knibbs, George H. Protogenesis and ex-nuptial natality in Australia [Sidney]. Journal and proceedings of the Royal society of New South Wales, v. 61, 1927, p. 73-114.

Based on data from the Bureau of census and statistics of the Australian commonwealth. For New South Wales and Victoria, combined, ratio of ex-nuptial births to total births, 1876-1925, can be computed from the data, as can the ratio for the whole of Australia from 1901 onwards. It is likely that the small percentage of ex-nuptial births in Australia "will decline still further. . . It has been falling from the beginning of this century." Frequency of ex-nuptial births according to age of mothers is given.

157. Kopp, Marie E. (The) Development of marriage consultation centers as a new field of social medicine. American journal of obstetrics and gynecology, v. 26, p. 122-34, July 1933.

A study made in Germany and Austria by the author, who plans to make a similar study in the United States.

Marriage consultation centers, of which there are more than a thousand in Germany and Austria, are a postwar development whose purpose is the betterment of national health in relation to the family. The first of these centers opened in Berlin in 1919, as a privately supported organization, and was later taken over as a government institution. The first under public control was started in Vienna in 1922. In 1929, an official marriage consultation center was established in Zürich, Switzerland.

Advice and guidance is sought chiefly in relation to family problems. The number of unmarried men and women applying at these centers is reported as one in three cases in Dresden and Hamburg, and one in five cases in Berlin-Friedrichshain. Consultation is free of charge.

No data have yet been published regarding the extent of the practice of abortion in Germany, but it is expected that these marriage consultation centers will lessen the present increasing number by education in sex hygiene and advice relating to birth control measures.

158. Kosmak, George W., M.D. Committee on obstetrical care of unmarried mothers. National conference of social work, Proceedings, 1920, p. 115-19.

"An important function of the State Charities Aid Association in New York is the supervision of abandoned and illegitimately pregnant women." The Maternity center association of New York City and a "number of other social welfare agencies in New York City have taken up the problem of illegitimacy and must be commended for their efforts to extend to these mothers the modern conceptions of appropriate obstetrical care."

159. Krische, P. Sociology of the illegitimate child. (Zur soziologie des unehelichen kindes.) Archiv für frauenkunde und konstitutionsforschung, v. 17, p. 69-74, May 1931.

"The author outlines the social, legal, and economic status of the ille-

gitimate child from primitive to modern times, and points out the tendency from irresponsible and uncontrolled breeding to responsible and controlled parenthood. (Graph.)"—[S.s.a.]
Quoted from Social science abstracts, v. 4, no. 4, p. 632, April 1932.

160. Lane, W. D. Just flickerings of life. Survey, v. 36, p. 157-60, May 6, 1916.

Summary and comment on George Walker's Traffic in babies.

161. Laughlin, Clara F. Condemned mothers and babies. Pearson's magazine, p. 227-37, February 1915.

The mother and child are condemned, but the father goes free. This is an article with a story foundation, contrasting conditions in Europe with conditions in the United States. In European countries and "even Japan" all births are recorded. "Making things hard for mothers and children does not check illegitimacy." Education, social ostracism, religion do not stop it.

162. Lawson, William. (The) Amendment of the law in Ireland as to the maintenance of illegitimate children. Statistical and social inquiry society of Ireland, Journal, v. 13, p. 182-206, 1914.

The article gives a paragraph on the difference between the law in England and in Ireland, the law of other countries; and proposed legislation for Ireland (Appendix).

163. League of nations. Report on the work of the League since the twelfth session of the Assembly. (A6, 1932.) 113 p. Geneva, The League, 1932.

Pages 82-83. Illegitimate children. The Child welfare committee "considered various means of improving the position of illegitimate children —among others, social insurance and official guardianship."

164. League of nations, Child welfare committee. Disclosure of illegitimacy in official documents. (C. 373. M. 184. 1933. IV.) (C. P. E. 399[I].) 8 p. Geneva, The League, 1933.

The Council in May 1933 approved the resolution adopted by the Child welfare committee, March 1933, in part as follows:
" 'Noting that several States have introduced provisions into their legislation or administrative practice with a view to avoiding any reference to illegitimacy in extracts from official documents;
" 'Considering that such measures deserve to be recommended;

" 'Draws the Council's attention to the importance of requesting the Government members and non-members of the League of Nations:

" '(1) To study the report by the Secretariat relating to official documents which do not disclose illegitimacy (see below);

" '(2) To examine the possibility of authorizing the issue of abridged birth certificates and other official documents which make no reference to parentage and which would be regarded as adequate in all cases where information regarding parentage is unnecessary.' "

Pages 1-8. Report of the Secretariat on the disclosure of illegitimacy in official documents. "At its eighth session, the . . . Committee's attention was drawn to the fact that certain States provide in their legislation for . . . abridged birth certificates, which do not disclose illegitimacy. The possibility offered by such legislation, which enables the fact of a person's illegitimacy to remain undisclosed e.g. when entering a school or competing for a post—is often of vital importance for children or young people born out of wedlock. For this reason the . . . Committee instructed the Secretariat to make a study of the question." This report comprises information from nineteen countries, including the United States. The situation in the various states of the United States is summarized.

165. —— Minutes of the sixth session, April 9-16, 1930. (C.337. M.137. 1930. IV.) (C.P.E., 6th session, P.V.) 96 p. Geneva, the League, 1930.

Pages 41-47. Illegitimate children: report of the Legal subcommittee.

Page 154. Illegitimate children: adoption of a draft resolution proposed by the Subcommittee, in part as follows: " 'The Child welfare committee therefore thinks that it would be valuable to study, in various countries, those social measures which are more directly concerned with the welfare of the illegitimate child, such as financial aid, guardianship, etc., and it requests the Secretariat . . . to prepare . . . a report on these questions.' "

" 'The Child welfare committee also thinks it would be useful to examine . . . the comparative mortality of illegitimate mothers and illegitimate children.' " In the resolution as adopted, "such as financial aid, guardianship, etc.," was omitted.

166. —— Official guardianship of illegitimate children. 16 p. Geneva [Switzerland], The Committee, 1932.

The position of illegitimate children in several countries which state they have a special system of official guardianship to which illegitimate children are subject is outlined: Austria, Finland, Germany, Portugal, Sweden, Switzerland, and the United States in so far as concerns Minnesota. Replies were received from all except Minnesota. The information shows that in Portugal there is no system of guardianship applicable to illegitimate children, and therefore Portugal is not included in the report.

167. —— Report of the work of the eighth session. (Series, League of nations, P.1932, IV. 4.) (C.395. M.221. 1932. IV.) (C.P.E., 351.) 16 p. Geneva, The League, 1932.

The session was held April 9-15, 1932.
Pages 9-10. Illegitimate children. Discusses: position of illegitimate child under social insurance law; official guardianship of illegitimate children.

168. —— Study of the position of the illegitimate child based on the information communicated by governments. (Annex 3 to document C.P.E. 141.) 110 p. Geneva, The Committee, 1929.

The report of the Committee to the Council in 1929. The first part of this study deals with the rights and obligations of the mother and father, legislation, legal, moral and material protection of the child by law. The data are drawn from thirty-seven countries. In the appendices, replies of governments to the questionnaire used, and extracts from the Swiss civil code on illegitimate children, are given.

169. League of nations, Health organization. Report on maternal welfare and the hygiene of infants and children of preschool age by the Reporting committee appointed to deal with these questions. (Series of League of nations publications, III, Health, 1931.) (C.H. 1060.) 75 p. Geneva, World peace foundation, 1931.

Page 17. "Pregnancy in the unmarried woman is not in itself more hazardous than in the married, but the desire to conceal the condition not only leads to attempted abortion, but may prevent the future mother seeking advice or making due preparation for the birth."
Page 29. "Statistics show more frequent cases of premature delivery among unmarried than among married women."

170. Leahy, Alice M. Some characteristics of adoptive parents. American journal of sociology, v. 38, p. 548-63, January 1933.

Adoption records of the Board of control, state of Minnesota, are summarized. The following abstract precedes the article:
"The adoptive parents of 2,414 illegitimate children in Minnesota have been characterized according to the presence or absence of certain attributes. Eighty-nine per cent are childless married couples. A larger per-

centage are native Americans than is true for adults in general, and their median age is older than that of comparable groups of true parents. An average of nearly ten years elapses between marriage and adoption of a child. This is five or six times the period preceding birth of the first child to parents in general. Girls are preferred to boys for adoption, although more boys are available, in a ratio of 104 to 100. The majority of adoptive parents are urban residents, which is related to the fact that most illegitimate children are born in the city. The median grade of schooling for adoptive parents is the eighth. The proportion of adoptive fathers in professional, business, and managerial occupations is three to four times that of adult males in general. The tendency is the reverse in lower occupational groups. The majority of adopted children are in homes of superior economic status. A larger percentage of older children than younger go into homes of farmers, indicating a possible preference by farmers for older children, or a selective placement."

171. ——— (A) Study of certain selective factors influencing prediction of the mental status of adopted children; or adopted children in nature-nurture research.[3] Pedagogical seminary and Journal of genetic psychology, v. 41, p. 294-329, December 1932.

Pages 294-96 (I). (The) Significance of selection in nature-nurture studies. Pages 299-304 (II). Scope of investigation and description of data. "In general, all available aspects of family history which would seem likely to carry implications as to the mental equipment of adopted illegitimate children will be presented. . . The data are drawn from the records of 11,742 unmarried mothers, known to the child-caring agencies of Minnesota during the period of 1918-1928, and on file in the Children's Bureau of the State Board of Control. Every living birth that survived the age of 2 years, and for whom the records revealed reasonably certain information as to placement, is included in the analysis. The number . . . is 9973 or 86.8% of the cases. Of this population, 4213 children were retained by their own mothers and 2875 were placed in adoptive homes." Representativeness of cases selected is discussed.

Pages 304-10 (III). Educational attainment of parents of illegitimate children. "To summarize, the mothers of adopted and retained children are similar in age, as are also the fathers; the parents of both groups of children resemble each other in race and nationality; the parents of adopted children reside in somewhat larger proportions in cities, in contrast to parents of retained children; the occupational status of the maternal grandfathers of adopted children is higher than that of the maternal grandfathers of retained children. . . From the available evidence we

[3]Pages 328-29. Abstracts of this article in French, and in German, by the author.

can conclude that a larger proportion of mothers and fathers of children who are relinquished for adoption attain higher levels of education than parents whose children are retained by their mothers. . . The theoretical significance of the above observation is highly important in nature-nurture investigations involving adopted children. The usual procedure is to assign the differences . . . to the influence of environment."

Pages 311-16 (IV). Occupational status of parents of illegitimate children. "From the available evidence it appears that when our data are examined for sampling errors due to age and residence, the relative superiority in occupational attainment observed for true parents of adopted children, in contrast to true parents of children retained by their mothers, is maintained."

Pages 316-19 (V). Cultural status of true parents and age at placement of adopted children. "A consistent tendency is apparent in these data for the occupation of parents of children placed at 3 months or earlier to be superior to that of parents of children placed at 21 months or over."

Pages 319-25. Selective placement of adopted children. The "trend of the evidence points directly to the conclusion that any direct study of children in adoptive homes cannot ignore the probability of selective placement."

References, p. 326-27.

172. Lee, Elizabeth A. Court procedure in securing support for a child of illegitimate birth. National conference of social work, Proceedings, 1922, p. 127-30.

Reforms are needed to do away with public hearings in Massachusetts. Comparison is made with the procedure in Pennsylvania.

173. Lenroot, Katharine F. Case work with unmarried parents and their children. Hospital social service, v. 12, p. 69-76, August 1925.

The child is to be "safeguarded from social censure, from the deprivation of parental love . . . and of a normal, happy childhood" only by the "slow, painstaking process involved in what we call 'social case-work,' and by the gradual education of the public to a more just attitude toward the problems of illegitimacy." Legislation in various parts of the country is discussed.

Bibliography, p. 76.

174. ———— For children of illegitimate birth. Survey, v. 44, p. 723-24, September 15, 1920.

The article discusses the drafting by the National conference of commissioners on uniform state laws, St. Louis, August 19, 1920, of a uniform act for the protection of children born out of wedlock.

175. ———— Social responsibility for the care of the delinquent girl and the unmarried mother. Journal of social hygiene, v. 10, p. 74-82, February 1924.

Psychiatric study of the unmarried mother is urged as a "basis for decisions as to whether or not she should keep her baby, what her mode of living should be, and what vocational opportunities should be opened to her. . . Case work with the illegitimate family and preventive measures should include the father as well as the mother. . ." Comparatively little is known about the fathers, but a summary of their ages and occupations is given.

176. ———— Social responsibility for the protection of children handicapped by illegitimate birth. Annals of American academy of political and social science, v. 98, p. 120-28, November 1921.

"It is only within the last ten or twelve years that a movement has developed which has already placed upon the statute books of several states more just and adequate laws, based upon the theory that the children . . . are entitled to the same benefits of home life and parental care as are enjoyed by children of more fortunate birth." The article discusses the hazards of illegitimacy: infant mortality, deprivation of parental care and support, hereditary handicaps and environmental difficulties; and points out the relation between illegitimacy and the problems of dependency and delinquency.

177. Lens. (The) Unmarried mother. New statesman, v. 14, p. 639-40, March 6, 1920.

Data regarding illegitimate births in England and Wales for 1917 and 1918 are given. Illegitimacy is increasing. There is a high rate in Scotland, but a low rate in Roman Catholic Ireland. The type of unmarried mother is "good" rather than "vicious" according to this article, which then goes on to discuss the proposed "bastardy" bill (1920), and raises the question of whether its passage would encourage illegitimacy. The new bill is described; in the main it concerns paternity and legitimation. The mother is considered the best guardian of her child if she is physically and mentally fit.

178. Levy, Julius, M.D. Prevention of foundlings. American city, v. 32, p. 179-82, February 1925.

The plan of the city of Newark, New Jersey, and throughout the state is that "in dealing with the unmarried mother situation it must make whatever special effort is necessary to keep the new-born baby with its mother, and breast-fed. If these two conditions are met, the high mortality rate usually found among illegitimate infants is considerably reduced." Hospitals should notify the health department of the admission of every unmarried mother.

179. [Los Angeles], Conference on the care of the unmarried mother and her child. [Study of 285 unmarried mothers in Los Angeles]. 4 p.[4] Los Angeles, The Council of Social Agencies, [1928]. (Typewritten.)

A study of the case work service of the six case working agencies handling unmarried mothers and their babies, in relation to the cases for whom the agencies "completed their services in 1928." Certain characteristics of the mothers and fathers studied are given. Among them, 71 percent came from unhappy or broken homes; 70 percent of the mothers were under 21 years, as were also 20 percent of the fathers.

The services given by the agencies indicate:

One hundred twenty-eight of 154 mothers known before confinement had prenatal care.

Seventy-six percent of the mothers were given Wassermann tests (6 percent of "all the mothers studied" had syphilis).

Sixty-three percent of the girls were given G.C. tests (9 percent of "all the girls" had gonorrhea).

Figures cited regarding physical examination are not clear and therefore not annotated here.

Thirty-seven percent of the babies had paternity established, 41 percent could not be established, 22 percent were not established. Support was secured for 60 percent of those whose paternity was established.

Eighty-three percent of the babies were born in hospitals or maternity homes.

Thirty-one percent were breast-fed for three months or over. Of the 140 mothers who did not breast-feed their babies, 34, or 38 percent, were physically unable to do so.

Sixty-six percent of the babies who lived remained in the custody of the mother.

180. Lowe, Charlotte. (The) Intelligence and social background of the unmarried mother. Mental hygiene, v. 11, p. 783-94, October 1927.

Report of a psychological study of unmarried mothers made by the Research bureau of the State board of control of Minnesota. The aim was to study all such mothers delivered during the year December 1924-

[4]The full tables are not included here, as no copy containing them was made available for this annotation.

November 1925 at all maternity hospitals in the Twin cities keeping the girls sufficiently long to ensure that their health was regained. Of 415 such cases, 71 were "unavailable" for various reasons; the study therefore comprised 344 cases. The author recommends that agencies "watch out" for the girls "leaving school to see what they do and where they go."

181. **Lummus, H. T., and W. Logan MacCoy.** Laws of Pennsylvania and Massachusetts relating to illegitimacy. Journal of American institute of criminal law and criminology, v. 7, p. 751-53, January 1917.

Failure to support an illegitimate child is a distinct offense, and the penalty is imprisonment at hard labor. The article further discusses the question of support from the father if he is a resident of Pennsylvania and the child is not begotten or born there.

182. **Lundberg, Emma O.** Child dependency in the United States; methods of statistical reporting and census of dependent children in thirty-one states. 149 p. New York, Child welfare league of America, [1933].

Foreword by C. C. Carstens.
A study undertaken by the author for the White House conference on child health and protection, (The) Handicapped (Section IV), in order to find some "method by which reliable and comparable data on dependent and neglected children might become available from the various States." The systems in use in the various states were studied, as was also the "value of the social statistics made available." An experimental census was made, which was a "demonstration of the practicability of obtaining complete census data in regard to dependent and neglected children under care in States using various methods of collecting social data."
"Suggestive" items for "cards used for current reports by institutions and agencies to State welfare departments," planned so that "duplicates may be used by local organizations for statistical cards" are presented by including a card [p. 39-40].
"The form was prepared mainly from the point of view of institutions and child-placing agencies, but the items to be recorded and the method of reporting to State welfare departments should be pertinent also to children's aid and protective societies, child-caring services of county welfare boards, juvenile courts, and town and county officials. Institutions primarily for other forms of service that undertake child care, such as maternity homes which engage in child-placing or have a department for the care of children apart from their mothers, would report on the cards their child-caring services only." Under Type of problem, Illegitimacy is one subdivision to be checked when applicable. Under Parent

status, Child illegitimate is one subdivision. Under Care first given unmarried mother are the following subdivisions: Before birth of child, After, Investigation for maternity home, Supervision in own home, Elsewhere (specify), Mother and child in boarding home, Other (specify). Suggestions follow for "periodic compilations by State welfare departments of the main facts that appear on the proposed statistical card," among which are various phases of illegitimacy.

183. ———— (The) Child-mother as a delinquency problem. National conference of social work, Proceedings, 1920, p. 167-68.

A study of 320 girls under eighteen years of age when they became mothers. One-fourth of these girls were fifteen years of age or under, five of them being thirteen and one being only twelve. Broken homes are an important factor. Almost three-fifths of the girls had been deprived of normal homes through the death of one or both parents, or divorce, separation, or desertion. "There is beyond question a definite relation between home conditions and delinquency of these girls."

184. ———— Illegitimacy in Europe as affected by the war. National conference of social work, Proceedings, 1917, p. 299-307.

"Statistics are incomplete but such figures as are available indicate . . . illegitimate births have decreased since the war. Most of the changes since the beginning of the war in regard to the status and support of children born out of wedlock have been made for the purpose of extending state aid to the children of soldiers."

185. ———— (The) Illegitimate child and war conditions. American journal of physical anthropology, v. 1, p. 339-52, July-September, 1918.

Since the war, emphasis of interest in illegitimacy is on the "anthropological side." The author discusses the data from European countries only, beginning with 1913, and presents illegitimacy rates and legislation.

186. ———— Progress in legal protection for children born out of wedlock. National conference of social work, Proceedings, 1922, p. 124-27.

The amendment to the Arizona law of 1921 declares "every child to be the legitimate child of its natural parents" but gives no adequate provision for the establishment of paternity. Advance has been made in several states: New York, New Jersey, and Illinois. The greatest advance has been the advocacy of a uniform illegitimacy act taken up by the Conference of commissioners on uniform state laws, headed by Ernst Freund.

187. ———— Progress toward better laws for the protection of children born out of wedlock. National conference of social work, Proceedings, 1920, p. 111-15.

Progress has been made by the studies of the [Federal] Children's bureau and of Ernst Freund, and by the regional conferences in Chicago and New York (1920) under the auspices of the [Federal] Children's bureau. The article gives the resolutions adopted by the two conferences [Intercity conference on illegitimacy] with discussion.

188. ———— Suggested new laws on illegitimacy. Mother and child, v. 1, p. 77-81, April 1920.

Refers to the Regional conferences in New York and Chicago (1920). Discusses existing laws and the resolutions adopted by the conferences.

189. ———— Unmarried mother. Survey, v. 43, p. 654, February 28, 1920.

A comment on "Final report . . . including a study of the records of the society of five hundred cases," of the Boston society for helping destitute mothers and infants. "The particular problem was that of the mentally subnormal mother and the incompetent, diseased or morally delinquent."

190. McCann, F. J. and others. Criminal abortion and measures necessary to reduce the sale of abortifacient drugs. Lancet, v. 216, p. 233-36, February 2, 1929.

"This is a summary report of several papers read before a joint meeting of the Medico-Legal society and the Maternity and Child Welfare Group of the Society of Medical Officers of Health . . . H. D. Roome felt that 'the real cure of abortion was a change in public opinion.' When there was more charity towards the unmarried mother, when maternity benefits were extended to the married and unmarried alike, then alone would a really permanent cure for abortion be found. . . Lord Riddell stated . . . 'There was no doubt that the disgrace attending the birth of an illegitimate child was responsible for a great many abortions and maternal and infant deaths, and a vast amount of invalidity. It was useless to shut our eyes to the fact that many women did not regard abortion as a moral offense'. . . "—[S.s.a.]
Quoted from Social science abstracts, v. 1, no. 10, p. 1312, November 1929.

191. McClure, W. E. Intelligence of unmarried mothers, II.[5] Psychological clinic, v. 20, p. 154-57, October 1931.

[5]This is apparently a continuation of W. E. McClure's and Bronett Goldberg's Intelligence of unmarried mothers.

"The problem of the unmarried mother is not serious among girls with intelligence below the moron level, nor with intelligence above the normal level. This was indicated by two studies of intelligence of unmarried mothers who had been admitted to a home for unfortunate girls. . . "—[S.s.a.]
Quoted from Social science abstracts, v. 4, no. 3, p. 440, March 1932.

192. McClure, W. E., and Bronett Goldberg. Intelligence of unmarried mothers.[6] Psychological clinic, v. 18, p. 119-27, May-June 1929.

"Eighty-seven girls from a home for unmarried mothers were referred for mental tests. Of this selected group, 19 per cent were normal mentally, the others below normal. The median I.Q. was 76, and the mean age 18.37 years. Only 13 per cent were above 21 years of age. . . "—[S.s.a.]
Quoted from Social science abstracts, v. 2, no. 3, p. 475, March 1930.

193. MacCoy, W. Logan. Law of Pennsylvania relating to illegitimacy. Journal of American institute of criminal law and criminology, v. 7, p. 505-29, November 1916.

The law of Pennsylvania recognizes "common law marriage." An illegitimate child must not only be "conceived out of wedlock" but must not have been "subsequently legitimated," or adopted.

MacCoy, W. Logan. joint author see entry 181.

194. McEvoy, M. F. (A) Diocesan program for the care of unmarried mothers and their infants; [I] from the administrative viewpoint.[7] National conference of Catholic charities, Proceedings, 1931, p. 100-108.

"The program must be so formulated that mercy toward the offender may never be mistaken for approval of the offense. This is the very essence of the problem as it presents itself to the Catholic worker. For him birth out of wedlock must always bear the stigma of society's condemnation. . . The parish we reject at once because it is too small a unit—too small to bear the cost, too small to afford the secrecy which the occasion demands. The maternity home, the foundling asylum and the protectory

[6]This is apparently continued as W. E. McClure's Intelligence of unmarried mothers.

[7]See A. Madorah Donahue's (A) Diocesan program for the care of unmarried mothers and their infants; [II] from the case work viewpoint, which is the complement of McEvoy's study.

offer specialized services, invaluable in themselves, but none of which meet the full requirements." There "should be in each diocese one agent and only one charged with complete oversight and control of all Catholic work for the unmarried mother. Where there is a bureau of charities this of course should be the agent because it is ex officio the mouth-piece of the bishop . . . within the bureau the unmarried mother department belongs more naturally in the children's division rather than in the division of families or of health. . . There is an advantage, it is true, in having specially equipped agencies render particular services such as protective care, confinement care or hospitalization, but the program should be directed and controlled by the central bureau. . . I would say that no diocesan program is complete that fails to provide at least an isolated ward for the care of unmarried mothers and their children. Whether the bureau maintains this ward itself or draws upon the resources of a neighboring hospital, I believe it should control the intake." There is a discussion of financial support of the program and of other administrative aspects, such as health facilities in general, education of the public to understand and appreciate modern case work methods, and discountenancing marriage during the period of adjustment except in occasional instances. "There is a growing recognition of the importance of religion in unmarried mother programs which more and more tends to push the bureau to the forefront in every community effort in this field."

(A) Discussion by Katherine Griffith, p. 109-13.

195. McGregor, (Mrs.) J. B. Social problems related to illegitimacy; the children of unmarried parents. National conference of social work, Proceedings, 1924, p. 151-57.

Regarding "public opinion in Canada on the problem of illegitimacy as it has been expressed, first, by legislation, and second, by the treatment of mother and child." The plan "which most workers find most satisfactory is the boarding of the baby apart from the mother."

196. Magee, Edith D. Illegitimacy as a medical social problem; a study of 176 cases. Hospital social service, v. 25, p. 287-306, April 1932.

Study of 176 cases of illegitimate pregnancy, during a period of one year beginning April 1, 1930, both ward and dispensary. Of these, 117 were colored and 59 were white. Stress is laid on the important position which the hospital social service department occupies in spite of the limitations it faces, because of the opportunity for "initial contact with the patient at perhaps the most crucial period in her life."

197. Mangold, George B., Ph.D. Children born out of wedlock; a sociological study of illegitimacy, with particular reference to the United States. 209 p. Columbia [Missouri], University of Missouri press, June 1921.

Illegitimacy in the United States is less common than in most of Europe. Our knowledge is dependent upon the development of a system of birth registration. Causes and present methods of treatment, care of unmarried mothers by commercial agencies, and means of prevention of illegitimacy are discussed. Tables show the age of the unmarried mother.
Bibliography, p. 196-201.

198. ———— Illegitimacy in St. Louis. Annals of American academy of political and social science, v. 125, p. 63-67, May 1926.

The annual number of illegitimate births in St. Louis is about 600. This is an understatement of the facts, as many births are never recorded. There is a large Negro illegitimacy. Tables show the age of the mother, the number of children born to each mother, and the occupation of the mother. The Missouri law is unsatisfactory and the differing policies of agencies cause difficulty.

199. ———— Problems of child welfare. 602 p. New York, Macmillan, 1924.

Pages 56, 408, 488-89, 507-11 deal with the mortality rate among infants born out of wedlock, the relation between delinquency and abnormal home conditions of children of unmarried mothers, studies of unmarried mothers in St. Louis and Baltimore and causes of illegitimacy, present care and recommendations, state supervision, registration of births, responsibility of the father, supervision of maternity homes, keeping the mother and child together.

200. ———— Unlawful motherhood. Forum, v. 53, p. 335-43, March 1915.

A statistical survey giving the extent of illegitimate births in certain states and cities of the United States, the age of the mother, and occupation (domestic service and factory employment). The reform suggested is to "make illegitimacy costly and burdensome and it will decline."

201. Mangold, George B., Ph.D., and Lou R. Essex. Illegitimate births in St. Louis. (Reports of social investigation, no. 4.) 27 p. St. Louis, St. Louis school of social economy, 1914.

Enforcement of the law for birth registration is discussed. Certificates are often inadequately filled out. Tables show the number of illegitimate births in St. Louis, the residence of the mother, her age, occupation, and previous illegitimate births, and the disposition of the child. Missouri has no "bastardy" law (right to establish paternity).

Mann, Delbert M. joint author see entry 268.

202. March, Jessie. Difficult daughters (and some of their problems). 47 p. London, John Bale, 1929.

A presentation of "rescue work."
Pages 5-11. (The) Unmarried mother. A general discussion of illegitimacy.

203. Massachusetts, Special commission on the laws relative to children. Report of the Commission established to investigate the laws relative to dependent, delinquent and neglected children, and children otherwise requiring special care, January 1931. 274 p. Boston, The State, 1931.

Pages 75-80 (Chapter 11). Adoption. "No less than nineteen States now require that before an adoption is allowed an investigation shall be made, and the court . . . shall be in full possession of all the facts regarding the child and his antecedents, and the adopting parents and their ability to provide a suitable home for him." Eleven states make "provision for a period of trial residence before the adoption petition is granted . . . the Commission believes that a period of trial residence is eminently desirable for the welfare of all concerned. . ." The Commission recommends that "adoption advertisements be permitted only when approved by the State Department of Public Welfare," as this will "undoubtedly enable many distressed mothers to keep their children through utilization of the community's social resources, and will prevent many unsuitable persons from obtaining adoption of children. . . Nor will it make harder or more difficult the lot of the unmarried mother. Rather it will serve to protect. . ."
Pages 81-87 (Chapter 12). Illegitimacy. "There is a growing recognition that the illegitimate child from the mere fact of his disadvantages, is entitled to special protection by the State, and that the more humane attitude of today demands the removal of every stigma so far as possible. . . The word 'bastardy' has fallen into such disfavor and is so objectionable that it is proposed to substitute the word 'illegitimacy' in the statutes. . ." Certain states have for years required that births of illegitimate children occurring in maternity hospitals should be promptly reported to the Department of Public Welfare. The Commission recommends that a similar safeguard be adopted in Massachusetts.
Pages 134-37 (Appendix D). Adoption statistics and charts. Adoption of illegitimate infants under one year in Massachusetts during 1928 were

80.7 percent of total adoptions under one year, and in 1929, they were 82.8 percent.

Pages 138-39 (Appendix E). Advertising for adoption. Results of the efforts of the [Boston] Council of social agencies to get in touch with those advertising to see whether they could be of service. "Contact could be established in only 37 of the 63 cases. Two children were accepted for care by the agency making the contact, 5 advertisers refused assistance, 4 children were already placed, 6 cases are pending, and so were transferred to other agencies in the hope" that a hasty adoption could be avoided.

Pages 140-48 (Appendix F). Illegitimacy in Massachusetts. "The general infant mortality rate has fallen from 105 per thousand live births in the year 1914 to 62 per thousand live births in 1929, whereas the mortality rate for illegitimate children has fallen from 290 per thousand illegitimate live births in 1914 to 130. . . Of the illegitimate live births during 1929, 1,431, or 75.7 per cent, took place in hospitals and maternity homes, and 457, or 24.3 per cent, of the illegitimate live births took place in residences. . . Of the 6,405 children under supervision and care of the Division of Child Guardianship, Massachusetts Department of Public Welfare, August 1, 1930, 1,929 children were of illegitimate birth or 30 per cent of the total . . . 'under three years of age,' 307, or 62 per cent, were of illegitimate birth."

Pages 149-55 (Appendix G). A brief study of illegitimate children born in Boston during the year 1928 and coming to the attention of twenty-three Boston public and private agencies. "As Massachusetts makes no mention of legitimacy or illegitimacy on the birth record, a count was made of those records where the name of the father was omitted. It was found that in 1928 there were 843 such records, and it was subsequently shown that 108 additional births known to the agencies to be illegitimate had the name of a father . . . also that twelve other births reported by the agencies could not be identified . . . the figures given above indicate that at least 968 of this number were illegitimate, or a rate of 5.15 per cent," instead of only 843, or a rate of 4.5 percent. "Thirty-two cases were known to agencies, and some 402 cases were known to maternity homes and hospitals before the birth of the babies. After the birth of the children, 672 cases were known to maternity homes and hospitals, and about 200 to other social agencies. Approximately 260 of the 782 cases in the group studied were reported by more than one agency, although not always as having received any degree of service. . ." Of the 782, "only 37 were reported as colored. Three of these children were recorded as 'white' on their respective birth certificates." There were 350 who were 21 years or under, and 418 over 21 years, the age not given for 14 mothers. "It was learned from the birth records that over one-half of the mothers . . . were non-residents of Boston, including forty-five who were non-residents of the State. . ." County of birth and marital status of the mothers are given. There were a "considerable number of second illegitimate pregnancies. . ." The figures given are:

First pregnancy 663
Second pregnancy 81
Third pregnancy 18
Fourth pregnancy 14
Not reported 6

782

"Disposition of the child, including adoption, is analyzed. Of the 968 births of illegitimate children in 1928, 876 occurred in maternity homes and hospitals, and 92 took place in private residences." A plea for increased provision for state care is made.

Pages 224-27 (Appendices XXXVI-XXXVIII). Drafts of bills submitted. Adoptions.

Pages 228-45 (Appendices XXXIX-XLVI). Drafts of bills submitted. Illegitimacy.

204. Massicotte, E. Z. How illegitimate children were cared for. (Comment on disposait des enfants du roi.) Bulletin de recherche historique, v. 37, p. 49-54, January 1931.

"An investigation into the methods of caring for illegitimate children during the French regime in Canada."—[S.s.a.]
Quoted from Social science abstracts, v. 4, no. 6, p. 888, June 1932.

205. Mathews, Catherine. Case work with unmarried mothers. Family, v. 13, p. 185-90, October 1932.

"As organized methods of care, we have first the foundling home, the maternity home, and then social case work." We must consider such questions as: Is it "best for the child to go with its mother? Is it best for the child to be taken away from the mother?" We can argue either way. "Only about 35 per cent of the children are adoptable." About 17 percent are placed by the agency described [unnamed] and about 60 percent are kept with their mothers. Fifty-two percent of the girls are under twenty. Among the girls cared for are school girls, domestics, and waitresses.

206. Mattingly, Mabel H. (The) Unmarried mother and her child; a fact finding study of fifty-three cases of unmarried mothers who kept their children. 80 p. Cleveland, Western reserve university, School of applied social sciences, 1928.

A study of fifty-three cases of unmarried mothers who kept their children. Tables show the age and sex of the children; the age of the mother compared with the age of the father.

207. Maxfield, F.N. (The) Social treatment of unmarried mothers. Psychological clinic, v. 9, p. 10-17, 1915.

A discussion of "some of the working principles that have been used in the Social Service Department of the University Hospital [Pennsylvania] . . ." Based on an analysis of the "ninety unmarried mothers and women illegitimately pregnant," referred from the "Woman's and Obstetrical Dispensaries to one worker in the Social Service Department" during the "period from January, 1912 to August, 1915."

208. Menken, A. D. (A) Social aspect of the unmarried mother. Journal of delinquency, v. 7, p. 99-103, March 1922.

A study of 306 women "(first offenders) who were convicted of prostitution and placed on probation in The Women's Court, Borough of Manhattan, New York City." The period 1914-19 was covered. Only "19 of the women were pregnant and only three of these 19, as unmarried mothers, proved to be unfit to retain their children." The desirability of keeping mother and child together is stressed.

Abstracted in Journal of social hygiene, v. 8, p. 350-51, April 1922.

209. Minnesota, State board of control. Standards for maternity hospitals of Minnesota adopted by the Board, March 5, 1928. 39 p. St. Paul, The Board.

As a result of the survey of the "specialized maternity hospitals of Minnesota" made by the [United States] Children's bureau in 1923 [United States, Children's bureau, Publication no. 167], the Conference on maternity hospital standards was organized in Minnesota and on January 4, 1928, presented to the State board of control "standards adopted by the organization with the hope that these standards may meet the approval of the Board. . ." A "large portion of the standards pertain only to the specialized maternity hospital" which limits its intake chiefly to unmarried mothers.

"Form S.B.C. 118 C is a combined social and medical record and is for maternity homes or hospitals caring for unmarried mothers and is to be filled out when the mother is discharged from the maternity home. This should be sent to the Children's Bureau."

Pages 32-35. Summary of state laws covering hospitals receiving maternity patients and the regulations of the Board of control. "The presence of an unmarried woman in any maternity hospital for purposes of confinement shall be reported to the Board of Control by the licensee of the hospital as soon as the facts are known to such licensee." Because of the "very large death rate among children born out of wedlock, the State Board of Control has declared:

"1. That it is the policy of the Board of Control that such illegitimate children shall be nursed by their mothers for a period of at least three months and as long thereafter as is advisable;

"2.   That it is agreed between certain properly equipped and specialized maternity hospitals in the state of Minnesota and the State Board of Control that such hospitals will receive women for their full term of maternity care and afford the mother and child full protection as well as aid and assistance at a reasonable cost; and

"3.   That it is the policy of such specialized maternity hospital and the State Board of Control that the consent of the mother to remain in such hospital for a period of at least three months after the birth of her baby, should be obtained before her admission thereto."

210.   Minnesota, State board of control, Children's bureau.   Biennial report of the Bureau, period ended June 30, 1930. 36 p. St. Paul, The Board.

Pages 9-11. (The) Child born out of wedlock. "The care and protection of the child born out of wedlock is a special responsibility of the Board of Control. All known cases are registered in the Children's Bureau. . . It is not possible to make an extended report on the 2,726 cases of this biennial, as in some cases the babies are not born, and for large numbers no plans have been made. . . It is interesting to note from the total of counties . . . that in many counties approximately the same number of unmarried mothers are found in the second biennium as in the first. Is this an index of the social condition of the county?" A study of "13,419 cases reported to the Board of Control from January 1, 1918, to December 31, 1927, is being made by the Department of Sociology and the Institute of Child Welfare of the State University. . . The University is attempting to measure the influence the Minnesota program has had on the future of the child born out of wedlock. . . As the study will include about 13,000 children who are now from three to 12 years of age, it is the most comprehensive study of its kind ever undertaken in the United States, and should yield information of value to all child-caring programs."
Pages 31-34. Tabular summary of unmarried mothers for this biennium is given a basis somewhat similar to that of the previous biennium, though it is less extensive as to topics covered (not including analysis of the children born). The total unmarried mothers reported for each biennium beginning with the period ending June 30, 1920 are given.

211.   ——— Biennial report of the Bureau, period ended June 30, 1932. 28 p. St. Paul, The Board.

Pages 8-10. (The) Child born out of wedlock. A marked increase in number of unmarried mothers registered in the Bureau in this biennial [3,171, as compared with 2,726 in the biennial immediately preceding], in view of a "decrease in the two biennials following 1926," raises a question as to the pertinent factors, which apparently are:

"1. As a result of the depression:

Idleness

Lack of job for man who puts off marriage

Lack of funds that has prevented an abortion or the mother from leaving the state

"2. Changes in industrial or commercial life:

Increasing number of construction crews of highways, telephone and electric lines, residing temporarily in a town aloof from home ties

Migratory men, as farmhands and wandering agents."

Data are given regarding the children: sex, "nationality and race," religion, paternity established, disposition of baby. The "economic depression has noticeably affected collections provided by court orders."

The study referred to in the Biennial report of the Bureau, period ended June 30, 1930, as being made by the Department of sociology and the Institute of child welfare of the University of Minnesota, "has not been completed. However, two major articles have been written and accepted for publication under the titles of 'Some Characteristics of Adoptive Parents,' to be published in the American Journal of Sociology, and 'A Study of Certain Selective Factors Influencing Prediction of the Mental Status of Adoptive Children,' to be published in the Journal of Genetic Psychology. The Institute of Child Welfare hopes to complete next year a monograph entitled 'Comparative Analysis of Family Background of Illegitimate Children According to Placement.' "

Pages 24-25. Tabular summary of work of Children's bureau [illegitimacy].

212. —— Report of the Director of the Bureau, biennial period ended June 30, 1928. 28 p. St. Paul, The Board.

"Because of its volume the report of the work of the Children's Bureau is herewith presented in statistical form. During the biennial the modern method of compiling statistics by punch machine was adopted. . ."

Pages 10-12. Compiled data concerning children born out of wedlock July 1, 1926, to June 30, 1928. There were 2,808 girls reported pregnant, with 2,398 "confined"; and 410 not "confined"; 2,699 fathers reported, and 109 fathers unknown ("girls promiscuous"); 2,423 babies born (25 twins). "Of the 2,808 cases reported, 331 were not born at close of biennium." For both mother and father, figures are given covering age, religion, nationality, illegitimacy of birth [42 of the girls illegitimate], marital status, education, occupation before birth of child, parents of other children [260 girls were mothers of other illegitimate children and 59 men were similarly situated]. For mother only, there are figures covering age at leaving school, reason for leaving school, reported cause of sex delinquency, occupation after confinement, paternity of first illegitimate child of girl.

For the family of the mother and father are cited occupation of parents, home history of parents, children in parents' family, home environment. Regarding the baby[8] are given: sex, disposition, "where born." Legal action is summarized under: to determine paternity, court order for support, to whom paid, criminal action, verdict. Summary of number of cases where paternity was established in 2,913 cases reported July 1, 1924, to June 30, 1926, is given. Reports by counties of unmarried mother cases are given, indicating for each county the numbers of the mothers and of the fathers with that legal address, and the number of cases reported.

213. Mix, Ruth R. Canada's unmarried mother. Welfare magazine [Illinois], v. 19, p. 475-78, April 1928.

Ontario, Canada has passed two acts, namely, the act for the protection of children of unmarried parents and the adoption act. Toronto has become a haven to which the unmarried mother flees. Here the unmarried mother and child are placed in foster boarding homes. The cost of this is about two-thirds less than institutional care would be.

214. Mohr, N. Emily. (A) Study of illegitimacy in Ontario; made under the direction of the Social service council of Ontario. 32 p. Toronto [Canada], Social service council of Ontario, 1921.

In 1920 visits were made to "as many centrally located municipalities as possible, covering those having facilities for the care of the unmarried mother and her child, those providing only such facilities as were available for any maternity case, and those having no facilities for care outside the girl's own home. As a study of illegitimacy was being conducted along casework lines in Toronto by the Neighborhood Workers' Association of that city, this largest centre of the Province was not touched [Neighborhood workers' association (Toronto), Illegitimacy in Toronto]." The basis was "children born of unmarried parents within the year immediately preceding the enquiry," some history being secured in regard to 374 children. Twenty tables and text cover the following subjects: extent of illegitimacy; education, age, occupation, mental health, and residence (urban or rural) of the mother; follow-up of the child; institutional delivery.

215. Morgan, Eugene. Safeguarding the rights of illegitimate children. National humane review, v. 7, p. 66-67, April 1919.

The author advocates the following imposition of penalty upon the

[8]Total of 2,477 babies is given ("does not include second twin"), apparently including births after the biennium.

father; reporting of the birth of the child within fifteen days; assigning as the legal name of the child that of his putative father; right of the child to inherit; right of schooling, care, and support by the father.

216. Morquio, Luis. Report on the tour, or turn-box. (Consultas sabre el Torno.) Boletin del instituto internacional Americano de protección a la infancia, v. 4, p. 270-80, October 1930.

"With few exceptions, all child protection is based on the protection of the mother through the direct or indirect and longest possible preservation of the mother-child relation. This is not only the most humane practice but also the surest guarantee of the child's life and health."— [S.s.a.]

Quoted from Social science abstracts, v. 3, no. 7, p. 1060, July 1931.

217. Morris, E. Sydney, M.D. (An) Essay on the causes and prevention of maternal mortality and morbidity. Medical journal of Australia, p. 301-45, September 12, 1925.

Page 313. The "statistics of the Commonwealth [Australia] show that extending . . . from 1909 to 1920 the combined number of illegitimate births and births occurring under nine months after marriage comprise over 54% of the total first births."

Bibliography on maternal mortality, p. 338-40, + 345.

218. Moutet, Anna, M.D. Illegitimacy in France. International conference of women physicians, Proceedings, 1919, p. 21-33.

Published by [New York City] Woman's press, 1920. A discussion of the legal situation of the illegitimate child in France.

219. Mudgett, Mildred D. For unmarried mothers in Europe. Survey, v. 57, p. 809-11, March 15, 1927.

"In Teutonic countries the protection of illegitimate children has been accepted as the responsibility of the state; in Latin countries the care of unmarried mothers and their babies is almost entirely under private auspices." The article describes the work being done in Germany, Austria, Czecho-Slovakia, Switzerland, and Holland. This shows a contrast with the attitude toward illegitimacy in Italy and France. "European child welfare work differs from ours in general in that more of it is supported by public funds than is the case here."

220. —— Marriages of unmarried mothers. Journal of social hygiene, v. 9, p. 193-99, April 1923.

A study of 133 unmarried mothers. In 79 cases the girl married the father of her child, in 54 cases other men. The ages of these girls were from 18 to 30, and their chief occupation was housework. The men were usually poorly educated and employed at low wages. Twenty-six of the marriages were apparently successful, and 45 parents or nearly 75 percent kept the child.

221. ———— (The) Social effect upon the family of forced marriage. Family, v. 5, p. 16-22, 1924.

By social effect is meant the effect on the stability of the family. The article raises the question of the permanency of forced marriages. A study of 134 cases gives the percentage of such families breaking down. The proportion of men who deserted their families after a forced marriage, over a period of 15 years, was 57 percent. The conclusion reached is that the forced marriage is not a good solution to the problem of illegitimacy.

222. Murphy, Ida Garrett. (The) Unmarried mother at work. Survey, v. 4) , p. 641-42, February 28, 1920.

An employer of an unmarried mother with her child shows the difficulty which confronts the unmarried mother in domestic service.

223. Murphy, J. Prentice. Illegitimacy and feeblemindedness. Mental hygiene, v. 1, p. 591-97, 1917.

Of the approximately eight hundred illegitimate births recorded by the Bureau of vital statistics in Boston "last year [1915]," about "one half were unknown to all the public and private charity organizations in the city. These unknown mothers, representing undoubtedly every condition, made their own plans which involved in most instances the placing of the babies apart from the mothers, frequently for adoption, and often under conditions which would not bear the searching light of careful inquiry." Problems of the feebleminded unmarried mother are discussed.

224. ———— Mothers and—mothers. Survey, v. 42, p. 171-76, May 3, 1919.

Should case work with the unmarried mother differ from case work with the married mother? "To make a distinction is, to say the least, professionally unsound . . . also undemocratic." Case work means individual treatment for each patient, which should be the same for unmarried and married.

225. ———— (The) Unmarried mother and her child. Ohio bulletin of charities and correction [Ohio board of state charities], v. 24, p. 50-54, June 1918.

The author decries the dual standard for the sexes, also the "very improper emphasis on the religious aspect" in maternity homes. Age and nativity of the unmarried mother have not been accurately known. "Because of privacy" some four hundred of the approximately nine hundred unmarried mothers, registered in one year [two years ago], had not availed themselves of the services of the "excellent organizations in Boston." There should be no hard and fast rule about keeping mother and child together. In general, breast-feeding is desirable. Marriage of the partners is not always desirable. "The Federal Bureau found that the question of responsibility rests very evenly between the father and the mother." Not every case should be prosecuted. The author advocates the state's entrance into inspection of maternity homes and children's organizations. The best maternity home should be small. Some of the most "promising mothers" have had more than one illegitimate child.

226. ——— What can be accomplished through good social work in the field of illegitimacy? Annals of American academy of political and social science, v. 98, p. 129-35, November 1921.

Higher standards in case work for unmarried parents, less hurried adoptions, adequate birth registration, elimination of the profiteering agency, interstate standards, health safeguards, control of feebleminded girls, social work in the schools, study of conditions in industry (as the relation between fatigue and sex delinquencies), sex education and improved legal procedure are suggested and discussed.

227. Myers, Earl D. (The) Illegitimate child in Germany. Social service review, v. 5, p. 258-75, June 1931.

Summary of legislation throughout Germany.
Abstracted in Child development abstracts and bibliography, v. 6, no. 1, p. 10, entry 39, February 1932 (from Social science abstracts).
Also abstracted in Social science abstracts, v. 3, no. 11, p. 1650, November 1931.

228. National [English] association for the prevention of infant mortality, English-speaking conference on maternity and child welfare.[9] Report of the proceedings of the third, 1924. 240 p.

Pages 46-55. Comparative legislation dealing with illegitimacy, by Letitia Fairfield, M.D.
The law of illegitimacy in England is associated very much with the English law of real property. The child has no right to inherit from either parent. In France, feeling has opposed any attempt to establish paternity and this can now be done only by strict evidence. In the new German

[9] Prior to 1926 entitled "English-speaking conference on infant welfare."

code, the child is made the legitimate child of its mother. In Norway, the equal responsibility of the mother and father is recognized by law. England is the only country where legitimation by subsequent marriage does not exist. Discussion of methods of legitimation closes the article.

229. ———— Report of the proceedings of the fourth, 1926. 210 p.

Pages 131-32. Homes for unmarried mothers and their babies, by Mrs. Leigh-Smith. An outline of the "attitude of the Catholic Church in England."

230. ———— Report of the proceedings of the fifth, 1929. 181 p.

Pages 33-36. Special difficulties in regard to illegitimate children, by Lady Gowers. The author, representing the National council for the unmarried mother and her child, states: "Day nurseries must play an important part in the care of the illegitimate, as well as the legitimate, child. . . Foster Homes for children up to five have proved their inestimable value as a sound and practical way of helping in this problem."
Pages 128-31. Venereal diseases in connection with maternity and child welfare, by Nora I. Wattie, M.D.
Discussion on p. 132: "Miss S. Musson said that in the work of the National Council for the Unmarried Mother and her Child, one part was making arrangements for the expectant mother during confinement. A difficulty about mothers suffering from venereal disease was that only a certain number of hospitals took a Wassermann test when the confinement was booked. It had been suggested that patients would resent such a test, but the Council's experience was that no objection was raised when the thing was done as a matter of routine. If all maternity departments would adopt such a course, her Council felt that a number of cases which at present escaped observation in the early stages, would be prevented from slipping through."

231. National [English] association for the prevention of infant mortality, National [English] conference on maternity and child welfare.[10] Report of the proceedings, 1919. 222 p.

Pages 8-19. Causes of ante-natal, intra-natal and neo-natal mortality, by Amand Routh, M.D. "Statistics point to at least a doubled stillbirth rate in unmarried mothers, and there is strong evidence that, including criminal abortion, the rate of miscarriages is also about double in illegitimate cases. The infantile death-rate of the children of both married and unmarried mothers is also known to be in the same proportions, being respectively 96 and 207 per 1,000 births in 1917, and the infantile deaths during the first month of life in the same year were respectively 37 and 72."

Pages 135-40. (The) Destitute unmarried mother, by Lady Nott-Bowers. A plea for some other choice of life for the mother than between the "Streets and the Workhouse."

Pages 140-45. (The) Illegitimate child, by the Bishop of Kensington. "The community must accept the responsibility for the standards of thinking which it adopts and encourages. . ."

Pages 145-49. (The) Legal position of the unmarried mother, by Robert Parr. Discussion of a "suggested Bill which it is hoped to introduce into Parliament. . ."

Discussion (of the three preceding papers), p. 149-66.

Pages 167-76. Parental responsibilities in relation to illegitimacy, by Mrs. Gotto. Figures from Australia are quoted showing a "decrease during the last ten years of the percentage of unmarried motherhood," and removing the "fear that in giving 'privileges' to unmarried motherhood we shall be encouraging illegitimacy." Mental defect of the mother in relation to illegitimacy is discussed, with a plea that social and legal steps be taken to standardize maternity and infant care in all areas, regardless of legitimacy.

Pages 176-83. Criminal abortion and abortifacients, with special reference to abortions and abortifacients, by William F. J. Whitley, M.D. That the "general reduction of the illegitimate birth rate" is not "an indication of a more favourable standard of morality" is the opinion of the author, who adds that the "general birth rate is decreasing, and this too from the same cause, namely, the use of contraceptives, and unfortunately, criminal abortion and contraceptives are closely allied." He suggests the "compulsory notification of every abortion and miscarriage to the local Sanitary Authority" and the "supression of all advertisements dealing with sexual weaknesses and complaints."

Pages 184-85. (The) Unwanted babe, by Adelaide Cox. A "few facts gathered" in the author's "experience as a Salvation Army officer" are cited. "We of the Salvation Army strongly advocate that mother and child should be helped together."

232. ——— Report of the proceedings, 1927. 218 p.

Pages 24-32. (The) Problem of the expectant unmarried mother, by A. F. G. Spinks, M.D. and others. A "debate."

Pages 24-27, by A. F. G. Spinks, M.D. Secrecy is "such an essential element of illegitimate pregnancy that voluntary notification" is "never likely to become a practical proposition. If every voluntary body however, made it a rule to appoint the Maternity and Child Welfare Medical Officer, or, if preferred, the Medical Officer of Health, as actual or nominal medical officer to their Homes for Unmarried Mothers, then the pregnancy of every

10Prior to 1930, entitled National [English] conference on maternity and infant welfare [1919, entitled National English conference on infant welfare].

woman entering such Homes would be notified automatically, and the vast machinery of public health could be applied."

Pages 27-29, by Miss Ronaldson. The author, a lady almoner, outlines the work of the almoner for the unmarried mother, in coöperating with agencies in the community, especially in relation to venereal diseases.

Pages 29-30, by Honorable Gerard Wallop. A discussion of the methods of poor law guardians in dealing with illegitimacy.

Pages 30-31, by Mrs. Young. A discussion of the work of the Bristol woman's aid association.

Pages 31-32, by Mrs. H. A. L. Fisher, of the National council for the unmarried mother and her child. "While something" has "been done towards helping the father to share in the upbringing of his child, very little" has "so far been done towards enabling the father to share with the mother responsibility for the health of the child before birth. The Council had been told by responsible people that the idea that the father should help the mother before the birth of the child was a new principle in law; apparently a principle that was not looked upon with favour in all quarters."

233. ———— Report of the proceedings, 1928. 180 p.

Pages 112-20. Fair play for the unmarried mother, by Robert A. Lyster, M.D. An "extension of sickness benefit during pregnancy," if made, "would result in substantial improvement and it would in practice, amount to an early notification of pregnancy."

234. ———— Report of proceedings, 1930. 184 p.

Pages 142-49. (The) Care of the illegitimate child in rural areas, by Patience Boggallay. Problems relating to illegitimacy in rural areas are discussed, together with a comprehensive program for meeting them. Among the problems surveyed are: high infant and maternal mortality, infrequency of prenatal care, failure to examine and treat for venereal diseases, separation of mother and child.

235. National conference of commissioners on uniform state laws. Uniform illegitimacy act. 14 p. [Chicago], The Conference, 1922.

Drafted by the National conference of commissioners on uniform state laws, "composed of Commissioners appointed by Legislative or Executive authority from the States, the District of Columbia, the territory of Alaska, and the Island Possessions of the United States. The Commissioners are chosen from the legal profession, and serve without compensation. . . When finally approved by the Conference, the Uniform Acts are recommended for general adoption through the jurisdiction of the United States," and represent the "experience and the judgment of a select body of lawyers chosen from every part of the United States." A resolution adopted by the Conference August 7, 1922, recommended the submission of this act to the legislatures of all the states for enactment at their next session.

Pages 5-6. Contents of Uniform illegitimacy act.

Pages 7-14. Text of Uniform illegitimacy act.

236. National conference of commissioners on uniform state laws, Committee on status and protection of illegitimate children. Report of the Committee to the thirty-first annual meeting of the National conference . . . including a first tentative draft of a uniform illegitimacy act. 18 p. New York, The Committee, 1921(?).

"1. In 1915 the Federal Children's bureau undertook an inquiry into illegitimacy as a child welfare problem. As part of this inquiry, it caused a study to be made of the illegitimacy laws of the United States, the result of which was published as Bureau Publication No. 42 in 1919.

"2. In 1920 conferences were held under the auspices of the Bureau in New York and Chicago, to consider standards of legislation and protection. These conferences were preceded by local deliberations on the part of about twenty groups representing different cities, thirteen of which reported their conclusions to the New York and Chicago Conferences . . . a report of these conferences was published as Bureau Publication No. 77.

"3. Following upon the two conferences the Children's Bureau appointed a committee to draft a memorandum embodying the principles agreed upon, and this committee adopted a syllabus of propositions to serve as a basis of a program for illegitimacy legislation which is printed in Bureau Publication No. 77, p. 20-23.

"4. It was deemed extremely desirable that these propositions should receive statutory expression . . . and the most effective way of accomplishing this appeared to be the framing of a uniform law by the National Conference.

"8. The Committee [on status and protection of illegitimate children] has deemed it wisest to prepare and present the draft of a law covering the entire subject. . .

"9. In preparing the draft, the Committee has endeavored to frame a measure which would have a prospect of being not only approved by this Conference, but also by the legislatures of the different states. In consequence it was unable to accept all the propositions endorsed by the Committee of the Children's Bureau. In particular the draft does not provide that the child shall have the right to inherit from the father even though not legitimated. . . Two other recommendations have not been incorporated . . . one, that an authorized public authority shall have the right to bring proceedings to establish paternity . . . the other, that a decree establishing paternity shall be accompanied by directions to make corresponding entries in the birth records; the subject of birth registration having been entirely omitted.

"10. The draft law submitted seeks to retain those provisions which have approved themselves by the experience of most of the states; particularly the coercive features of the support proceedings have been preserved and strengthened. The changes prepared seek to advance the interest of the child . . . by recognizing every possible benefit not offered by a strong adverse interest; by strengthening the support obligation which at present is lamentably inadequate; and by aiding enforcement by new remedial and coercive measures and by removing jurisdictional limitations which now unduly favor evasion of liability."

237. National [English] council for the unmarried mother and her child. National [English] council for the unmarried mother and her child (and for the widowed or deserted mother in need). 16 p. London, The Council, 1918.

The aims of the Council: "To obtain reform of the existing Bastardy acts and Affiliation orders act; to secure the provision of adequate accommodation to meet the varying needs of mothers and babies throughout the country; such provision to include hostels with Day Nurseries attached, where the mother can live with her child for at least two years, whilst continuing her ordinary work." Statistics of England and Wales show that the rate of infant mortality is excessive on the first day of life.

238. ——— (The) Unmarried mother and her child in England and Wales. 22 p. London, Welbecson press, 1924.

The Council, whose objects are legislative and propagandist, presents the subject under the following captions: (The) Illegitimate child and its mother; (The) State and the illegitimate child; Residential accommodation; Arrangements for mother and child who are not admitted to a residential institution; Abnormal cases.

239. National council of women of Great Britain and Ireland. (A) Compendium of the Norwegian laws concerning illegitimate children, by Mrs. Edwin Gray. 4 p. London, The Council, 1922.

Establishment of paternity, maintenance, legal status of the child, and dissolution of marriage, as provided for in three laws which became effective January 1, 1916.

240. Neighborhood workers' association [Toronto]. Illegitimacy in Toronto. 16 p. Toronto, The Association, 1920.

A survey of illegitimacy in Toronto (period covered not given) comprising 232 cases. Data on the mother include residence, age, previous illegitimacy, mentality, physical condition, education, religion, occupation, marital status, and nationality. Data on the child include birthplace, physical condition, and disposition of the child. On the father there are the same data (less complete) as on the mother, except that they do not include previous illegitimacy, physical condition, or education. Rural *vs.* urban illegitimacy rates are discussed.

The Illegitimate children's act of the Province of Ontario is quoted and discussed.

241. Neville-Rolfe, S. (The) Social aspect of the illegitimacy problem. Contemporary review, v. 125, p. 358-64, March 1924.

Pertains to England. We are conscious today of the responsibility of the people for the welfare of the next generation and recognize the equality of men and women as, for example, in our divorce laws. The article discusses the new Legitimation bill before Parliament (1924) providing for legitimation of children born out of wedlock by subsequent marriage of the parents.

242. Newman, Herman. (The) Unmarried mother of border-line mentality. National conference of charities and correction, Proceedings, 1915, p. 117-21.

Seventeen private agencies in five years worked on this case. There is no adequate state law for dealing with feebleminded adults in Illinois.

243. New York academy of medicine, Committee on public health relations. Maternal mortality in New York City; a study of all puerperal deaths 1930-1932. 290 p. New York, Commonwealth fund, 1933.

A study directed by Ransom S. Hooker, M.D. Every death was "investigated by personal interview, often by several interviews, with those connected with the case. The evidence was analyzed and was carefully studied by experienced obstetricians." It was decided to pattern the study "somewhat on the lines of the similar survey being made by Dr. Fred L. Adair and his associates, with the cooperation of the Children's Bureau at Washington—the so-called 'Fifteen States Study'—and to adopt their questionnaire, in order that satisfactory comparisons might be made . . . the committee was able to enlist the cooperation of the Department of Health in obtaining weekly reports on the deaths from puerperal causes occurring during the previous week, thus making it possible to obtain the material for the questionnaires while the cases were still fresh in the minds of the attendants." With respect to social problems, their "magnitude is so overwhelming and their ramifications so extensive that separate and intensive study would be required to give a thorough and satisfactory representation of the situation in those aspects." Comparisons with other areas may be very important "but they must be . . . based upon entirely similar situations. . . In New York City the puerperal death rate is calculated per 1,000 live births . . ." Variations in the general maternal mortality rate and in the septicaemia rate, from those of the Department of health, are explained.

Pages 52-58. Abortion. "Any consideration of the subject of abortion is necessarily a most inaccurate and unsatisfactory one. . . The difficulties surrounding the study and evaluation of abortion are, in many instances, those surrounding criminal activity. . . Willfully false reporting is the main source of error . . . such cases, of course, do not appear in our figures, as they cannot be classified as puerperal deaths but are included in the general rates. Nor have proven criminal abortions been included in our figures. . . The deaths following abortion represented 15.5 per cent of all the deaths among the women legitimately pregnant and 44.9 per cent of the deaths among those illegitimately pregnant. This is a reliable figure, since it is based not on the report on the death certificate but on information obtained by investigations. A figure derived from the death certificates would be smaller than the actual total, since the attendant frequently falsified this item under pressure from the family."

Pages 58-62. Ectopic gestation. "One hundred and four of the 120 cases were legitimate pregnancies and 16 were illegitimate."

Pages 72-89. Puerperal septicaemia. "It is not at all unexpected to find a great disparity evident between the death rates from septicaemia following legitimate and illegitimate births—1.42 and 4.27 (Table 31). . . The difference is the same when the deaths from sepsis are divided with reference to caesarean operations. The frequency with which women who are illegitimately pregnant enter hospitals late in labor after a totally unsupervised pregnancy no doubt contributes to this result."

Literature cited, p. 273-75.

244. New York [State], Commission to examine laws relating to child welfare. Second report of the New York State Commission to examine laws relating to child welfare. 2 v. 460 p. Albany, J. B. Lyon, 1923.

Pages 5-110 (Part I). Legislation recommended in regard to: boards of child welfare; "binding out" of children; county children's court act; New York City children's court law; placing out and boarding out; adoption.

Pages 111-460 (Part II). Manual of child welfare laws.

Pages 403-23 (Chapter 14). Illegitimacy. This chapter deals with: "bastardy" proceedings; criminal code; support of "bastards"; poor law; prosecution and jurisdiction of certain courts.

245. New York [State], State charities aid association. How foster children turn out. (Publication no. 165.) 239 p. New York, The Association, 1924.

Foreword by Homer Folks.

"A study of the State charities aid association, made under the direction of Sophie Van Senden Theis. . . There are available but few carefully collected data regarding the success or failure in adult life of foster children." After a quarter of a century of child placing by the Association, "there were 910 children who had passed the formative stage and were mature enough to give some indication of their development." The agency's records of those children, supplemented by "personal interviews with the children themselves, the foster parents and such other persons as might be advisable," were studied. "There were recorded as legitimate 529, or 76.3%; illegitimate 101, or 14.6%, and unknown 63, or 9.1%." Many aspects of foster care are presented, together with recommendations for further studies; there is not much space, however, devoted to illegitimacy in particular. There are 217 "foundlings" to the special consideration of whom a chapter is devoted.

246. Nims, Elinor. (The) Illinois adoption law and its administration. (Social service monograph no. 2.) 127 p. Chicago, University of Chicago press, c1928.

Pages vii-ix. Editor's preface. A study attempting to "set out the situation in Illinois with reference to the use of adoption procedure authorized under the statutes of the state. . . The absence of the social worker in so many of the cases in which children born out of wedlock are given in adoption suggests . . . a feature of the act that should probably be radically amended."

Parliament's First report of the Child adoption committee, 1925, is cited: " '. . . it is desirable that there should be some safeguard against the use of a legal system of adoption as an instrument by which advantage may be taken of the mother's situation to compel her to make a surrender of her child final in character, though she may herself, if a free agent, desire nothing more than a temporary provision for it. Further, there are many who hold that a system of adoption, so far as it tends to encourage or increase the separation of mother and child, may of itself be an evil. . .' " Identification of cases known to the State department of public welfare, often originating with agencies not clearing with the Social service exchange, was difficult, as the records of investigation of the State department on these cases are not "open to public scrutiny." Of the children adopted in the county and circuit courts in Cook county in 1925, 434 were illegitimate, 414 legitimate, 9 not reported as to status.

Pages 52-60 (Chapter VI). Children adopted by relatives in Cook county. "In this study 30 illegitimate children as against 190 legitimate children were adopted by relatives. . . As in the case of the illegitimate child, adoption [of legitimate] by stepfathers has first rank."

Page 61-80 (Chapter VII). Children adopted by strangers in Cook county. One hundred and sixty-five children were unknown to social agencies. "Of these 165 children, 64, or 39 per cent were known to be illegitimate, while the status of other children was not reported." The "illegitimate child is, on the whole, younger at the time of adoption. . ." Of 472 children known to social agencies, 340 children or 72 percent were illegitimate. "The adoption problem with which the social agencies dealt grew largely out of the problem of illegitimacy."

Bibliography, p. 99-100.

247. O'Grady, John. Ethical aspects of illegitimacy. Catholic charities review, v. 11, p. 12-16, January 1927.

Social attitude favors a monogamous family. As to ethical aspects, it is better to acquaint the prospective employer with the unmarried mother's situation. Agencies should not advise the mother to change her name.

248. Ohio, Public welfare department. Illegitimacy as shown by a study of birth certificates from Franklin county in 1924, by Julia Griggs. 18 p. Ohio welfare bulletin, v. 3, p. 1-18, March 1927.

The extent of illegitimacy in Franklin county, Ohio, in comparison with that of other counties, is given. The Negro is an important factor, as are the age of mother, place of birth of baby, number of other children, and residence of mother and father.

249. Ottenberg, Louis. Fatherless children of the national capital. Survey, v. 33, p. 459-60, January 30, 1915.

The author acted as volunteer counsel for the Associated charities and secured several convictions under the "bastardy" law of the District of Columbia. He points out the need of changing the registration law, and states that 10 percent of the births in the District of Columbia for 1912 and 1913 were illegitimate. The age of the mother is in most cases under 25 and in a large number below 18. Negro illegitimacy is four times that among whites.

250. Padua, Regino G., M.D. Incidence of illegitimate births among Filipinos. Journal of the Philippine Islands medical association, v. 12, p. 430-39, September 1932.

Analysis of official data from eleven localities—ten "representative provinces," and the city of Manila—selected as "submitting fairly reliable returns." The data comprise the births of 1923-27, the percentage of illegitimacy based on total births each month being computed. The "total birth rates by months and by years do not seem to have any relation with the percentage of illegitimates. . ." Proposed legislation is discussed.

251. Parker, Ida R. "Fit and proper"? A study of legal adoption in Massachusetts. 130 p. Boston, Church home society, 1927.

Of 852 individuals studied, there were 810 minors, of whom 303 were legitimate children and 490 were illegitimate.

252. ———— (A) Follow-up study of 550 illegitimacy applications. 8 p. Boston, Research bureau on social case work, 1924.

To what extent were the needs of the 550 unmarried mothers and their children met? Which agencies were assuming responsibility? These questions were raised by the study. Considerable shifting, passing on, or transferring of applications among the different agencies was noted. Tables show the ages and occupations of mothers.

———— joint author see entry 113.

253. Parmenter, Laura S. Case of an unmarried mother who has cared for her child, and failed. National conference of social work, Proceedings, 1917, p. 285-87.

Few cases fail. This case failed because of the mother's frequent change of position, lack of supervision by agency, willingness of the mother to have her child adopted, and final disappearance of the mother. Supervision requires three to four years.

254. Peck, Emelyn. Justice for the fatherless child. Survey, v. 50, p. 236-38, May 15, 1923.

The North Dakota law of 1917 declares that children whether born in or out of wedlock are the legitimate children of the natural parents and so entitled to support and education. In 1921 a similar law was passed in Arizona. Abandonment laws have been passed in several other states applicable to illegitimate children. The North Carolina law of 1917 opposes the separation of the mother and child under six months of age unless the physical defect of the child demands it.

255. Pedersen, V. C., M.D. Gonococcal infection in its relation with bastardy; social problem study with case report. Medical times, v. 55, p. 227-28 + 243-44, October 1927.

A case discussion with medico-legal aspects.

256. Pendleton, Ora. New aims in adoption. Annals of American academy of political and social science, v. 151, p. 154-61, September 1930.

This article discusses the social work involved in adoption of illegitimate children and considers the requirements for successful placement. A criticism of the commercial maternity home is included. The actual legal process of adoption varies in different states. "Adoption is fundamentally an American institution."
Footnote references.

257. Pennsylvania, Commission appointed to study and revise the statutes of Pennsylvania relating to children. Report to the General assembly meeting in 1925; part one of the Report of the Commission, with appendices containing the results of the study of the practice of adoption in Pennsylvania.[11] 252 p. Harrisburg, The Commission, 1925.

Pages 61-136 (Appendix I). Study of the practice of adoption in Philadelphia county, January 1, 1919-June 30, 1924. Illegitimacy is discussed in relation to each of the chapters, I-V.
Pages 65-75 (Chapter I). The adoption of children in Philadelphia county.
Pages 76-89 (Chapter II). Children adopted by relatives.
Pages 90-103 (Chapter III). "Private" adoption by strangers.
Pages 103-17 (Chapter IV). "Private" adoption by strangers (continued).
Pages 117-32 (Chapter V). Adoption of minors in which social agencies participated.
Pages 132-36 (Chapter VI). Conclusions.
Pages 137-58 (Appendix II). Summary of a study of the practice of adoption in Alleghany and twelve other counties in Pennsylvania. The study comprises "1187 adoptions, granted in thirteen counties of the State during 1922-23," which together with the Philadelphia county study totalled 2,209 adoptions. Comparison is made with the findings in the study of Philadelphia county.
Pages 159-78 (Appendix III). Questions and answers on legal adoption in Pennsylvania.

[11]The principal findings are summarized in Neva R. Deardorff's "The Welfare of the said child. . ."

Pages 179-84 (Appendix IV). Typical adoption petition and decree and deed of adoption.

258. Philadelphia, Bureau of municipal research. Unmarried mothers in the Municipal court of Philadelphia; a report . . . prepared by E. O. Lundberg. (Philadelphia municipal court survey series.) 177 p. Philadelphia, Thomas Skelton Harrison foundation, 1933.

A report by the Bureau of a "study made by it as agent" of the Foundation, being a "part of the survey of the municipal court of Philadelphia undertaken by the Bureau. . . This report presents a study of the work of the women's criminal division with unmarried mothers. The field work on the study was done in January and February of 1926." Much of the tabular material in the report was built up from "225 sample cases . . . the first 25 in each of nine months . . ." and 60 cases were selected from this larger group for more detailed study. From the reports of the Division of vital statistics of Philadelphia, 1914-25, the prevalence of illegitimacy in Philadelphia is outlined. "The number of applications to the court has averaged approximately two-fifths of the total number of illegitimate births reported" by the Division of vital statistics. The "number of unmarried mothers reaching the court before delivery is about equal to the number reaching it after delivery. Birth registration "must be fairly complete for at least four-fifths of the illegitimate births and undoubtedly also for a considerable portion of the remainder. This does not imply, of course, that all the births are correctly registered as illegitimate. . ." So far as references of cases to the court is concerned, the figures indicate a "very small degree of cooperation between social agencies and the court. The agencies dealing with families and child welfare do not avail themselves of the work of the court in establishing paternity and holding the father liable for the support of the child."

"The fact that the court deals with such a high percentage of very young unmarried mothers is surprising in view of the small amount of reference by social agencies." Detailed analysis is given of the work of the court on these cases, and of the results of court action. Coöperation with private agencies was studied through information from "four child-caring or protective societies, two maternity homes, and eight hospital social-service departments." Supervision by the Division of child hygiene of Philadelphia was studied through records of the latter. The "ultimate outcome" to mother and child of "all the steps taken, within and without this court, in their behalf" was studied through the follow-up of 33 cases in which the "collection of support orders had been reasonably successful. . ." Summary and recommendations comprise the concluding chapter. Appendices cite case illustrations.

259. Philadelphia, Municipal court. Annual report [1915]. 320 p. Philadelphia, The Court, 1915.

Pages 54-103. Court work with illegitimate families, by Louise Stevens Bryant, Ph.D. The article describes the procedure to establish paternity and to secure support from the father of the child. There were 640 unmarried mothers who came to the Municipal court and this report shows the help given to these women, what was learned about them and the fathers of their children. Thirty-six tables are given.

260. ——— Sixteenth annual report, for the year 1929. 190 p. Philadelphia, The Court.

Compiled by the Statistical department.
Page 152 (Table 2). Volume of work done in illegitimacy cases, 1923-29. "Office interviews" in 1929 totalled 12,612.

261. Philadelphia, Seybert institution, Bureau for social research. Unmarried girls with sex experience, by Carol Aronovici. 48 p. Philadelphia, Seybert institutions, n.d. (Bulletin no. 1.)

The author draws a distinction between the "immoral girl" and the girl prompted by strong sex instinct or sense of the romantic, and points out the danger of the spread of moral as well as physical contamination from the first type. The investigation of the problem of immorality in Philadelphia is based on the records of certain agencies: the Magdalen home; the Midnight mission; Sleighton farm; the House of correction. The mentality of the girls, their home life before coming to these institutions, and the number of prostitutes among them are studied.

262. Piddington, Marion. (The) Unmarried mother and her child. 16 p. Sydney Moore's bookshop, 1923.

An "appeal with regard to the Status of the Unmarried Mother and her Child" based on the importance of "sex training of the young," and of a "general change of personal attitude" toward the unmarried mother.

263. Popenoe, Paul. Some eugenic aspects of illegitimacy. Journal of social hygiene, v. 9, p. 513-27, December 1923.

"Births outside of wedlock are steadily decreasing in almost all civilized countries." The article discusses legislation in North Dakota (1919) and Arizona (1921). The author states that the mothers are mostly young, and are, to a large extent, of inferior mentality. The effects of "ostracism of illegitimate mothers" and of "callous indifference often manifested toward the fate of their children" are "eugenic in a crude, harsh, and drastic way," because the "typical illegitimate child" is the "offspring of a young mother of inferior status mentally, morally, and economically; and of a father who is probably a little superior to the mother in age, mentality, and economic status, if not in morals." Legislative changes requested in behalf of illegitimacy the author finds not desirable eugenically. He suggests the following eugenic measures; birth registration, establishment of paternity, responsibility of the father, inheritance rights, care by the mother, state supervision.

264. Potter, Ellen C., M.D. How shall we plan for children of unmarried mothers in correctional institutions? Hospital social service, v. 23, p. 403-12, April 1931.

Because the "courts were sending unmarried mothers with increasing frequency" to a girls' correctional school, the author, in charge of the school, undertook a study of forty-two young mothers who had been in the institution but paroled previous to the study. The case conference committee concluded: "First: The child born of an unmarried mother . . . should receive primary consideration. . . Second: A careful case-work study (physical, social, psychiatric, psychologic) should be made of every pregnant woman or girl who is brought into conflict with the law. . . Third: . . . only in those [cases] in which the expectant mother is a serious menace to the community and where there is no other agency to which she can be committed should" she "be committed to a correctional institution. . . Fourth: . . . the actual birth of the child should be arranged for outside the correctional institution when possible. . . Fifth: . . . it is essential that the institution provide facilities for the pre-natal, delivery and post-natal care as adequate as 'Class A' hospitals outside of the institution would provide. . . Sixth: . . . the social case work study must be relied upon to determine when this separation is indicated [of mother and child]. . ."

265. President's research committee on social trends. Recent social trends in the United States, v. 2. New York, McGraw-Hill, 1933.

Page 771. This volume devotes apparently only one paragraph to illegitimacy: "Increasing concern for the illegitimate child is shown by improved illegitimacy laws, public provision for protective work for mother and child, requirement of financial support from the father and the policy of discouraging the separation of mother and child. In view of the apparent increase in the number of illegitimate births these steps are important in the protection of such children."

266. Preston, Clarence R. Good care of unmarried mothers as an important phase of preventive and protective work. Journal of social hygiene, v. 17, p. 94-98, February 1931.

More "emphasis should be placed on prevention and protection than on rescue and restoration." Preventive work in illegitimacy means good medical care and social service. The unmarried mother should have adequate prenatal, natal, and postnatal care. With "good social case work the majority of them (probably 85 per cent at least) would have become self-supporting and self-respecting members of society once more."

267. Prettenhofer, Emerich. (The) Legal status of illegitimate children in civilized states. ([Die] Rechtsstellung des unehelichen kindes in den kulturstaaten.) Soziale praxis, v. 39, p. 1175-80, December 11, 1930.

"The youth section of the League of Nations has published in 1929 the results of an inquiry into the legal status of illegitimate children in the different countries. . ."—[S.s.a.]

Quoted from Social science abstracts, v. 3, no. 8, p. 1200, August 1931.

268. Queen, Stuart A., Ph.D., and Delbert M. Mann. Social pathology. 690 p. New York, Thomas Y. Crowell, 1925.

Pages 153-76 (Chapter VIII). (The) Illegitimate family. One case study is given. Extent, causes and factors of illegitimacy; problems of the mother and handicaps of the child; agencies that serve the unmarried mother and the kind of service rendered; prevention of illegitimacy: these are discussed generally.

269. Reed, Ruth. Illegitimacy among Negroes. Journal of social hygiene, v. 11, p. 73-91, February 1925.

The high percentage of Negro women gainfully employed (both single and married), the occupations in which they are employed, are presented, with an analysis of domestic service as contributory to illegitimacy. The problem of "illegitimacy in rural communities and small towns is apparently as great as that existing in all but the largest cities." The "majority of unmarried mothers are derived from the more ignorant and illiterate groups, and may be presumed to be influenced directly or indirectly in their conduct by environmental conditions growing out of ignorance or illiteracy." There was no illegitimacy among Negroes before the Civil war. Because Negroes have been "subject to different forces in our social and economic history, the problem of unmarried parenthood among them presents very different aspects from those existing among the whites."

270. Reed, Ruth, Ph.D. Modern family. 182 p. New York, Alfred A. Knopf, 1929.

Pages 135-46 (Chapter XV). (The) Unmarried mother and her child. The economic status of the unmarried mother is usually low. Repeated illegitimacy and support from the father of the child are discussed.

271. ——— Negro illegitimacy in New York City. 136 p. New York, Columbia university press, 1926.

"500 cases of negro illegitimacy from the records of social and philanthropic agencies in New York city are studied in relation to: the attitude of society toward the unmarried mother; the attitude of the mother toward her child; the conditions which foster illegitimacy; and the social readjustment of the mother."—[B.r.d.]
Quoted from Book review digest, v. 23, 1927, p. 614.
Bibliography, p. 133-34.

272. Rentoul, R. R., M.D. Infant murder or foundling hospitals? Medical press and circular, v. 99, p. 420-22, April 28, 1915.

A discussion, based on the number of illegitimate births registered in England and Wales, Scotland and Ireland, 1892-1911, urging the establishment of several "foundling" hospitals in Great Britain to lessen the problems of illegitimacy.

273. Richmond, Mary E. Social diagnosis. 511 p. New York, Russell Sage foundation, 1917.

Pages 95, 144, 190-92. Case work involving problems of illegitimacy.
Pages 413-19. Suggested questionnaire (unmarried mother), prepared by Mrs. Ada E. Sheffield.

274. Richmond, Mary E. and Fred S. Hall, Ph.D. Child marriages. 159 p. New York, Russell Sage foundation, 1925.

Pages 74-82. Exceptions in pregnancy cases. The special provisions in the law of the various states for marriage below the minimum marriageable age, in case of pregnancy, are outlined.

275. ——— Marriage and the state. 395 p. New York, Russell Sage foundation, 1929.

"Based upon field studies of the present day administration of marriage laws in the United States."
Pages 155-62. A discussion of "forced" marriages.

276. Robbins, Horace H. and Francis Déak. (The) Familial property rights of illegitimate children; a comparative study. Columbia law review, v. 30, p. 308-29, March 1930.

A historical summary of legislation relating to the illegitimate child with a discussion of the modern laws of France, Germany, Norway, and the United States.

277. Roror, Emily F., M.D. (A) Survey of illegitimacy of unmarried Negresses who were delivered at the Lying-in hospital of Philadelphia, 1927-1928. The Medical woman's journal, v. 39, p. 8-13, January 1932.

A study, undertaken during the author's neuropsychiatric service of one hundred unmarried Negresses, ranging in age "from fifteen to thirty years." The purpose of the study was to determine the "factors responsible for the delinquency, and to suggest remedies."

278. Rowlands, E. Bowen. Legitimation by subsequent marriage. Fortnightly review, v. 107, p. 514-24, March 1917.

The law of England in 1917 did not permit legitimation by subsequent marriage, but certain legislation existed regarding the illegitimate child. The author does not believe that the "legitimation would prove a check upon immorality" or reduce illegitimacy, but he does maintain that a "sense of justice demands such reform" for the sake of the child.

279. Schiff, Mary. Jewish unmarried mothers and the fathers of their children; a study of the records of 77 unmarried mothers known to the Jewish social service bureau of Brooklyn. 128 p. New York, 1932. (ms.)

A prefatory note indicates that the draft is "an unrevised first draft of a thesis project submitted in partial fulfillment of the requirements for the Certificate of the Graduate School for Jewish Social Work in June, 1932... No study has been made exclusively of Jewish unmarried mothers, within the knowledge of the writer, nor has an intensive study of the fathers of illegitimate children been attempted." The present study is a "comparative study of both the men and the women," of all cases of unmarried Jewish mothers active at any time in the period 1930-32, "where the man had actually been seen by the worker." In 1931, the man had been interviewed in 51 percent of the (unmarried Jewish mother) cases. In each section "comparisons have been made between the findings of the girls and men . . . as well as between the findings of this and other studies." The cases studied represent the "dependent and delinquent groups" and are a "highly selective group of all those known" to the Bureau. Percentages are based in each instance on the number of cases which have information on the item in question. The "median age of the men studied was 26, or five years higher than that of the girls." There is little material on the ages of the fathers or on their intelligence to be obtained from other authors. The findings in the present study indicate that the "girls are subnormal on the average, while the men are slightly more intelligent," tending to have "about average intelligence [based on psychological tests of the girls, but only on the workers' judgments in the men]." On the "whole the men come from wealthier families than the girls."

The study has too little data on nativity of the men's cases "for statistical purposes." Of the men involved, 63.1 percent were Jewish. "These figures disprove the general impression that Jewish men do not seek Jewish girls for illicit relationships." Of the men, "64.4% . . . were single; 23.6% married, and 11.7% widowers, divorced, separated, or deserted. . . Practically all unmarried mothers are single. . ." There are not sufficient data to warrant conclusions, but there seems to be a "tendency for the men to be better educated than the girls." Only 1.4 percent of the cases were "assaults." In 14.5 percent of the cases there was a single instance of intercourse, and in "41.9% more, the intimacy lasted for less than six months. . . The median period of time for the friendships was from 1-2 years; and for the intimacies, under 6 months." The "fathers are not yet required to assume financial or social responsibility for their illegitimate children to any appreciable extent. . . The three studies which mention the rate of Jewish illegitimacy . . . stress the fact that it is lower than in the general group," but the "question . . . still remains open to decide just why. . ."

Pages 103-17. Case summaries.
Bibliography, p. 122-28.

280. Schreiber, Adele. (The) Actual situation of the unmarried mother in Germany. 8 p. Berlin, German Red Cross, 1925.

A general summary of the situation in Germany, with special reference to legislation, both present and future.

281. ———— Status of the illegitimate child in Germany. Maternity and child welfare [London], p. 8-9, January 1923.

The substance of an address dealing with the rights of the illegitimate child under the new child welfare law, and the private work carried on for mothers by the Red Cross. State insurance for unmarried mothers is recommended.

282. ———— (The) Unmarried mother in Germany. Maternity and child welfare [London], v. 10, p. 213-14, July, 1926.

A plea for "protection for both mother and child during the whole important physiological period, with full opportunity for the child's physical and intellectual development."

283. Schumacher, Henry C., M.D. (The) Unmarried mother; a

sociopsychiatric viewpoint. Mental hygiene, v. 11, p. 775-82, October, 1927.

We "must be careful not to assume, though there be high correlation, that there exists a causal relationship between illegitimacy and mental defect and disease. . . Approaching the problem in a scientific way, one at once seeks for causes within the individual herself." Normal inhibitions may be lacking in both the girl with abnormal sex drive and the girl with normal sex drive. "In this latter case, moreover, we would expect to find a definite causal relationship between her weak inhibitions and her intellectual level. And chiefly because of this causal relationship we do find a high correlation between mental defect and illegitimacy." The higher grades of mental defectives have "come in for the greatest share of discussion in this problem of illegitimacy." Besides the "normal physiologically and intellectually," there are those who "engage in illicit sex relationships as an expression of a definite behavior tendency. Frequently such an individual uses her sex life to overcome or to compensate for thwartings of desires or of activities in other directions, or to gain consideration and through it expression of other desires and interests," but there are such individuals without "mental conflict" who are merely choosing to gratify passions. Psychoneuroses and psychoses as underlying causes of illegitimacy are also discussed. Better laws and a "more enlightened view" by judges are urged, but especially important is the "careful study" of each case by "social worker, psychologist, and psychiatrist."

284. Scotland, Registrar-general. Annual report, 1931. 163 p. Edinburgh, His Majesty's stationery office.

Includes a few standard tables on illegitimacy. Illegitimate births per hundred total births in Scotland, and its group of public health districts in 1931, p. xi; births by legitimacy, in Scotland, 1855-1931, by quinquennial averages, p. lxvii; births in Scotland, 1921-30, by quarter of year, and legitimacy, p. lxix; birth-rates in Scotland, its counties and large burghs in 1931, by illegitimacy rate, p. lxx-lxxi; in the small burghs, p. lxxii-lxxv; in the landward areas, p. lxxvi; birth-rate among married and among unmarried women in Scotland, 1931, p. lxxvii-lxxviii; births, by legitimacy, in Scotland, its counties and large burghs, 1931, p. 2-3.

285. Scotland, Scottish board of health. Maternal mortality; report on maternal mortality in Aberdeen, 1918-1927, with special reference to puerperal sepsis, by J. Parlane Kinloch, M.D., J. Smith, M.D., and J. A. Stephen, M.A., M.B. 60 p. Edinburgh, His Majesty's stationery office, 1928.

Page 9. "Puerperal mortality in relation to illegitimacy. In Aberdeen about one-tenth of all the births during the 1918-27 period were births of illegitimate children." The death-rate "among the mothers of illegitimate children for 1918-27 was also, like that for their infants, fully twice as great as among the other mothers, viz. 13.2 as against 6.0 per 1,000 births. Further, the death-rate from sepsis, excluding septic abortions, was three times as high in unmarried mothers, the difference being still greater for non-septic abortions. The difference for sepsis in abortion cases was even more pronounced. Deaths from albuminuria and convulsions were also distinctly higher, but the reverse was true with regard to hemorrhage. . . Some part of the difference must be attributed to the much higher proportion of first pregnancies among the illegitimate cases than among the legitimate. Our experience over the ten year period, however, has led us to the conclusion that a considerable part of the higher mortality among unmarried mothers is due to the deliberate endeavor to procure abortion."

286. Scotland, Scottish departmental committee on puerperàl morbidity and mortality. Report. 39 p. Edinburgh, His Majesty's stationery office, 1924.

Page 12. Illegitimacy. "Illegitimate births appear to be associated with a maternal death rate above the average. While this is partly due to a higher proportion of primiparous births, there is every reason to believe that unmarried mothers—apart from those dealt with by Parish Council institutions—suffer specially from lack of antenatal care. The natural tendency to concealment makes this inevitable, and we are unable to suggest any special measures towards overcoming this difficulty."
Page 26. Illegitimacy. "In the large towns of Scotland the proportion of illegitimate births is usually about six or seven per cent. . . Several factors which we have found to be of importance in relation to maternal morbidity, e.g. illegitimacy itself, primiparity, venereal disease, etc., are frequently concurrent in the unmarried mother."

287. Seagrave, Mabel, M.D. Causes underlying sex delinquency in young girls. Journal of social hygiene, v. 12, p. 523-29, December, 1926.

The article treats delinquency in its larger aspects, but attitude toward abortion in the illegitimately pregnant woman is discussed under "lack of any idealism."

288. Semachko, N. Social insurance in the Union of Soviet Socialist Republics. International conference of social work, Proceedings, v. 1 of 1928, p. 546-54.

Page 548-49. Maternity insurance. This "insurance includes an allowance at the birth of the child, and during eight weeks preceding and eight weeks following confinement. No distinction is made between registered marriage and irregular union. . ."

289. Shaw, H. L. K., M.D. (The) Problem of the institutional infant. American journal of public health, v. 3, p. 1100-1103, 1913.

Statistics "on the subject of infant mortality in institutions in the United States are extremely unsatisfactory" but are discussed in contrast to infant mortality in the home, as are also types of care in infant asylums and hospitals, the more individual the care, the better the outcome of the infant. Infant "asylums" should be done away with, the "foundling and motherless baby should be provided with a suitable home with wet-nursing, and the mother and her infant should never be separated."

290. Sheffield, Ada E. Is "stigma" removable? Social hygiene, v. 7, p. 49-54, January 1921.

The question of monogamy is involved. "A society which aims to conserve all these values which go with married maternity must necessarily disapprove their violation."

291. ———— Nature of the stigma upon the unmarried mother and her child. National conference of social work, Proceedings, 1920, p. 119-22.

"The cruelty of the old mode of expressing the stigma through punishment was not alone that the forms of punishment adopted were extremely harsh, but that they often inflicted a public humiliation . . . The thing we should aim for then is not to remove the stigma . . . but to give the unmarried mother ample opportunity to win back her good name . . . The stigma on the child differs from that of the mother in that it is undeserved."

292. ———— Program of the Committee on illegitimacy; Committee report. National conference of social work, Proceedings, 1919, p. 74-81.

The Committee on illegitimacy proposes to formulate progressive standards for dealing with unmarried parents and their children. The aim of the Committee is to get the consensus of opinion as to which methods are best to give the mother and child an opportunity to make the most of their situation, and to impress upon the father a sense of obligation to his child and to society. The formation of five subcommittees was suggested to consider: prenatal, obstetrical, and convalescent care; after-care; the unmarried mother as human material; enactment and enforcement of laws; construction and education.

293. Shuman, Cora V. (The) Good girl with a first baby, who is not feebleminded. National conference of charities and correction, Proceedings, 1915, p. 114-15.

The case of a girl who refused to marry the father of her child because of a difference in religious beliefs is presented.

294. Slingerland, William H. Child-placing in families; a manual for students and social workers. 261 p. New York, Russell Sage foundation, 1919.

Introduction by Hastings H. Hart.
Pages 33, 34, 89, 90, 158, 159, 165-77. Illegitimate birth rates in Germany and Austria; status in Missouri and the proposed code; results of social ostracism; social program.

295. Smill, Eva. Unmarried mother. Family, v. 9, p. 240-42, November 1928.

The problem of illegitimacy in New Orleans is greatly intensified by the large surrounding rural territory. The age of the unmarried mother in this area is usually sixteen to nineteen.

296. Smith, Edith Livingston. Unmarried mothers. Harper's weekly, v. 58, p. 22-23, September 6, 1913.

Study of conditions in hospitals, factories, and department stores, and the prevalence of illegitimacy among shop girls, waitresses, factory girls, maids, chorus girls, stenographers, and governesses.

297. Smith, Edith Livingston and Hugh Cabot, M.D. (A) Study in sexual morality. Journal of social hygiene, v. 2, p. 527-47, October 1916.

A comparative study of forty women who were all "normal" women, giving "causes" for their sexual difficulty. A discussion of the personal factors in illegitimacy is given.

298. Smith, Lillian R., M.D. Maternal mortality. Michigan public health [Michigan department of health], v. 18, p. 148-59, July 1930.

"A field study of 1,627 deaths of women in Michigan from causes connected with childbirth from July 1, 1926 to December 31, 1928 has just been completed by the Michigan Department of Health. . ." Of these deaths, 465 were "deaths from abortions. . . We usually think of abortions as being performed to prevent the birth of an illegitimate child. While this was a factor in some cases, there were only 45 single women, 8 divorced, and 9 widowed, or 62 cases where the birth of a child would have affected the reputation of the mother. Four hundred and three of the women were married and we therefore must look for another cause of the abortions."

299. Smith, Mary Frances. Changing emphases in case work with unmarried mothers. Family, v. 14, p. 310-17, January 1934.

"Letters, speeches, and pamphlets covering these years [last four decades] give such an interesting story of the growth of certain lines of thinking, and the popularity and decline of others, that one seems warranted in attempting a brief resumé. . . The passages quoted certainly do not represent all the thinking of their authors. . . Some of them were not writing with an idea of publication. . . They have been chosen because they seem to show rather clearly how the ideas of each era were transmitted by a process of discarding unworkable elements, adapting to increasing resources and needs, and experimenting with new approaches."

In 1890 we "find an interest in working out something constructive . . . through a wholesale placement of unmarried mothers in domestic service positions with their babies. . . In the writings of the next decade or so it is accepted without much question that a 'healthy young woman can usually maintain herself and her child in a home. . .' In the period from 1910 to 1920 this simple and natural solution begins to be questioned." However, "domestic service continued to be accepted for a time as the orthodox plan. . . In the best practice of today, placement at domestic service with the baby would hardly be considered unless it was the mother's own plan and one for which she was willing to take responsibility."

In 1900 social workers are saying: " 'Four parties are to be considered, the child, the mother, the father, and the community. Too often the child is considered last but rightfully it is entitled to first consideration'. . . The practice of the time seems to have been standardized to a series of rules: The mother should invariably, when capable, he required to nurse the child. Babies should not be segregated, they should not be given away through baby farms, their placement should be supervised by competent state agents." Concern for "working out a better social order, probably . . . prompted social workers in the period from 1910 to 1920 to enter extensively into research studies dealing with large groups of unmarried mothers, to form a nation-wide organization of social workers. . ." Results of this interest were undoubtedly "changes in legal status, and in increased provision for care of unmarried mothers and their babies. The work of the Federal Children's Bureau during these years was particularly constructive. . ."

Difficulties in "building up from individual conduct a group picture" as well as of finding "again in the total picture a resemblance to the individual," are cited. Toward the end of the decade are shown a "broader attitude, an interest in viewing the whole problem objectively and in utilizing the constructive elements to their best advantage. But it is nevertheless standardization which is sought. . ."

"In 1921 the Philadelphia Conference on Parenthood compiled a report on General Standards of Case Work with the Illegitimate Family which summarized the findings of these years of social research, emphasized their practical application, and recommended some next steps. . . The emphasis was on variety in treatment and on discovering individual abilities and needs of the client. However, as worded, the standards put the responsibility for decisions on the agencies interested rather than emphasizing an active rôle for the mother or father." At the same time, however, another pamphlet presented "what seems to be a really new emphasis on personality. . . First of all she [the unmarried mother] is a human being who needs an opportunity to develop. . . And this can never entail a program which has been thought out in advance, or even a choice from four or five possible plans for herself and her baby. . . It took much of the period 1920 to 1930 to catch up with some of the ideas which have been quoted. . . In the last ten years there has been classification. . . The unmarried mother appears less often in our writings and discussions but we know more about her. . . ." A 1930 "passage concludes that the separate character of work with the unmarried mother is not being emphasized except in improvement of law and court procedure, and that the problem of treatment is being taken over in general case work agencies, family, children's, or medical." The rôle which the case worker assigns himself at different stages is outlined.

300. Smith-Rossie, C. (The) Love child in Germany and Austria. English review, v. 11, p. 435-44, June 1912.

Refers to the works of Professor Othmar Spann and other German works on the subject of "unhonoured" children, which have received little attention in English, and also mentions the works of District-Judge Franz Janisch of Austria. "The child is to become a future citizen and it is not good for the State to permit its father to neglect it."

301. Snow, Francis H. Unmarried mother. Current history, v. 15, p. 433-40, December 1921.

The article discusses what Great Britain and the United States are doing to remedy the injustice of the ages, and Russia's radical change in regard to children born out of wedlock.

302. Social work year book, edited by Fred S. Hall, Ph.D., v. 1. 600 p. New York, Russell Sage foundation, 1929.

Pages 73-75. Children born out of wedlock, by A. Madorah Donahue. A summary of legislation which has been passed by various states: Wisconsin, New Jersey, Michigan, Wyoming, New York and Pennsylvania. Bibliography, p. 75.

303. Social work year book, edited by Fred S. Hall, Ph.D., v. 2. 680 p. New York, Russell Sage foundation, 1933.

Pages 75-78. Children born out of wedlock, by A. Madorah Donahue. Partially a repetition of the article in volume 1, but in addition points out the social significance of birth out of wedlock, which, the author states, "is far-reaching and is reflected in the factors which bring many of these children to the care of private and public agencies." Bibliography, p. 78.

304. Spinks, A. F. G., M.D. (The) Problem of the unmarried mother. Medical officer [London], v. 38, p. 197, October 29, 1927.

A suggestion that the "sympathy of local authorities" be enlisted, "by appointing their medical officials to the staffs of all institutions dealing with unmarried mothers," as a means toward better prenatal, natal, and postnatal care.

305. Stark, Morris. Illegitimate and adopted children under workmen's compensation acts. Cornell law quarterly, v. 16, p. 587-90, June 1931.

"Generally the mother is permitted to recover for the injury or death of an illegitimate child, while the father is not. But since under the common law the illegitimate child could not inherit, it is still common to hold that recovery by or for an illegitimate child must depend on a definite statement of statute law. So also foster mothers have been permitted to recover for the death of adopted children, under adoption statutes. But since step-parents are under no legal obligation to support their minor step-children, they are not allowed to recover either under workmen's compensation acts or under wrongful death statutes."—[S.s.a.]
Quoted from Social science abstracts, v. 4, no. 1, p. 91, January 1932.
Also abstracted in Child development abstracts and bibliography, v. 6, no. 3, entry 628, p. 226, June 1932 [from Social science abstracts].

306. Stöcker, Helene. Twenty-five years struggle for mother protection and sexual reform. (Fünfundzwanzig jahre kampf für mutterschutz und sexual reform.) Neue generation, v. 26, p. 47-55, March-April 1930.

"In 1905 the Organization for the Reform of Sex Ethics was created in Berlin. Out of this in 1911 grew the International Union for the Protection of Mother and Reform of Sex Ethics. . . The primary aim of the organization was to protect children born out of wedlock and their mothers. . . Homes and clinics for unmarried mothers have been established. . ."—[S.s.a.]

Quoted from Social science abstracts, v. 2, no. 12, p. 1966, December 1930.

307. Stöcker, Lydia. Illegitimate maternity of teachers. (Über die uneheliche mutterschaft der lehrerin.) Neue generation, v. 27, p. 18-23, January-February-March 1931.

"Despite the fact that article 121 of the new [Weimar] constitution granted legal equality to illegitimate children . . . there are yet many hardships and serious problems confronting the mothers of such children, especially those in the teaching profession. She is often ostracized by others on the teaching staff or in the community. . . Some teachers try to overcome these difficulties by placing the child with others. . ."—[S.s.a.]

Quoted from Social science abstracts, v. 4, no. 2, p. 281, February 1932.

308. Stoneman, A. H. Social problems related to illegitimacy; safeguarding adoptions, legally and socially. National conference of social work, Proceedings, 1924, p. 144-51.

A discussion of child-placing and adoption. The author suggests that there be a law that children of unmarried parents may not be removed from the mother until three months (preferably six months) after birth, except by special order of the state department upon recommendation of two physicians of good and regular standing.

309. Storck, Dr. (The) Protection of women with dependent children. International bulletin of social work, no. 2, p. 27-37, May 1931. International bulletin of social work, no. 3, p. 25-38, December 1931.

The second article[12] is the "conclusion" of the first.

Abstract of first article. The five classes into which German law divides women with dependent children are discussed together and separately. Unmarried mothers make up one class. The discussion gives the provision made for the unmarried mother by law, by state organization, and by private welfare organizations. The "father, in 25% of cases [unmarried] pays the full amount required for the maintenance of his child, and in 50% of cases, a portion of these costs." Unmarried mothers, "if they keep their child with them . . . either marry the father of their child within the first few years following its birth (33%), start a home by marrying another man, or undertake the child's education single-handed in their own home or in that of their parents." The effects of illegitimacy on

[12]Entitled "(The) Protection of destitute mothers in Germany.

family life, the desirability of keeping together mother and child, the length of such period, and the opportunity of day nurseries, are outlined. The desirability of having the foster mother relationship to the child not exclusive of the mother-child contact is stressed. The support of the child is treated from many angles. Dr. Gertrude Bäumer points out that "legitimization occurs more frequently when the mother is living with her parents. . ." Legislation, existent and proposed, are discussed.
Abstract of second article. Housing and material assistance are discussed.

310. Storck, G. Fr. (The) Draft concerning the legal position of illegitimate children. ([Die] Reichstagsvorlage über die rechtliche stellung der unehelichen kinder.) Zentralblatt für jugendrecht und jugendwohlfahrt, v. 20, p. 257-62, January 1929.

"This article is a thorough discussion of the second draft of a law for illegitimate children. . ."—[S.s.a.]
Quoted from Social science abstracts, v. 2, no. 8, p. 1367, August 1930.

311. Taylor, Eleanor. Nobody's child. Woman's journal, v. 15, p. 20-21, 35-36, May 1930.

There is a new spirit toward the illegitimate child. "Juster laws, kinder treatment and friendly help hold out new hope for mother and child." The father's obligation and legislation thus far established in various states to determine paternity are discussed. Ideals formulated by the [Federal] Children's bureau are presented, with a brief reference to legislation in European countries.

312. Thomas, William Isaac. (The) Unadjusted girl. 261 p. Boston, Little, Brown, 1923.

Pages v-xvii. Foreword, by Mrs. W. F. Dummer. A discussion of psychological and sociological aspects of marriage and the unmarried mother. Pages 98-150 (Chapter IV). Largely a case presentation of sexually delinquent girls, a number of whom are unmarried mothers.

313. Tinney, Mary C. Illegitimacy. National conference of catholic charities, Proceedings, 1920, p. 99-104.

The author states: "that all these girls were feebleminded is not based on fact and that barely ten per cent can be considered below the line of normal intelligence. State supervision and protection, mothers' or widows' pension funds should be available for the children of unmarried mothers, on the same conditions of fitness of the mother to care for her child as in the case of legal mothers." The decrease of illegitimate births in New York City means that abortions are increasing.

314. Tönnies, Ferdinand. Illegitimate persons and orphans among criminals; studies on criminality in Schleswig-Holstein. (Uneheliche und verwaiste verbrecher; studien über verbrechertum in Schleswig-Holstein.) Kriminalistische abhandlungen, no. 16, p. 48, 1930.

"The author studied data referring to 3,174 male convicts sentenced to death or penal servitude in Schleswig-Holstein. Among them were 470 or 14.8% of illegitimate birth. . . A still more surprising result of the investigation is that there were among the 3,171 convicts, 1,393 persons (44%) who had lost one or both parents before reaching the age of 20. Tönnies also shows the association of conviction for crime with certain environmental conditions and considers the possibilities of reducing illegitimacy and orphanhood."—[S.s.a.]

Quoted from Social science abstracts, v. 3, no. 11, p. 1647-48, November 1931.

315. Townley-Fullam, C. Moral and social aspects of illegitimacy in Hungary. Forum, v. 50, p. 618-30, November 1913.

"The Hungarian child belongs to the state." The father may legitimize the child by acknowledgment of paternity or by adoption. Child murders and abortions have thus been decreased.

316. Trounstine, Helen S. Illegitimacy in Cincinnati. (Studies from the Helen S. Trounstine foundation, v. 1, no. 6.) [42] p. Cincinnati, The Foundation, 1919.

The new trend in "bastardy" legislation (Maryland, Massachusetts, Norway) and suggestions for a model law on "bastardy,"precede the major part of the article, devoted to the work of the local social agencies.

317. United States, Census bureau. Birth, stillbirth and infant mortality statistics for the birth registration area of the United States, 1929. Washington, Government printing office, 1931.

Pages 13-20. Includes standard tables on illegitimate births in each annual issue, as in this volume, the following:

Table P. The number of illegitimate births with ratio to thousand total births, by sex and color, for each registration state.

Table Q. The number of live illegitimate births, with ratio to thousand total births, by age and country of birth of mother, for the total registration area of the United States.

Table R. The number of live legitimate and illegitimate births, by color, and general nativity of mother, with ratio to illegitimate births, in urban and rural districts of each registration state.

Table X. Number of births and stillbirths, with ratio of stillbirths to hundred live births, by legitimacy, for urban and rural districts of each registration state.

318. ────── Mortality statistics, 1929; thirteenth annual report, 531 p. Washington, Government printing office, 1932.

Pages 36-39. Puerperal causes. "The rates for mothers under 20 years of age were considerably higher than the rates for mothers 20 to 29, and a partial explanation, at least, is the comparatively large number of illegitimate children involved and the lack of care so common in such cases."

319. United States, Children's bureau. Analysis and tabular summary of state laws relating to illegitimacy in the United States, in effect January 1, 1928, and the text of selected laws, by Marietta Stevenson, M.D. (Bureau chart no. 16.) 49 p. Washington, Government printing office, 1929.

Dr. Stevenson cites the number of illegitimate births in the United States exclusive of California and Massachusetts (statistics not available) in 1917 as 55,134. The modern aim is to care for and protect the child by registration of births and proceedings to establish paternity. The texts of selected laws and the proposed uniform illegitimacy law are given.

320. ────── (A) Brief treatment of the prevalence and significance of birth out of wedlock, the child's status and the state's responsibility for care and protection (with bibliographical material), by Emma O. Lundberg and Katharine F. Lenroot; Part I of Illegitimacy as a child-welfare problem. (Bureau publication no. 66.) 105 p. Washington, Government printing office, 1920.

Discusses the extent of the problem in the United States and the prevalence in foreign countries. The article further discusses infant mortality and care of the child.
Bibliography, p. 57-95.

321. ────── Child dependency in the District of Columbia, by Emma O. Lundberg and Mary E. Milburn. (Bureau publication no. 140.) 160 p. Washington, Government printing office, 1924.

Pages 4-5. A paragraph devoted to unmarried mothers and children of illegitimate birth who are cared for by the Board of children's guardians in the District of Columbia.

322. —— Children deprived of parental care, by Ethel M. Springer. (Bureau publication no. 81.) 96 p. Washington, Government printing office, 1921.

A study of children under the care of Delaware agencies and institutions. The records for 513 children under 18 were studied. More than two-thirds of the children were of illegitimate birth.

323. —— Children of illegitimate birth and measures for their protection, by Emma O. Lundberg. (Bureau publication no. 166.) 20 p. Washington, Government printing office, 1926.

A discussion of the infant mortality rate and its causes, of legislation, and of illegitimacy as a dependency problem.

Page iv. "Other publications of the Children's bureau relating to illegitimacy."

324. —— Children of illegitimate birth whose mothers have kept their custody, by A. Madorah Donahue. (Bureau publication no. 190.) 105 p. Washington, Government printing office, 1928.

Suggests means of keeping the mother and child together, such as affiliation of maternity homes with children's agencies, provision by social agencies for temporary care in a boarding home or institutions for unmarried mothers, greater willingness to aid the mother in caring for her child, and more intensive attempts to establish paternity in order to provide support for the child.

Also abstracted in Child development abstracts and bibliography, v. 4, no. 1, p. 98-99, entry 242, February 1930.

Also abstracted in Social science abstracts, v. 1, no. 10, p. 1340, November 1929.

325. —— Child-welfare conditions and resources in seven Pennsylvania counties, by Neva R. Deardorff, Ph.D. (Bureau publications no. 176.) 305 p. Washington, Government printing office, 1927.

The Letter of transmittal states: A "report . . . made at the request of the Pennsylvania Children's Commission."

Pages 246-52. Support and protection of children of illegitimate birth. A discussion of: "Births of unmarried mothers in the seven counties," "Legal procedure for securing support in Pennsylvania," "Illegitimacy cases in courts in the seven counties," "Outcome of illegitimacy proceedings," "Settlements outside of court," "Illegitimacy as related to dependency and mental defect," "Illegitimacy and standards of family life," "Exposure of children of illegitimate birth to unusual hazards," "Questionable placements for adoption of children of illegitimate birth." The author states: "The perecentage of illegitimate to total live births for the seven counties was 3.2. Allowance should be made for the fact that in one of the counties there was a large commercial maternity home," to which non-residents of the county, as well as residents, were admitted. "Only about 45 per cent of the mothers . . . filed complaints, and an even smaller percentage of men were held. The relation of the number of illegitimate births to the number of complaints varied widely in the seven counties. For the counties with more than 50 illegitimate births the percentage of complaints varied from 84 in the bitmuinous-coal county to 20 in the commercial county. . . In the commercial county the small proportion of cases coming before the courts was accounted for by the statement that public sentiment was generally against the girl and it was difficult for her to prove the man guilty. . . In the bituminous-coal county 71 of 81 complaints were returned to court. . . Very little information could be obtained regarding the settlements made in the cases withdrawn from court. . . The dangers to these babies range from actual murder to early separation of mother and child and careless placement of them with any one who will take them. . . Adoption is used as a method of disposing of children of illegitimate birth in ways that suggest that sometimes the child, sometimes the adopting family, and sometimes both, are chosen most unwisely. The children of feeble-minded mothers are placed for adoption in all kinds of families, apparently without thought of results. Children with other questionable backgrounds likewise are given to unsuspecting persons."

326. ——— Child welfare in selected counties of Washington [State]. (Bureau publication no. 206.) 111 p. Washington, Government printing office, 1931.

"Six counties were selected as typical of the varying social, economic, and geographical conditions existing throughout the State."

Pages 28-42. Care of dependent children away from their own homes. Protective legislation regarding transfer of guardianship of a child is discussed. "The largest group of children needing the protection which such legislation affords are children of illegitimate birth. Under the emotional strain which the unmarried mother suffers, her natural affections are submerged by her immediate problems, and she often signs a release from guardianship she later regrets. . . Only 87 of the 322 children involved in adoption proceedings were reported as having been under agency care before the filing of petitions for adoption. The reason for agency care was given for 62 children, 35 being of illegitimate birth and 27 otherwise dependent."

Pages 43-44. Care of children presenting special problems; children of illegitimate birth. In the six counties studied, the birth-registration records showed 209, out of 10,241 children born in 1926, as of illegitimate birth. "This group of children constituted only a small proportion of children in institutions but more than one-third of those under care of child-placing agencies, and the majority of those placed in homes by individuals and other agencies. . . In the counties visited in Washington no adequate program had been undertaken by either private or public agencies for case work with unmarried mothers. Records were obtained of only 16 cases in which complaint had been filed during the year to establish paternity and to provide support for the child. . . In striking contrast to these figures are those reported by one State department. . . The biennial reports of this department for the four years ended June 30, 1928, show that complaints for establishment of paternity had been filed in about one-third of the cases of unmarried mothers. . ." Agencies, both public and private, are increasingly endeavoring to have the mothers keep their children during the early months of infancy, as this policy "usually results in the assumption of responsibility for his permanent care by his mother or other relatives. With willingness . . . to assume care of her child usually comes willingness to obtain, if possible, some support for him from his father. . . There is need in Washington for the development of public sentiment in regard to the adequate care of children of illegitimate birth as well as for legislation placing responsibility for their care on some public agency."

327. ——— Foster-home care for dependent children. (Bureau publication no. 136, revised.) 289 p. Washington, Government printing office, 1926.

Pages 17-31. Conserving the child's parental home, by J. Prentice Murphy. Illegitimacy is touched on as follows: "In regard to children born to unmarried parents, the trend is definitely in the direction of continued care and responsibility for the child by the parents. If good reception methods are followed, if social backgrounds are sought and social causes are looked for, separation of unmarried parents from their children is usually found to be unwise and undesirable; yet many children's agencies and many organizations working with unmarried mothers countenance such separations as soon after birth as they can safely be effected."
Pages 193-204. Psychoclinical guidance in child adoption, by Arnold Gesell, M.D., Ph.D. Part I. (The) Adoption of infants. Part II. (The) Child-adoption case illustrations.

328. ——— Illegitimacy laws of the United States and certain foreign countries, by Ernst Freund. (Bureau publication no. 42.) 260 p. Washington, Government printing office, 1919.

A discussion of the history of English legislation relating to illegitimacy;

legislation in various states showing the relation between divorce and illegitimacy; legitimation by subsequent marriage allowed in many American states; the law of Louisiana recognizing the special status of the natural child; the law of various states relating to registration of illegitimate births; the law of Florida and Illinois relating to support-enforcing legislation; courts having jurisdiction over "bastardy" proceedings and the procedure in various states; possible changes in state laws. A reference index is given, and also the text of the illegitimacy laws for each state and for France, Germany and Switzerland.

329. ——— Maternal deaths; a brief report of a study made in 15 states.[13] (Bureau publication no. 221.) 60 p. Washington, Government printing office, 1933.

Page 11. Illegitimacy. A summary of the presentation of illegitimacy in the larger report.

Pages 33-36. Abortions. Among the findings is given a brief summary of the presentation of illegitimacy in the larger report.

330. ——— Maternal mortality in fifteen states. (Bureau publication no. 223.) 234 p. Washington, Government printing office, 1934. (Page proof.)

A study made under the "supervision of . . . the former director of the maternity and infant-hygiene division . . . and of the Bureau's obstetric advisory committee. . . The plan for the study was outlined by its chairman. . . The material was analyzed and the report was written by Dr. Frances C. Rothert . . . all deaths assigned to puerperal causes in 13 States in 1927, and in these same States and two others in 1928 were studied," in coöperation with the state departments of health. "The 15 States included in the study are fairly well distributed geographically and are fairly typical of the sections in which they are located. . . The physicians or other persons signing the death and birth certificates were . . . visited, as well as other physicians or midwives to whom the interviewers were referred. Except in very rare instances . . . families were not visited. Hospitals and clinics in which the patient had received care were visited and . . . the case records were studied."

Pages 36-38. Illegitimacy. "The deaths of 509 unmarried women are included in the study." Fifty-one percent "died of puerperal septicemia, as compared with 39 percent among the married women, and of the deaths from septicemia among the unmarried almost two thirds . . . occurred before the women had reached the last trimester. Puerperal albuminuria

[13]A brief report of the Bureau's larger report: Maternal mortality in fifteen states (Bureau publication no 223).

and convulsions, also, caused a larger proportion of the deaths of un-married than of married women." Of the 509 unmarried women, 263 were colored, "as compared with 18 percent colored in the entire study. Of the women for whom parity was reported primiparae made up 85 percent of the 474 who were unmarried and only 30 percent of the 6,366 who were married. The single women were a much younger group than the married women. . . Of the 506 unmarried women for whom the period of gestation was reported, 219 (43 percent) died before reaching the last trimester, as compared with 2,152 (32 percent) of the 6,819 mar-ried women. . . This larger proportion of early terminations of pregnancy among the unmarried women who died was confined, however, to the white women. . . Few of the unmarried women had had any prenatal care. . . There was less prenatal care among the colored than among the white women and less among those who died in the rural areas than among those who died in cities of 10,000 or more population. . . There was practically no difference in the hospitalization of the unmarried women and of the total group . . . 18 percent of the unmarried women, as compared with only 9 percent of the total group, had had medical attention only when dying or not at all. . . Live births were recorded as legitimate or illegitimate in all the States included in the study except California. The maternal mortality rate of unmarried mothers in all the States combined, exclusive of California, was 143 per 10,000 illegitimate live births; for married mothers it was 60 per 10,000 legitimate live births . . . for white unmarried mothers was 137, for colored 149, for urban 162, and for rural 129—all much higher than the corresponding maternal mortality rates for the entire group of mothers."
Pages 103-16. Abortions.
Page 108. Abortions; illegitimacy. "Married women made up 90 percent of the women whose deaths followed abortions; but abortion was a more frequent cause of death among unmarried than among married mothers, as abortions preceded the deaths of about one fifth of the married mothers in the study and of more than one third of the 509 unmarried mothers. . . For every 10,000 legitimate live births in the States of the study except California there were 14 deaths of married women following abortions . . . 50 deaths of unmarried women following abortions. . ."

331. ——— Mental defect in a rural county; a medico-psycholog-ical and social study of mentally defective children in Sussex county, Delaware, by Walter L. Treadway, M.D. and Emma O. Lundberg. (Bureau publication no. 48.) 96 p. Washington, Government printing office, 1919.

Pages 33, 47-48, 56-60, 62-65, 75, 78, 80-88, 90. Illegitimacy and mental defect.

332. ———— Methods of care in selected urban and rural communities; Part III of Illegitimacy as a child-welfare problem. (Bureau publication no. 128.) 260 p. Washington, Government printing office, 1924.

Pages 13-94. Philadelphia's problem and the development of standards of care, by Amey Eaton Watson. There are sixty-six agencies in Philadelphia which deal to some extent with the illegitimate family, giving social treatment of which the provisions include maternity care and legal assistance. A study of the characteristics of the father and mother and the disposition of the child is included.

Pages 95-141. Care of children born out of wedlock in Milwaukee, by Louise Drury and Mary E. Milburn. The total number of illegitimate births in Milwaukee in 1916 and 1917 was 793. The care given illegitimate children by agencies and institutions, history of the child's parents and legal action for the support of children born out of wedlock are discussed.

Pages 143-62. Securing employment for unmarried mothers in New York City, by Mary E. Milburn. A study of the parental home, age, schooling, and employment of the unmarried mother. Tables show housework as an employment for mothers with young children, previous and subsequent employment at housework, age of the child when placed and length of time the child lived with the mother at housework, number of positions held by the mother, first employment of the mother after the birth of her child.

Pages 163-79. Illegitimacy in eighteen counties of New York State, by H. Ida Curry. Special emphasis is given here to rural problems. Eighteen counties which were chosen had some social organization for dependent children. One hundred and twenty-five cases of illegitimacy were studied covering the period from October 1, 1916 to September 30, 1917. Children less than one year at the beginning of the period and at least six months at the end of the period were included.

Pages 181-236. Results of Minnesota's laws for protection of children born out of wedlock, by Mildred Dennett Mudgett. Public administration of such work by the state on an extensive scale is unique. Minnesota has thirty-five laws in all dealing with this problem.

Pages 238-39 (Appendix A). Illegitimacy in various states and cities of the United States.

Pages 240-45 (Appendix B). Comparative data from studies of illegitimacy.
Pages 246-50. Schedule forms for study of illegitimacy.

333. ———— Minimum standards for child welfare; adopted by the Washington and regional conferences on child welfare, 1919.

(No. 2, of Conference series [Bureau publication no. 62].) 15 p. Washington, Government printing office, 1919.

Pages 10-14. Resolutions on standards relating to "children in need of special care."
Page 12. Care of children born out of wedlock. "The child born out of wedlock constitutes a very serious problem, and for this reason special safeguards should be provided. Save for unusual reasons both parents should be held responsible for the child during its minority, and especially should the responsibility of the father be emphasized. Care of the child by its mother is highly desirable, particularly during the nursing months. No parent of a child born out of wedlock should be permitted to surrender the child outside its own family, save with the consent of a properly designated State department or a court of proper jurisdiction. Each State should make suitable provisions of a humane character for establishing paternity and guaranteeing to children born out of wedlock the rights naturally belonging to children born in wedlock. The fathers of such children should be under the same financial responsibilities and the same legal liabilities toward their children as other fathers. The administration of the courts with reference to such cases should be so regulated as not only to protect the legal rights of the mother and child, but, also to avoid unnecessary publicity and humiliation. The treatment of the unmarried mother and her child should include the best medical supervision, and should be so directed as to afford the widest opportunity for wholesome, normal life."

334. —— Norwegian laws concerning illegitimate children. (Bureau publication no. 31.) 37 p. Washington, Government printing office, 1918.

Introduction and translation by Leifur Magnusson. A "translation of certain Norwegian statutes passed in 1915, bearing upon the rights of children born out of wedlock, together with an historical introduction.
Pages 7-14. Introduction.
Pages 14-37. Text of the laws regarding illegitimate children in Norway.

335. —— Protective case work for young people and maternity homes, by Glenn Steele. (Separate from Publication no. 209.) 16 p. Washington, Government printing office, 1932.

Pages 1-7. Protective case work for young people. Statistics for the whole field so designated are analyzed. The case work departments of eight maternity homes submitted service reports for the year.
Pages 9-16. Maternity homes. "Monthly reports from 72 maternity homes representing 30 metropolitan areas were received during 1930 by the

Children's Bureau. . . Although the primary purpose of institutions in this field is to shelter and protect unmarried mothers and their children, the homes sometimes receive married women and legitimate infants in cases of distress. More than 8,000 girls or women and about 6,600 babies were cared for during 1930 in the homes which reported." The rate of those served per 10,000 women 15 to 44 years of age residing within the area, is given, though it is granted: "Rates that are relatively higher in proportion to the population group may reflect a territorial service which is broad."

"In 13 of the 27 areas for which information on this subject was reported, all, or practically all, of the delivery service was given at the maternity homes." In 3 areas "all mothers under the care of the maternity homes were sent to hospitals for delivery, and in the 11 remaining areas both home and hospital deliveries were reported. Of these only 2 reported that the "majority of deliveries occurred in hospitals." Table 6: Number of live births and stillbirths, and number of deaths of infants and women reported by maternity homes in 27 specified metropolitan areas during 1930. "In the absence of information as to how long the infants stayed in maternity homes subsequent to birth, no definite conclusions regarding the relative extent of infant mortality can be drawn."

336. ——— (A) Social study of mental defectives in New Castle county, Delaware, by Emma O. Lundberg. (Bureau publication no. 24.) 38 p. Washington, Government printing office, 1917.

Pages 14, 15, 23, 26, 35 deal with the relation between mental defect and illegitimacy.

337. ——— Standards of child welfare; a report of the Children's bureau conferences, May and June, 1919. (No. 1 of Conference series [Bureau publication no. 60].) 459 p. Washington, Government printing office, 1919.

Pages 211-18. French experience, by Dr. Clothilde Mulon. There is a brief reference to illegitimacy in relation to the World war, as follows: "Not only did the practice of criminal abortion become more common, but the proportion of illegitimate births reached much higher figures than formerly."

Pages 307-12. The responsibility of the state, by Robert W. Kelso. There is a brief reference to the state and the illegitimate child.

Pages 353-62.(including discussion, p. 360-62). Standards of child placing and supervision, by Edmond J. Butler. In discussion Mrs. Ada E. Sheffield raised two questions regarding unmarried mothers: "Is it better that pregnant girls should be placed in maternity homes up to the period of confinement, or is it better that they should be boarded out or placed out. . . The second question is: Should the mother and child be placed together—dual placement—or should they be supervised separately, the mother at her work and the children in a foster home?" Mr. William Hodson discusses the Minnesota law.

Pages 440-44. Minimum standards for the protection of children in need of special care.

Pages 442-44 [Minimum standard 7]. Care of children born out of wedlock.

338. ———— Standards of legal procedure for children born out of wedlock; a report of regional conferences held under the auspices of the United States Children's bureau and the Inter-city conference on illegitimacy [Chicago, Illinois, February 9-10; New York, N. Y., February 16-17, 1920]. (Bureau publication no. 77.) 158 p. Washington, Government printing office, 1921.

Resolutions and proceedings of the two conferences.

339. ———— (A) Study of maternity homes in Minnesota and Pennsylvania, by Ethel M. Watters, M.D. (Bureau publication no. 167.) 92 p. Washington, Government printing office, 1926.

Pages 27-29. Special provisions in Minnesota for unmarried mothers and their children. Public versus private care (child-placing agencies) is discussed.

340. ———— (A) Study of original records in the city of Boston and in the state of Massachusetts, by Emma O. Lundberg and Katharine F. Lenroot; Part II of Illegitimacy as a child-welfare problem. (Bureau publication no. 75.) 408 p. Washington, Government printing office, 1921.

For interpretation of the report, see Katharine P. Hewins' Study of illegitimacy, Hazards in illegitimacy, Illegitimacy in a rural community.
Pages 74-264 (Section I). The report deals with the problem in Boston and in the state. The problem in Boston includes a study of the infant born out of wedlock with information regarding his parentage and background; children of illegitimate birth under care of social agencies; legal action for the support of children born out of wedlock.
Pages 266-69 (Section II). The problem in the state includes a comparison of the problem in certain sections of the state and discusses illegitimacy as a rural problem.

341. —— Welfare of infants of illegitimate births in Baltimore as affected by a Maryland law of 1916 governing the separation of mothers of children under six months old. (Bureau publication no. 144.) 24 p. Washington, Government printing office, 1925.

Pages 3-9 (Part I). Mortality among infants born out of wedlock in 1915 and 1921, by Rena Rosenberg. Tables of infant mortality rates by color of the mother and age of the child at death.
Pages 11-21 (Part II). Effect of the law on the policies and work of social agencies, by A. Madorah Donahue. A discussion of the agencies that care for the unmarried mother and changes in their policies due to the law.

342. Unsigned. Boston conference on illegitimacy. Survey, v. 30, p. 707-8, September 13, 1913.

Conference of workers on problems of illegitimacy. Their plan is to keep mother and child together where possible, if the mother is reasonably capable of bringing up the child. Feeblemindedness is discussed as the greatest single cause of illegitimacy.

343. —— Cuban demography for 1928. (Datos cubanos. Demografía cubana de 1928.) Revista bimestre cubana, v. 25, p. 293-96, March-April, 1930.

"There were 88 fewer marriages in 1928 than in 1927 but 508 more births, or a total of 60,176. Of the white births, 41,383 were legitimate and 6,182 illegitimate. Of the colored births, 6,330 were legitimate and 6,281 illegitimate. Illegitimacy increased among both whites (283) and colored (440). The infant death rate is declining."—[S.s.a.]
Quoted from Social science abstracts, v. 3, no. 11, p. 1641, November 1931.

344. —— (The) Effect of statutes altering the position of illegitimate children on judicial construction of wills. Harvard law review, v. 45, p. 890-96, March 1932.

The position of the illegitimate child has been radically altered by legislation. The article discusses whether the word "children" when used in a will includes illegitimate children; some courts have held that it does.

345. —— Home for unmarried mothers. Modern city, v. 4, p. 21-22, June 1919.

"Newark, New Jersey, is on a fair way to solve the social problem of the unmarried mother." The policy of reclamation of these women has led to the establishment of a home under the charge of Dr. Julius Levy. This is the first municipal institution of its kind in the country, and houses one hundred mothers and their infants. The ages of the mothers are 18-22. A study by Dr. Levy shows that the proportion of illegitimate births in Newark is 2 percent, whereas in some states it is as high as 18 percent.

346. ——— (A) Humane measure for the protection and care of certain children. Journal of American institute of criminal law and criminology, v. 8, p. 117-25, May 1917.

The article refers to legislation in Illinois.

347. ——— Illegitimacy in California. Journal of the American medical association, v. 65, p. 453, July 31, 1915.

Editorial states that in a "study of 163 cases [illegitimate children], 25 per cent. of the mothers were the only children in the family, and the percentage of illegitimacy gradually decreased as the size of the family increased. This was regarded as testimony to the value of large families."

348. ——— Illegitimacy in Europe. Journal of social hygiene, v. 13, p. 242-44, April 1927.

A summary of Mildred D. Mudgett's For unmarried mothers in Europe, discussing social work in Austria, legal procedure in Czecho-Slovakia, guardianship of the illegitimate child in Switzerland, the work of agencies in Holland, hospital social service in France, and private social work in England.

349. ——— Illegitimacy legislation. Journal of social hygiene, v. 9, p. 112, February 1923.

"Norway and North Dakota have enacted revolutionary legislation designed to place the burden where it rightfully belongs. Legislation in most other countries is inadequate.

350. ——— (The) Illegitimate child. Survey, v. 43, p. 654-55, February 28, 1920.

A comment on the [United States] Children's bureau's Illegitimacy laws of the United States and certain foreign countries.

351. ——— Legislation for children born out of wedlock. Survey, v. 43, p. 747, March 13, 1920.

The article refers to the regional conferences held in Chicago and New York in 1920. The purpose of these conferences proposed by the Children's bureau was to discuss principles of legislation. The resolutions adopted by the two conferences are given in full.

352. ——— Marriage and the law of bastardy. Edinburgh review, v. 222, p. 155-72, July 1915.

Reference is made here to (The) Laws of England (1907-1915), edited by Lord Halsbury, which contains information regarding the existing "bastardy" law in England amended in 1915 to throw the burden on the parents rather than on the child.

353. ——— New Swedish legislation concerning illegitimate children. (Translated from the original by Mr. Oscar Gustafson.) Journal of American institute of criminal law and criminology, v. 11, p. 284-88, August 1920.

Pertains to Swedish legislation, giving the provisions of earlier laws; 1734, 1866, 1905, 1917.

354. ——— 1933 census. Child welfare league of America, Bulletin [monthly], v. 12, p. 1, November 1933.

A brief announcement: "A census of dependent children cared for away from their own homes will be taken by the United States Census Bureau as of December 31, 1933."

355. ——— Nobody's children. Nation, v. 119, p. 135, August 6, 1924.

England's new illegitimacy bill. By its provisions, a child born out of wedlock becomes legitimate through the subsequent marriage of its parents. Legislation for the welfare of the child in Russia and in Scandinavia is in advance of legislation in England.

356. ——— Notes and notices. Eugenics review [London], v. 12, p. 135-36, July 1920.

A summary of the Swedish law of 1918 for the protection of illegitimate children.

357. ——— (The) Paternity of children. United States law review, v. 64, p. 518-23, October 1930.

The question of property rights and divorce cases often brings up the question of paternity. It is "presumed" that a child born to a married woman is the child of her husband. Illegitimacy may be proved sometimes if the child has certain racial characteristics that the husband has not, but this is not often allowed.

358. ——— Paternity of illegitimacy. Boston council of social agencies, Bulletin, v. 8, p. 9, July 1929.

A summary of a "current study of 565 cases of illegitimacy undertaken by the Boston Conference on Illegitimacy . . . the paternity of the child was adjudicated by court action in only one-third of the cases," in half of which "court action was initiated by the mother of the child, and in one quarter by private social agencies. . . In 100 cases, the reason for not going into court was the unwillingness of the mother; in 108 more, the alleged father could not be found. Insufficient evidence and the unstable character of the mother are reasons in another 100 cases. . . The total number of mothers receiving some financial assistance was 257, while 308 received none."

359. —— Social work in Sweden. International conference of social work, Proceedings, v. 1 of 1928, p. 500-22.

Page 507. "Assistance to unmarried mothers . . . is mostly provided by private charity." A "Welfare Guardian shall be appointed for each child born out of wedlock, who shall aid the mother . . ." and "shall, in particular," endeavor to secure maintenance from the father for the child throughout childhood.

360. —— (The) Unfathered child. Woman citizen, v. 3, p. 1128, May 24, 1919.

This is a comment on Emma O. Lunberg's (The) Illegitimate child and war conditions.

361. —— (The) Uniform illegitimacy act and the present status of illegitimate children. Society of comparative legislation, Journal, Series 7, p. 33-40, February 1925.

The uniform law has been adopted in four states: Nevada, North Dakota, South Dakota, and New Mexico. The provisions of the law are stated and comparisons made with the illegitimacy laws of Germany, France, and Switzerland. "Within its rather limited sphere, the uniform illegitimacy act is a well-drawn statute; but it is restricted in scope of bastardy proceedings, and the important topic of the legal status of the child in relation to its parents, its collateral relatives and society in general, is not treated."

362. Vansant, Martha. (The) Life of the adopted child. American mercury, v. 28, p. 214-22, February 1933.

An adopted child looks up the histories of nine adopted children she has known, and with these as illustrations discusses problems of adoption. "The danger that threatens an adopted child is not his uncertain heredity, his obscure background or doubtful illegitimacy, but the fact that his foster-parents take him ready-made, and then expect him to grow and evolve according to specifications which they set down. . . The successful ones among them today are those who in childhood were treated as rational beings who could safely be told that they were adopted, and not as mere emotional entities who had to be controlled by unthinking affection."

363. Van Waters, Miriam. Youth in conflict. 293 p. New York, Republic publishing company, 1925.

Pages 54-57 (Case XII). Case presentation of an "unmarried mother and her baby."
Page 61. General summary of "unmarried mother problem."

364. von Borosini, Victor. Problems of illegitimacy in Europe. Journal of American institute of criminal law and criminology, v. 4, p. 212-36, July 1913.

"In some countries in Europe there is an increasing number of unmarried mothers and their children. It is not possible to check illegitimacy to any extent but it is possible to prevent its fearful consequences, especially the appalling infant death rate." The article discusses the relation of illegitimacy to crime in later life. There is more illegitimacy where there is a surplus of women over men. Economic reasons for not marrying increase illegitimacy.

365. Waite, E. F. Placement of child born out of wedlock; is it an exclusive public function? Minnesota medicine, v. 15, p. 509-13, August 1932.

An abstract of statutory provisions for the illegitimate child in Minnesota. "On paper the scheme is quite complete, but it does not always work perfectly. The chief obstacle is the attending physician and especially the family doctor. . . I am thinking of the kind and honest doctor who . . . assumes the functions which the state reserves to itself, and privately places the child, directly or indirectly, for adoption in a home he believes to be a desirable one." Attempts to answer the desirability of "interference" by the state are given.

366. Wakefield, Charles Cheers. (The) Care of the unmarried mother and her child. Child [London], v. 9, p. 241-44, March 1919.

A plea for aid to help the work of the National council to provide protection for the unmarried mother and her child. The author explains the purpose of the Council.

367. Walker, George. (The) Traffic in babies; an analysis of the conditions discovered during an investigation conducted in the year 1914. 156 p. Baltimore, Norman, Remington, 1918.

An investigation comprising two institutions [unnamed] in Baltimore caring for infants including those of illegitimate birth. The results show a high rate of mortality. The law of Maryland (1916) is given in the appendix.

368. Warner, Charles H. Suggested changes in our adoption laws. New York State conference of charities and correction, Proceedings, 1922, p. 191-99.

Keeping the child with the mother even for the first six months is not always advisable.

369. Watson, Amey Eaton. Attitude of married parents and social workers toward unmarried parents. National conference of social work, Proceedings, 1918, p. 102-8.

An "analysis of the factors involved in parenthood as a constructive force in human society."

370. ———— (The) Illegitimate family. Annals of American academy of political and social science, v. 77, p. 103-16, May 1918.

Outline for a minimum investigation for a study of illegitimacy. The article recommends individual treatment and work for the unmarried mother to enable her to live a normal life, but states: "After all it is the child that is our real interest."

371. Weidensall, Jean. (The) Mentality of the unmarried mother. National conference of social work, Proceedings, 1917, p. 287-94.

"This paper reports the percentage of feeble-mindedness, as determined by two supplementary systems of mental tests, among an unselected series of the unmarried mothers, from the obstetrical service of the Cincinnati General Hospital." The conclusion is that "not more than 20 per cent. of the unmarried mothers can be safely pronounced normal. Of married mothers about 50 per cent. may be so considered."

372. Weiss, Egon. (The) Legal position of illegitimate children in the Roman empire. (Zur Rechtsstellung der unehelichen kinder in der Kaiserzeit.) Zeitschrift der Savigny-stiftung für rechtsgeschichte, Romanistische abteilung 49, p. 260-73, 1929.

A historical summary of the legal status of the illegitimate child in the

Roman empire. The article refers to the discovery of a tablet in Egypt dated 145 A.D. stating that illegitimate children were not entitled to enrollment in the register of births.

From Social science abstracts, v. 2, no. 7, p. 1169, July 1930.

373. **White House conference on child health and protection.** White House conference 1930; addresses and abstracts of committee reports. 365 p. New York, Century, 1931.

Pages 324-25. (The) Handicapped (Section IV). Socially handicapped (Committee C1). Children born out of wedlock (Subcommittee). Report.

374. **White House conference on child health and protection,** (The) Handicapped (Section IV), Socially handicapped (Committee C), Dependency and neglect (Subcommittee 1). Dependent and neglected children. 439 p. New York, D. Appleton-Century, c 1933.

The final published report of the White House conference, Subcommittee IV-C1.

Pages 14-17. General report; children born out of wedlock.

Pages 251-75. Children born out of wedlock. "The general principles, discussed here, are workable only when adapted to individual needs. Sensitiveness to the whole situation of mother, father and child, in relation to their social and physical environment, will determine the flexibility of any good social case work program. Respect for personality, however trivial it may seem, usually develops personality, and upon such development depends fulfilment."

Pages 251-53. Vital statistics. Illegitimate births. The extent of illegitimacy in the United States birth registration area for each year 1922-29 inclusive is indicated, separate for native white, foreign white, and colored mothers, with the exception of California and Massachusetts, which do not require on the birth certificate a statement concerning illegitimacy. This estimate of the extent is an "under-statement," but shows "consistent differences between the rates for the several racial groups. Birth registration is nearly complete in European countries, and illegitimacy statistics have there been given very much more attention than in the United States. . . Because of different methods of registration and definitions of illegitimacy, the figures for these countries are to be considered with certain reservations and modifications for purposes of comparison with the illegitimacy rates of the United States."

Pages 253-54. Vital statistics. Infant mortality. "It is not the practice in vital statistics bureaus to differentiate between infants born out of wedlock and those born in wedlock in tabulating infant deaths for mortality statistics. . . Certain indications as to the problem are found in the results of extensive field studies by the Children's Bureau. These studies show rates three times as high for children born out of wedlock as for those born in wedlock, in Boston in 1914; in New Bedford in 1913, 2.7 times as high; in Milwaukee in 1916 to 1917, 2.3 times as high; in Baltimore in 1915, 3.3 times as high for white babies, and 1.8 times as high for Negro babies." The desirability of breast-feeding and of retention of the child by the mother, are stressed.

Pages 254-59. Social data. The [United States] Census bureau publishes certain detailed information annually regarding illegitimacy. "A higher rate of illegitimate births is found, generally, in urban centers than in rural areas. Those states with a large Negro population have higher rates than other states. Among colored women the rate is eight or nine times higher than among white women, and the number of illegitimate births to Negro women is considerably higher than to other colored women. Among white mothers, those of American birth outnumber those of foreign birth by about three to one. . . The great majority of mothers are under twenty-five, and nearly half of them, under twenty-one. While most of the fathers of these children are young men, their age groups generally fall somewhat higher than those of the mothers. Some idea of the burden carried by the community for the maintenance of children born out of wedlock is indicated in the findings of a study in one city and state made by the Children's Bureau [United States, Children's bureau, Publication no. 75]. . . This study also reports, for Massachusetts for 1914, 7,526 children under care of the Division of State Minor Wards, of whom 1,721, or 23 per cent, were born out of wedlock. Twenty-two per cent of all the children receiving prolonged care were born out of wedlock. . . The findings suggest that children born out of wedlock, deprived of care by their own people, are placed in correctional institutions at an earlier age and for less serious offenses than children who have the advantage of normal home life. Of th 2,863 children born out of wedlock under care of the Boston agencies, the histories of 2,178 gave social data sufficient for study of the extent to which paternal responsibility was assumed or compelled. . . The proportion of cases in which no support was available from the fathers of the children, nearly two-thirds, is a telling indication of the extent to which the community must carry the burden of support for this group of children. It is regrettable that no later data comparable in scope are available. The absence . . . calls attention to the need for inclusion of the status of children as regards birth in such statistics on dependent, neglected and delinquent children as are compiled by the Bureau of the Census and by the Children's Bureau." Recent figures from the "Child Welfare Division . . . of the District of Columbia" show "disproportion with the rates for children of legitimate birth requiring" care 'for dependency and neglect."

"The social factors that led to unmarried parenthood in the past have increased in our changing life. Broken homes, unhappy family life, lack of education or trade training, and insufficient recreation, still figure largely, but in addition there is the automobile. . . There also is slackening of standards in sex relations due somewhat to universal craving for self-expression and depreciation of the virtue of self-control . . . respect for traditional conventions, which to some extent safeguarded wholesome companionship between the sexes, has in some instances broken down. The attitude of society is changing slowly but perceptibly due . . . largely to the careful thought which is being given to improve legislation in behalf of the child born out of wedlock; to research studies on child welfare problems; to the skilled social workers in their many case work contacts; to the interpretation of social conditions in the press, and to gradual elimination of the words 'bastard' and 'illegitimate.'"

Figures are given, showing that mothers of illegitimate children are chiefly young, the colored especially (see Child welfare league of America. Unpublished study of child welfare work in Cincinnati, 1929-30; Unpublished study of child welfare work in Richmond, 1924). "Minnesota statistics . . . offer convincing evidence that girls who go to school only up to the last grades of grammar school, and then go into unskilled employment, are more likely to get into difficulty than those who have had better opportunity for education and professional training. . . We know from studies made by the Children's Bureau and others, that a large proportion of the unmarried mothers under fifteen years of age, and the recidivists, are frequently subnormal mentally."

Pages 259-70. Social treatment. "Every unmarried mother, whether she has money or not, whether she has a family or not, needs someone who will understand her particular problem, see her through her immediate trouble and help her face the future. This usually can be done better by someone outside the family who sees all the factors involved objectively but sympathetically. . . As the social disgrace seems more unbearable to the more intelligent and well-to-do persons, the physician often . . . arranges for immediate adoption or placement of the baby. . . It would seem as if carefully selected trusteeship, even among strangers, should be the lot of the unwanted child of good inheritance. The social agencies would like to offer their services . . . but in most instances it is assumed that persons with money need no advice or assistance."

A "maternity home, which is perhaps the best type of care for many unmarried mothers . . . should give prenatal care, the best obstetrical service in or out of its own building, postnatal and convalescent care to mother and baby for at least two or three months. Careful placement and follow-up should be given every mother and baby when they return to the community. . . .The mother and baby's rehabilitation in society is the real test of complete service. . . By the end of the nursing period the mother has had time to face the facts and with wise assistance may decide to keep her baby. . . Reports and surveys consistently state that ideally the mother and baby should be kept together. How far is society, through its social agencies and its public opinion, making this possible. . . Children, in general, should not be separated permanently from their mothers to save the family name or social position."

Figures from several studies are cited indicating about 60 percent of adoptions are of illegitimate children. "Child and adopting parents ought to be safeguarded by a social investigation . . . and no legal action should be taken until a trial period of six months to a year has passed." In Minnesota, "where all adoptions are investigated and approved by the State Board of Control," it would seem that "hasty and secretive adoptions have been abolished."

"It is generally admitted and advised that no money should be accepted for confinement expenses or support of the child without establishment of paternity by the court, or without a signed agreement made out of court, acknowledging paternity . . . every effort should be made to improve and enforce the various state laws," regarding paternity. "Marriage to a good man," not forced, is urged as "undoubtedly the happiest solution of the unmarried mother's problem."

Pages 271-72. Conclusions and recommendations.

Pages 273-75. Bibliography (Children born out of wedlock).

Pages 418-19. Bibliography (General references. Children born out of wedlock).

375. White House conference on child health and protection, Medical service (Section I), Prenatal and maternal care (Committee B). (The) Address of the chairman (Fred L. Adair, M.D.) of the Committee on prenatal and maternal care. American journal of obstetrics and gynecology, v. 21, p. 767-83, June 1931.

A summary of the conclusions of the Committee. "In the Children's Bureau's study" 89 percent of the women "whose deaths followed abortions were married." The "problem of illegitimacy alone opens up a wide range of activity which has been inadequately handled from the standpoint of both mother and infant."

376. White House conference on child health and protection, Medical service (Section I), Prenatal and maternal care (Committee B), Subcommittee on factors and causes of fetal, newborn, and maternal morbidity and mortality. Fetal, newborn, and maternal morbidity and mortality; report of the Subcommittee. 466 p. New York, Appleton-Century, 1933.

Pages 439-45. (The) Importance of complete and accurate certificates of birth and death in the prevention of maternal and early infant mortality; report of Richard A. Bolt, M.D. There are "differences of completeness, definition, classification and interpretation in the vital statistics as tabulated in various countries and even in the United States. . . It is especially desirable that general agreement should be reached as to what items should appear on the standard certificates of birth and death, especially as related to maternal and early infant mortality. . . It is urged that all state bureaus of vital statistics accept the revision of the International Classification of Causes of Death as set forth in the new manual of the International List of Causes of Death or Diseases of Pregnancy, Childbirth and the Puerperal State." A "few minor changes" are suggested regarding the birth and maternal death certificates, as "preventability of death calls for suggestions for possible improvement." Length and quality of prenatal care should appear on the birth certificate, and in a "supplementary questionnaire" desirable for all maternal deaths.

Pages 446-72. Abortion in relation to fetal and maternal welfare; report of Fred J. Taussig, M.D. Abortion is defined as the "previable expulsion of the human ovum." Statistics on abortion are inadequate "due not merely to the fact that the early abortions offer considerable diagnostic difficulty, but more especially to the efforts of the patients to conceal the truth for fear of scandal or criminal prosecution. . . Only in Russia, where abortions are legalized, can one expect to find any appreciable percentage of cases recorded." A communication from the Children's bureau to the author stated that the Bureau "had absolutely no data on the frequency of abortions in this country."

"The increase in the number of abortions which has been observed generally throughout the world has been due less to a laxity of morals than to underlying economic conditions. This is seen by the fact that the majority of criminal abortions occurred in married rather than unmarried women. Among younger individuals, however, this is not the case." Ofderdinger's findings in Hamburg, Germany, are cited. "Riechelt found in Breslau, Germany, that abortions were more frequent among the unmarried, 1,179 of the patients being unmarried and 691 married. Dame Louise McIlroy, in July, 1929, stated that in England criminal abortions before the war had been resorted to mainly by unmarried women, but that at the present time abortion was most frequent among married women. In the United States based on the maternal mortality statistics of the 1,824 women who died following abortions, 186 were unmarried whereas 1,638 women were married. . . Distribution of legitimate abortions to pregnancies" comprises Table 3 and 4, from which "it would appear that legitimate abortion occurs much more frequently among multigravidas. . ."

Bibliography on abortion, p. 471-72.
Bibliography (general), p. 23-24.

377. White, James Dundas. Legitimation by subsequent marriage. Law quarterly review, v. 36, p. 255-67, 1920.

The material is historical and deals with proposals for legitimation in England.

378. Williams, C. V. (The) Unmarried mother in the maternity hospital. Hospital social service, v. 20, p. 266-71, October 1929.

The author outlines a procedure which carries out the principles of the White House conference of 1909, reaffirmed in the regional and Washington conferences in 1919, and "insisted upon by the Child Welfare League of America."

379. Willoughby, W. G., M.D. (The) Unmarried mother and her child. Journal of the Royal sanitary institute [London], v. 40, p. 136-39, November 1919.

The number of illegitimate births registered in England and Wales in 1918 was 41,153, an increase over the previous year of 1,444. The mortality rate was high, particularly on the first day of birth. The author suggests preventive measures to lessen the high rate of infant mortality: sex education of older children; a woman's hostel where a friendless girl can go; "rescue" homes; greater penalties and responsibilities for the father; prenatal and postnatal clinics; economic provision for the unmarried mother; homes for mothers and infants; foster-mothers and infants' homes if the child has been abandoned.

380. Wise, L. W. Mothers in name. Survey, v. 43, p. 779-80, March 20, 1920.

"Jewish sentiment is peculiarly intolerant of an unmarried mother . . . not in one case in a thousand will she be taken back into her parents' home. . . A mother's pension should be given to every mother, though unmarried, who will keep her child. The stigma too long attached to the unmarried mother should be removed. . . Must we not think primarily of the future of the child? The child of the unmarried mother rarely has a chance." The article argues for the adoption of such children, as many unmarried mothers have no understanding of their duty and obligation to society.

381. Wolbarst, A. L. (The) Unmarried mother and the Wassermann reaction. Hospital social service, v. 5, p. 281-88, May 1922.

There is no "unanimity among physicians as to the exact values that may be placed on this test and its findings in the diagnosis of syphilis." The positive reaction should be "supported by other evidence of active syphilis." The author's object is to secure for this test a correct "appraisal . . . in its application to the status of the unmarried mother and her infant."

382. **Workum, Ruth I.** (The) Cincinnati illegitimacy plan. Hospital social service, v. 7, p. 247-55, April 1923.

A description of the Cincinnati plan of handling illegitimacy: case work including physical treatment and social treatment, court action, and child-placing.

383. **Worthington, George E.** Stepping stones to an improved law for children born out of wedlock. Journal of social hygiene, v. 10, p. 164-76, March 1924.

The present New York laws on this subject are termed "bastardy" laws. They are part of the poor law, and have remained virtually unchanged for over a hundred years. There is need for improved legislation. Early in the summer of 1923, a group representing many of the social agencies of New York City met to discuss the subject of illegitimacy.
Pages 168-76. Suggestions drafted in the form of a proposed bill.

384. **Young, Evangeline W., M.D.** Progress in the treatment of illegitimacy. Medical review of reviews, v. 21, p. 284-89, May 1915.

A discussion of the history and significance of the Norwegian act passed March 7, 1915, and of illegitimacy in general, with special comment on the illegitimate father.

385. **Zahorsky, John, M.D.** Problems of the foundling home. American journal of obstetrics, v. 71, p. 826-44, May 1915.

A study of the care, feeding, and death rate of "infants in asylums" based on the meager data the author could obtain from the literature, from several physicians in different large cities, and from inquiries from the boards of health in ten states known to have one or more "infant asylums."

NOTES

An attempt was made to include all references appearing in English, from January 1912 to May 1933, presenting significant data on illegitimacy, or new or stimulating points of view, available through the sources consulted. "Illegitimacy," "Bastardy," "Unmarried Mother" are not extensively indexed subjects, especially in the periodical literature, partly because the most significant contributions are often merely small sections of discussions of more comprehensive fields. This may account for certain unintentional omissions from the bibliography. Only such references in foreign languages are included as appeared in Social Science Abstracts, 1929-32. No consistent search was made for publications appearing later than May, 1933, though such pertinent references as chanced to come to hand subsequently were included.

Listings of students' theses by the Russell Sage Foundation Library were consulted, and, when it could be determined that a thesis satisfied the preceding requirements for inclusion, it was entered in the bibliography. A few unpublished documents available for reference were included.

Government publications, national, state, and local, were included, but the search for them is particularly difficult because very few indexes list government publications; even when they are indexed, usually only gross subject classifying is done. There are therefore probably omissions of some governmental material.

Excluded from the bibliography are routine annual reports of institutions and agencies, and compilations of texts of laws (though annotations may mention texts).

Unsigned articles are arranged under "Unsigned," in lieu of author, alphabetically by title.

Card catalogues of the following libraries were consulted: Columbia University Library; Metropolitan Life Insurance Company Library; National Health Library; New School for Social Research Library; New York Academy of Medicine Library; New York Public Library; Russell Sage Foundation Library; Woodrow Wilson Memorial Library. All were very helpful. The Russell Sage Foundation Library and the National Health Library especially gave many valuable suggestions involving expenditure of much time on their part, regarding bibliographical procedure.

Thorough search was made of the following publications:

Child Development Abstracts and Bibliography; Encyclopaedia of the Social Sciences; Index-Catalog of the Surgeon General's Office; Proceedings of the International Conference of Social Work; International Index to Periodical Literature; Proceedings of the National Conference of Social Work; Publications of the President's Research Committee on Social Trends; Public Affairs Information Service; Quarterly Cumulative Index Medicus; Readers' Guide to Periodical Literature; Social Science Abstracts; Social Work Year Book; Publications of the United States Children's Bureau; Publications of the White House Conference on Child Health and Protection.

INDEXES

TOPICAL INDEX TO ANNOTATED BIBLIOGRAPHY
ON ILLEGITIMACY

References are to reference document numbers in the Annotated Bibliography; cross references are to other topics in this index.

1. Social significance of illegitimate family.

    a) Abandonment of children: 11, 69, 153, 245, 254, 272, 289, 385. See also 6.*a*)(2)(*a*).

    b) Abortions: 20, 84, 87, 119, 157, 169, 190, 231, 243, 285, 287, 298, 313, 315, 330, 375, 376.

    c) Dependency: 32, 77, 93, 130, 132, 176, 213, 231, 309, 321, 323, 340. See also 4.*h*), 5.*i*), 6.*a*)(1)(*c*), 7.*b*)(3), 8.*j*).

    d) Effect on family life: 62, 105, 146, 176, 221, 247, 290.

    e) Eugenics: 97, 159, 263. See also 4.d)(2)(*a*), 5.c), 9.a).

    f) Extent of illegitimacy: 4, 15, 22, 28, 31, 40, 46, 53, 55, 67, 68, 75, 80, 82, 84, 92, 96, 100, 104, 106, 110, 111, 118, 125, 127, 132, 135, 138, 147, 156, 177, 184, 185, 197, 198, 200, 201, 203, 210, 211, 212, 214, 217, 223, 231, 240, 243, 248, 249, 250, 258, 265, 268, 269, 271, 272, 279, 284, 285, 294, 313, 317, 319, 320, 323, 325, 326, 330, 332, 337, 340, 343, 345, 360, 364, 374, 379.

    g) Infant mortality and morbidity: 9, 11, 13, 16, 42, 44, 59, 72, 84, 85, 88, 90, 92, 93, 94, 108, 109, 111, 116, 121, 122, 123, 130, 138, 143, 144, 146, 160, 169, 176, 178, 190, 199, 203, 231, 234, 237, 272, 285, 289, 315, 320, 323, 335, 340, 341, 343, 364, 367, 374, 376, 379. See also 1.*h*), 4.d)(1), 6.

    h) Maternal mortality and morbidity: 4, 110, 111, 165, 190, 217, 234, 243, 285, 286, 298, 318, 329, 330, 335, 376. See also 1.g), 4.d)(1), 4.e).

    i) Prostitution: 42, 105, 144, 152, 208, 261. See also 1.*j*), 4.*i*), 8.*a*)(2), 8.*b*), 8.*e*).

    j) Venereal diseases: 20, 22, 24, 72, 109, 111, 230, 232, 234, 255, 261, 286, 381. See also 1.*i*), 4.d)(1), 4.*i*), 7.*a*)(5), 8.*a*)(2).

i) Prostitution: 1, 151, 208. See also 1.*i*).

j) Color: 1, 15, 25, 31, 46, 55, 75, 96, 196, 198, 203, 248, 249, 258, 269, 271, 277, 317, 330, 341, 343, 374.

k) Religious and cultural connections: 40, 51, 76, 118, 139, 140, 141, 148, 171, 194, 210, 212, 225, 229, 240, 279, 283, 293, 380.

l) Repeated illegitimacy: 1, 24, 64, 73, 132, 145, 179, 201, 203, 212, 225, 240, 270, 340.

m) Types of unmarried mother: 104, 151, 177, 283. See also 4.*d*)(2)(*a*), 8.*e*), 8.*i*), 8.*k*), 9.*d*).

n) General: 332.

5. Unmarried father.

a) Age: 50, 52, 55, 75, 100, 171, 175, 179, 206, 210, 212, 240, 258, 279, 374.

b) Country of birth of foreign-born: 55, 171, 212, 240.

c) Health, mental: 39, 240. See also 1.*e*), 7.*a*)(5)(*b*).

d) Identity: 15, 27, 33, 35, 37, 45, 52, 71, 107, 123, 128, 143, 175, 177, 239, 258, 259, 263, 311, 319, 324, 357, 384.

e) Marital status: 24, 210, 212, 240, 258, 279.

f) Occupation: 55, 171, 175, 210, 212, 220, 240, 258.

g) Color: 258.

h) Religious and cultural connections: 40, 139, 140, 141, 210, 212, 240, 258, 279, 293.

i) Responsibility to child: 8, 24, 27, 33, 35, 37, 38, 42, 47, 50, 56, 69, 77, 93, 116, 128, 136, 148, 168, 179, 181, 199, 210, 211, 212, 232, 236, 239, 258, 259, 263, 265, 270, 279, 300, 309, 311, 326, 327, 333, 337, 358, 359, 374. See also 1.*c*), 7.*b*)(3).

j) Other: 258.

k) General: 332.

6. Illegitimate child. See also 7.*a*)(2).

a) Disposition of child.

(1) Retention with mother.

GENERAL INDEX

Abandonment, 15, 16

Abortions, 196

Adoption, 66, 87, 88, 90; *see also* child placement

Age, of unmarried fathers, 166; of unmarried mothers, 49, 78, 113

Agencies, coöperation of, 96; for delinquents, 80; preventive, 72; protective, 71, 73; records of, 6, 33, 103; sectarian, 73; specialized, 52, 140

Application for help, 150

Association for Improving the Condition of the Poor, 71

Baltimore, illegitimacy in, 9, 18, 19; infant mortality in, 21

Birthplace of illegitimate children, 193

Birth rate, 25

Boarding homes, 89

Breast feeding, 81, 89

Brooklyn Bureau of Charities, 71

Brooklyn Society for the Prevention of Cruelty to Children, 77

Care of the illegitimate child, 200, 207

Case records, 93, 94

Case work, 54, 75, 78, 161

Charity Organization Society, 71

Chicago, illegitimacy in, 18

Child dependency in New York State, 95

Child placement, 51, 87, 92

Children, of unmarried fathers, 181; of unmarried mothers, 144; of unmarried mothers, living, 149

Church Mission of Help, Brooklyn, 73

Church Mission of Help, New York, 73

Cities Census Committee, 137

Cleveland, illegitimacy in, 18

Committee on Public Health Relations, 9

Coöperation of agencies, *see* Agencies

Correction Hospital, 80, 81

Davis, Michael M., 195

Day nurseries, 67

Deardorff, Neva R., 93

Delinquents, 80; institutions for, 80

Dependency, 10

Discrimination, in hospitals, 58

Domestic service and illegitimacy, 130, 139

Drachsler, Julius, 170

Education, in institutions, 85; of unmarried fathers, 176; of unmarried mothers, 131

Employment, in maternity homes, 62

European illegitimacy rates, 123, 124

Family in America

AN ARNO PRESS / NEW YORK TIMES COLLECTION

Abbott, John S. C. **The Mother at Home:** Or, The Principles of Maternal Duty. 1834.

Abrams, Ray H., editor. **The American Family in World War II.** 1943.

Addams, Jane. **A New Conscience and an Ancient Evil.** 1912.

The Aged and the Depression: Two Reports, 1931–1937. 1972.

Alcott, William A. **The Young Husband.** 1839.

Alcott, William A. **The Young Wife.** 1837.

American Sociological Society. **The Family.** 1909.

Anderson, John E. **The Young Child in the Home.** 1936.

Baldwin, Bird T., Eva Abigail Fillmore and Lora Hadley. **Farm Children.** 1930.

Beebe, Gilbert Wheeler. **Contraception and Fertility in the Southern Appalachians.** 1942.

Birth Control and Morality in Nineteenth Century America: Two Discussions, 1859–1878. 1972.

Brandt, Lilian. **Five Hundred and Seventy-Four Deserters and Their Families.** 1905. Baldwin, William H. **Family Desertion and Non-Support Laws.** 1904.

Breckinridge, Sophonisba P. **The Family and the State:** Select Documents. 1934.

Calverton, V. F. **The Bankruptcy of Marriage.** 1928.

Carlier, Auguste. **Marriage in the United States.** 1867.

Child, [Lydia]. **The Mother's Book.** 1831.

Child Care in Rural America: Collected Pamphlets, 1917–1921. 1972.

Child Rearing Literature of Twentieth Century America, 1914–1963. 1972.

The Colonial American Family: Collected Essays, 1788–1803. 1972.

Commander, Lydia Kingsmill. **The American Idea.** 1907.

Davis, Katharine Bement. **Factors in the Sex Life of Twenty-Two Hundred Women.** 1929.

Dennis, Wayne. **The Hopi Child.** 1940.

Epstein, Abraham. **Facing Old Age.** 1922. New Introduction by Wilbur J. Cohen.

The Family and Social Service in the 1920s: Two Documents, 1921–1928. 1972.

Hagood, Margaret Jarman. **Mothers of the South.** 1939.

Hall, G. Stanley. **Senescence:** The Last Half of Life. 1922.

Hall, G. Stanley. **Youth:** Its Education, Regimen, and Hygiene. 1904.

Hathway, Marion. **The Migratory Worker and Family Life.** 1934.

Homan, Walter Joseph. **Children & Quakerism.** 1939.

Key, Ellen. **The Century of the Child.** 1909.

Kirchwey, Freda. **Our Changing Morality:** A Symposium. 1930.

Kopp, Marie E. **Birth Control in Practice.** 1934.

Lawton, George. **New Goals for Old Age.** 1943.

Lichtenberger, J. P. **Divorce:** A Social Interpretation. 1931.

Lindsey, Ben B. and Wainwright Evans. **The Companionate Marriage.** 1927. New Introduction by Charles Larsen.

Lou, Herbert H. **Juvenile Courts in the United States.** 1927.

Monroe, Day. **Chicago Families.** 1932.

Mowrer, Ernest R. **Family Disorganization.** 1927.

Reed, Ruth. **The Illegitimate Family in New York City.** 1934.

Robinson, Caroline Hadley. **Seventy Birth Control Clinics.** 1930.

Watson, John B. **Psychological Care of Infant and Child.** 1928.

White House Conference on Child Health and Protection. **The Home and the Child.** 1931.

White House Conference on Child Health and Protection. **The Adolescent in the Family.** 1934.

Young, Donald, editor. **The Modern American Family.** 1932.